W0044090

THE POLITICS OF HINDI CINEMA IN THE NEW MILLENNIUM

'I think a failed state is the responsibility of the people who have made that state fail, and those are generally the people of that country.'
—Lakhdar Brahimi, Algerian public servant and UN diplomat

M.K. Raghavendra

THE POLITICS OF HINDI CINEMA IN THE NEW MILLENNIUM

BOLLYWOOD AND THE ANGLOPHONE INDIAN NATION

OXFORD
UNIVERSITY PRESS

OXFORD
UNIVERSITY PRESS

Oxford University Press is a department of the University of Oxford.
It furthers the University's objective of excellence in research, scholarship,
and education by publishing worldwide. Oxford is a registered trademark of
Oxford University Press in the UK and in certain other countries

Published in India by
Oxford University Press
YMCA Library Building, 1 Jai Singh Road, New Delhi 110001, India

© Oxford University Press 2014

The moral rights of the author has been asserted

First published in 2014

All rights reserved. No part of this publication may be reproduced, stored in
a retrieval system, or transmitted, in any form or by any means, without the
prior permission in writing of Oxford University Press, or as expressly permitted
by law, by licence, or under terms agreed with the appropriate reprographics
rights organization. Enquiries concerning reproduction outside the scope of the
above should be sent to the Rights Department, Oxford University Press, at the
address above

You must not circulate this work in any other form
and you must impose this same condition on any acquirer

ISBN-13: 978-0-19-945056-5
ISBN-10: 0-19-945056-0

Typeset in Goudy Oldstyle Std 10.5/14
by The Graphics Solution, New Delhi 110 092
Printed in India by G.H. Prints Pvt. Ltd, New Delhi 110 020

For
Ashis Nandy,
who discovered before almost everyone else what
an intellectual adventure popular cinema was.

Contents

Acknowledgements

This book would not have been possible without help and suggestions from people, the nature of which is too varied and difficult to enumerate: Sharadini Rath, Usha K.R., Rammanohar Reddy and the *Economic and Political Weekly*, and the editors at Oxford University Press, who have been deeply understanding, helpful, and prompt. The book also owes a deep debt of gratitude to the anonymous readers whose perceptive and useful suggestions I promptly implemented.

Introduction

This is an introduction to a collection of essays devoted to mainstream Hindi cinema after 2000. If the impact of globalization began to be experienced almost universally in India in the new millennium, a principal vehicle utilized to propel a largely pre-modern society into the global age was the English language. This being the case, it is logical to suppose that the social impact of English would be registered by mainstream Hindi cinema which after 1947 had been instrumental in the imagining of India by its citizens as a cohesive community.

The thrust of the essays in this book is broadly political, which has been the approach of much of the writing on the subject in India. Where the present approach differs, however, is in the analysis offered being almost entirely textual. The tendency in the most ambitious academic writing on film in India has been to examine its 'effects',[1] that is, the uses to which cinema has been put and the consequences of its interactions in the public space. While this is certainly legitimate, it cannot be unrelated to scholars being uncomfortable with admitting that the popular film text is anything but innocuous. But the Indian popular film has been a treasure trove of signifiers and I hope to show not only that politics has had a bearing on cinema but also that cinema[2] shows us new ways in which political issues can be understood.

This book is primarily a work of film interpretation but this needs clarification since different kinds of meaning can be made of any film. The meaning of a film to the audience which consumes it locally is not the meaning that a national film jury would ascribe to it, and an academic studying it would construct a third kind of meaning. It is now a truism to say that media texts are not only authored by their creators but also 'co-authored' by audiences.[3] If one supposes that there is a 'natural selection' of patterns and motifs in the popular cinema of any period depending on their pertinence,[4] the role of the consumer co-author is made more significant and this places a greater value upon popular cinema. Popular cinema can therefore be broadly considered an utterance by the constituency it is addressing and interpreted accordingly. This is not to assert that this interpretation is the same as the one that audiences will voice but neither is it the kind of meaning that academic studies of Indian cinema have generally excavated. While the most sensitive of cinephiles will ascribe a surface meaning to any film, Indian audiences perhaps respond most readily to the 'relayed meaning' of popular cinema[5] and academics seek out deep meanings. It should be noted here that 'depth' in the context of deep interpretation has little to do with profundity. While 'surface' interpretations presume that authors as agents are still in some privileged position with regard to what the representations are, deep interpretations presume that they have no such privilege.[6] Deep interpretations, apart from being symptomatic, seek to get at the structure underneath. They are not content with establishing and interpreting relationships within texts and are reliant on pre-existent theoretical approaches in psychology and the social sciences with which they align themselves.

My own interpretation of popular films in this book will be 'symptomatic' but it diverges from that of most academic writing on Indian cinema inasmuch as it is not theory-down.[7] Interpretive approaches have been psychoanalytical (Freudian or Lacanian) or have relied on post-Marxist theory (usually cultural studies) and the tendency has been to understand Indian cinema as an instance in a broad generality. Sometimes the pressure to find interpretive models has been so strong that doubtful descriptions of individual films[8] have been offered and many of the resultant interpretations widely accepted as wisdom on the meaning of Indian popular cinema. I hope to demonstrate in the course of this book that while Hindi cinema is political and ideological, its political significance can be understood more sharply through local developments in India than through overarching notions like 'class struggle' or 'patriarchy'.

While the relationship between Hindi cinema and its constituency is crucial, a question also of key importance is whether the constituency addressed by mainstream Hindi film has not changed in the new millennium and whether—considering that it was the closest that India had to a pan-national cultural artefact—this does not point to the Nation itself being constituted more asymmetrically than in the past, because 'Bollywood' is not 'mainstream Hindi cinema' as we once understood it.

Hindi Cinema and Bollywood

The term 'Bollywood' is loosely used today to denote mainstream Hindi cinema from Mumbai but there is evidence that the term became a widely accepted parlance only in the new millennium, when Bollywood became a brand. The overseas spectator profile of Indian cinema changed substantially between 1988 and 2001 and if the Gulf and USSR were the largest overseas markets in 1988 (35.16 per cent and 14.17 per cent, respectively),[9] USA and UK together accounted for 55 per cent in 2001.[10] The share of exports in the total earnings of a successful mainstream film has also changed and this can be gauged from the example of Om Shanti Om (2007) which grossed around USD 24 million worldwide out of which USD 8 million—or approximately 30 per cent—was accounted for by overseas receipts.[11] The changing spectator profiles also suggest that the diaspora is now the largest contributor to Indian cinema's export earnings. This has gone along with the increasing importance of Indians abroad with People of Indian Origin (PIO) becoming increasingly visible inside India. By and large, Hindi mainstream cinema is addressing the global Indian in a much larger way today than it did when it was only 'mainstream Hindi cinema'.

The term 'Bollywood' was, as late as in the new millennium, resisted by doyens of the film industry in India because they took the term to be pejorative, since it seemed to indicate that mainstream Hindi cinema simply aped Hollywood.[12] It has been argued that there are two types of cultural nationalism at work with regard to the meaning of popular cinema today. The older one insists that mainstream Hindi cinema is first and foremost located at 'home', that is, in India. The second sees a distinct cultural constituency including not only audiences within India but a crossover segment as well. It would appear that the term 'Bollywood', shorn of its pejorative implications, is promoted by the second kind of 'cultural nationalists'. The indications are that the term 'Bollywood' first became acceptable currency not within India but in the UK and USA, in places like Bradford, Leicester, and Birmingham, where Hindi films are marketed as a brand, with 'Bollywood' being a kind of label.[13] I would like to stretch the argument to suggest that, since a part of the overseas audience consuming mainstream Hindi cinema would be South Asians without being Indian, the term 'Bollywood' may have even become a more acceptable label than 'Indian' because it does not signify a specific national identity which might invite hostility.[14]

What makes Bollywood a brand is not the content of cinema—as constituted by film narrative[15]—but a certain kind of allure produced by a characteristic visual excess brought in by spectacle, choreography, costume, and music. It is this visual excess that allows Bollywood to become a 'lifestyle statement' and enables it to be employed in areas outside cinema itself. It is Bollywood and not mainstream Hindi cinema that has assisted in Indian capital becoming conspicuous abroad through Indian restaurants/food, clothing, and décor. Well-known instances are the moderately successful musical *Bombay Dreams* (2004) produced by Andrew

Lloyd Webber with music by A.R. Rahman and the various selling campaigns used partly by clothing stores and restaurants. The well-known British departmental store Selfridges had a month-long focus on the theme of Bollywood in May 2002 with Indian clothes and items of décor exhibited in its London and Manchester stores. During this period a broad-based promotion of South Asian film, dance, music, and theatre—called 'Imaginasia'—was also undertaken in Britain.[16] With this transformation in the spectator profile of the mainstream Hindi film, one might anticipate a transformation in its political role within India as well and it may not be doing what it once was.

The Political Role of Mainstream Hindi Cinema after 1947

It is now a truism to say that mainstream Hindi cinema assisted in the imagining of the Indian Nation. The growth of cinema in the former colonies went through several stages. In the first stage, located between 1910 and 1915 usually, there was an explosion of locally produced cinema that was soon wiped out by mass entertainment from the West.[17] Even in India, which was to later dominate its domestic market, 85 per cent of the screen time in the 1920s was occupied by foreign imports.[18] Some of these local commercial cinemas reasserted themselves later but they also provoked reactions of a predominantly negative kind among 'Third World' critics and theorists, and the critical writing or the theoretical speculation that Hollywood generated was absent. It was perhaps as a response that the first wave of 'national' film-makers emerged from the former colonies: Youssef Chahine from Egypt, Satyajit Ray from India, Lester James Peries from Sri Lanka, Leopoldo Torre Nilsson from Argentina, Tomás Gutiérrez Alea and Humberto Solás from Cuba, and Fernando Birri from Brazil.

While the 'national' film-makers were largely from the Western-educated elite of the former colonies and their films were often officially designated as representing national culture, the more successful of the local entertainment cinemas—especially Indian and

Egyptian—also took up the task of building nationhood in earnest. If Egyptian cinema went on to represent 'Arab' rather than 'Egyptian' cinema, it has been shown by film theorists that Hindi entertainment cinema, which had been suturing cultural differences and producing a homogeneous mass culture even before 1947, became a useful tool in defining and maintaining the Indian Nation.[19] The Hindi film was intended to appeal to people spread over a wide territory and it kept its language simple and accessible, much more so than the Hindi of All India Radio (AIR) or Doordarshan.[20] The Indian Nation is therefore discernibly 'inscribed' in mainstream Hindi filmic texts after 1947. Theorists have broadly noted that Independence acquires 'figurability' in mainstream Hindi films after 1947.[21] But Jawaharlal Nehru, who perhaps looked upon the mainstream film as a cultural embarrassment, declared that the film industry was not a priority and the Nehruvian state declined to do for the film industry what it did for the other industries.[22] Mainstream cinema therefore assisted in the collective imagining of the Nation despite the state's apathy towards its development.

Much work has been done with regard to Hindi cinema's ideological/political role and the more influential approach has been post-Marxist. M. Madhava Prasad's approach to Hindi cinema immediately after Independence depends on two key arguments. The first is that Parsi theatre, which was apparently the original model for mainstream Hindi film, took inspiration from the romance which preceded the advent of realist fiction in the West. The romance was typically a tale of love and adventure in which a high-born figure, usually a prince, underwent trials that tested his courage, at the end of which he returned to inherit his father's position and to marry.[23] But there are problems in tracing Hindi cinema through the medium of Parsi theatre of the early twentieth century because the attributes of Parsi theatre are not rigorously documented and much wisdom on what it was like rests on hearsay. Also, if Parsi theatre uses the model of the romance, the model hardly finds correspondence in Hindi cinema of the 1940s and 1950s. In fact, one would be hard-pressed to find films in this period in which the protagonist 'inherits his father's position'. The films cited as examples—Mehboob Khan's *Andaz* (1949) and Raj Kapoor's *Awaara* (1951)—feature enormously wealthy fathers but both films conclude on a tragic note with the 'heirs' also being handed prison sentences. Neither film concludes with the affirmation of a 'feudal order'[24] as one would expect from conjectures. The motifs familiar to us from the typical films of the same period are those of the legal profession (*Aag*, 1948; *Mahal*, 1949), orphans (*Anokhi Ada*, 1948; *Dastaan*, 1950), and shadowy criminals (*Baazi*, 1951; *Jaal*, 1952). It will take some effort to detect 'feudal' motifs in many of these films and a factor is the absence of a landowning class.[25] The protagonists of the Hindi films of the 1940s and 1950s, when they own land, usually till it themselves. While it must be acknowledged that wealth in these early films is usually inherited, the protagonists are wealthy only in some films and, even here, the wealthy live in cities. While acolytes are characters in many of these films, there may be other explanations for them. The rich protagonist's dealings with his acolyte friend in *Andaz* may appear like an endorsement of 'feudal' relationships but it owes more directly to Sanskrit dramatics with its reliance on the *vidhushaka* or clown. Still, a key aspect of Hindi cinema which might make it appear 'feudal' is that binding relationships are centred on familial associations (and genealogy) and rarely on work. Even in avowedly Marxist works like *Dharti Ke Lal* (1946), there is little sense to be found of workers coming together through labour and the family is the essential binding force. Still, one wonders whether applying the epithet 'feudal' bestows any kind of helpful understanding upon a rapidly transforming society. The thrust of this enquiry will therefore be towards identifying the actual political decisions, happenings, and processes which readings of cinema suggest to be the determining factors in social transformation.

Allegory of the Nation

A more helpful understanding of mainstream Hindi cinema's political role after 1947 can perhaps be arrived at through an older study[26] which is generally not cited by film scholars today. A study of audience reactions to Hindi cinema testing several independent hypotheses on popular cinema's social role concluded that it was largely an instrument of 'cultural continuity'. Hindi films apparently stabilize the social system by representing new needs and mythologizing 'tradition'. New needs are historically created and an 'instrument of cultural continuity' needs to bridge the gap between the expectations created by traditional belief and the actual dispensations of history. Popular film narrative problematizes the experience of history in a language familiar to tradition and then provides fictional resolutions. This implies, as one might expect, that it is the immediate expectations of the present which are the key to what is problematized. As an instance, the economic liberalization of 1991–2 aroused apprehensions in the public about how the moral fabric of the nation might be affected with the end of Nehruvian socialism and non-interventionism by the state. A key film of the period, *Baazigar* (1993), responded by portraying the struggle between two families for the control of a business empire as a fight to the death between the scion of one family and the patriarch of the other, with the police hesitating to intervene. As argued elsewhere[27] the amorality of the anti-hero of this film was engendered by the distance of the moral state, and his amorality shows itself in the way he takes advantage of and betrays a defenceless woman. At the basic level, therefore, it would seem that popular cinema proceeds by allegorizing the historical circumstances of the present in the language of familiar myth.[28] This finds agreement in Frederic Jameson's well-known contention that 'Third World' texts should be read as national allegories although Jameson approaches the issue from another perspective.[29]

A principal way in which the Nation is inscribed in Hindi cinema after 1947 is by allegorizing it as a community. In *Mother India* (1957), the community is the village and in *Hum Aapke Hain Koun...!* (*HAHK*, 1994), Kailash Nath's family gatherings represent the community. In *Border* (1998) the community is a battalion in the military, while in *Lagaan* (2002), it is the cricket team. In each of these films the community is constituted to include religious minorities, different castes, and social classes. The community, like the Nation, commands loyalty and betraying it or its creed merits punishment.[30] This sanctity accorded to the community means that it has a greater significance than suggested by its physical constitution. To elaborate, the village in *Mother India* is not merely an Indian village just as the cricket team in *Lagaan* is not merely a village cricket team. The community as the Nation in microcosm also means that the deepest conflict in the narrative is arranged within and not caused by agencies external to it. The character(s) at the moral centre of the narrative as well as those creating discord are therefore part of the community—as in *Mother India*, *HAHK*, and *Lagaan*. While the community is a convenient way of representing the Nation, the narrative may also invoke it explicitly and without resorting to allegory. *Upkaar* (1967), for instance, not only allegorizes India and Pakistan as estranged brothers and Partition as the division of their ancestral land but also introduces the military, war, and the defence of the Nation as motifs. The 'community' is only one way in which the Nation may be inscribed because there is a more fundamental motif—an issue brought into crisis by Hindi melodramas after 1947 which is 'loyalty'.

Melodrama and the Nation

It is generally accepted that melodrama is the form chosen by popular cinema to emphasize its concerns but the relationship between Hindi cinema's ideological side and melodrama is still uncertain. The tendency among Indian film theorists is to rely on Western theories of melodrama to explain Indian popular cinema.[31] The key underlying work here is perhaps by Peter Brooks, who traced it to the aftermath of the French Revolution when the traditional sacred (Church and Monarch) lost their centrality.[32] The 'moral occult' within melodrama, that is, the metaphysical system that rewards and punishes, is considered a corollary to the democratization of society (the Republic becoming the agent of morality instead of the King and the Church) and this gives melodrama special value. While Indian film theorists appear, generally, to be in agreement about melodrama being a consequence of the democratization of society, they decline to explain how a narrative form regarded as a repository of 'feudal' values is also a vehicle for the 'democratization of society'.[33]

Not only is there no evidence that Indian film melodrama owes in any way to European history, but it is also very different from standard Western melodramas in which the spectator is brought to a state of recognition.[34] Western melodrama allows for point of view and the spectator is encouraged to follow the same emotional trajectory that a focal character might have taken. In Douglas Sirk's *All That Heaven Allows* (1955), for instance, we are gradually led to the same recognitions that the woman played by Jane Wyman makes. The narrative follows the dictum that melodrama finds the way to introduce the unexpected into the action, violating the course of events as grasped by the spectator and turning it in new unforeseen directions[35] and it is the unexpected element that makes us take the same trajectory. In contrast, Indian film narrative chooses the omniscient eye.[36] This means that when gaps of knowledge are created, they are only for the characters, the audience being privileged with complete information at every juncture. Instead of forcing recognitions, consequently, the Indian film melodrama chooses to affirm truths which are familiar. The affirmation of familiar truths introduces a sententious element into Indian popular cinema and the sentiments expressed usually have the sanction of tradition. This means that it has no capability to be other than socially conservative[37] although, as I shall show, it has sometimes found the means to get out of this bind through adroitness.

It can also be argued that since many traditional tales like that of 'Raja Harishchandra' preceded Western melodrama, the stories exhibiting some of Western melodrama's features is not due to any Western influence.[38] In 'melodramas' like *Raja Harishchandra* (1913) the protagonists are not endowed with agency and the gods themselves intervene to set matters right. Hindi films like *HAHK* often rely on divine intervention in a comparable way.

The 'social' (or the domestic) melodrama originated in the colonial period and post-Independence melodrama may be understood as a continuation of the social melodramas of the earlier period but there are nonetheless key differences. Some of the differences in the films after 1947 noted by scholars pertain to the tone of the films, especially a new viscerality not in evidence earlier[39] but there are significant narrational contrasts as well, and these will be more helpful in my investigation. A key difference between the 'reformist' films of the 1930s and early 1940s and their counterparts around 1947 (and after) is that the melodrama in the later cinema is of a much more heightened kind. There is apparently a greater degree of 'moral polarization' in films like *Anmol Ghadi* (1946) and *Awaara* inasmuch as the film places an object of immense love/veneration at its centre (the mother) and gets heightened effects entirely through this placement. Indian popular cinema never took an ambivalent position with regard to right and wrong (which find correspondence in 'good' and 'bad') but in *Anmol Ghadi*, we also see an individual denoted as 'good' conducting himself in a way judged as 'wrong' and this seems to be without precedent. My own understanding is that 'wrong' conduct is towards a new entity introduced into the narrative, and the subsequent redefining of the moral framework to admit a reference to this entity. The new entity demanding loyalty in *Anmol Ghadi* is the mother and an association can be made between the figure of the mother and the future Nation.[40] The idea of the Nation therefore plays a part in redefining the moral framework within film narrative around 1947.

A new moral issue, namely 'loyalty' comes into evidence with Independence and it is usually possible to read the involvement of the Nation into melodramas whenever loyalty is the central issue—whether to a community or a relationship. It is the issue of 'loyalty' which implicates the Nation or an affiliated notion (like the land, the state, or even tradition) morally and helps inscribe the Nation in any popular Hindi film after 1947.[41] This argument ties in with the earlier proposition that popular films are allegories of the Nation: 'loyalty' towards persons or groups is prescribed when they mean more than themselves, that is, they represent an allegorized entity.

But the inscription of the Nation does not mean that the Nation is a constant in cinema. It waxes and wanes depending partly on the exigencies of the historical moment. In the years after the disastrous Sino-Indian War of 1962, for instance, the Nation is weakest in cinema. Loyalty is still an issue in a film like *Mere Mehboob* (1963) but not the central one. Much of this book engages with the weakening of loyalty as a notion in the cinema of the new millennium.

An examination of some of the most celebrated Hindi melodramas after 1947—films like *Andaz, Awaara, Mother India, Sangam* (1964), *Deewaar* (1975), and *HAHK*—reveals that loyalty is the issue which comes under test each time although the apparent object of loyalty varies. A narrative ploy is a sacrifice of some sort in which a course of action is taken as a way of affirming a loyalty. In *Mother India* and *Deewaar*, for instance, the mother sacrifices her son when he becomes a threat to the community. In *Sangam*, a man kills himself because his relationship with his childhood friend demands it. The factor significant here is that the sentiment of loyalty in each of these films is a 'universal'. To elaborate, it is a sentiment which does not address a single class or segment but an undifferentiated audience. *HAHK* may be dealing with an affluent class but when the protagonists agree to marry against their personal choices and in accordance with the wishes of their families, they affirm that the joint family is a transcendental object of loyalty and this sentiment is familiar enough to be a 'universal' among Hindi film audiences. There is, for instance, never a case in which a merchant is loyal to his business partner because of an agreement, since this would specify a class. The allegorical side of Hindi film melodrama coupled with the 'universality' of the loyalties it affirmed, it can be argued, made the Nation—that Hindi cinema helped to imagine—a largely inclusive one and this is true of Hindi cinema until the early years of the new millennium.

'Loyalty' as a virtue in Indian film narrative does not always imply the Nation because the notion finds a place in regional language cinema which, because it addresses local identities, is not a pan-national cinema. The 'community' in regional language cinema is therefore not the Indian Nation but a smaller one circumscribed by people who speak the same language. As an instance of how loyalty appears in regional cinema, Kannada cinema originally addressed audiences in the erstwhile princely state of Mysore. This being the case, the 'nation' addressed by Kannada cinema in the 1940s was a monarchy in which loyalty to the King was valorized. B. Nagendra Rao's *Harishchandra* (1943), which is a film version of the same tale cited earlier, affirms the loyalty of the Queen and the Prince to the King—they are prepared to bear any distress for his sake since he is their King.[42] In examples from early Kannada cinema, wife and/or child are often 'loyal subjects' of the father and this is not an allegorical representation familiar to us from Hindi cinema.

While the 'affirmative' aspects of Hindi cinema—towards the Nation and the state—were traditionally obligatory, there were moments when the state was publicly viewed more ambivalently than at other times and Hindi cinema was able to respond to this ambivalence. *Deewaar*, which carries echoes of *Mother India*, is still very different from the latter in one crucial way. *Mother India* was made in a period of great national optimism,[43] while *Deewaar* came out during the Emergency when Prime Minister Indira Gandhi had armed herself with dictatorial powers and the state was viewed with apprehension. In both *Mother India* and *Deewaar* the male protagonist has a disadvantaged childhood, embarks on an unlawful path as an adult, and in both the films his mother plays a key role in his killing. But important here is that in *Deewaar*, the audience's sympathies are deliberately channelled in another direction when the criminal protagonist upstages both his mother and his lawful brother—even as the film nominally upholds the latter.[44] If the sentiments the film expresses are still familiar, its 'insincerity' now comes to its assistance.

While the poorest people in India may never have constituted the bulk of Hindi film clientele, mainstream Hindi cinema not only helped an undifferentiated mass audience to imagine the Nation but also provided mechanisms by which the state could be interrogated although the underlying sentiment was affirmative. This interrogation sometimes took the shape of the judge being tried or made to answer in court as in *Awaara* and *Dhool Ka Phool* (1959). With mainstream Hindi cinema becoming Bollywood and the diaspora becoming a key commercial factor, its address has become more asymmetric, and Bollywood is perhaps not even as 'Indian' as Hindi cinema once happened to be.

A Period of Transition

The 1990s represent a period of transition for Hindi cinema because 'Nehruvian socialism' ended with the economic liberalization of 1991–2 and Hindi cinema changed track significantly after that. Nehruvian 'socialism' was, of course, largely rhetoric because it was without a strong redistributive programme and the term 'statist' may be a more appropriate term to describe it.[45] Still, the rhetoric was effective enough to take hold of the popular imagination in such a way that the poor became a moral concern for Hindi cinema after 1947 and lasted until the early 1990s. It took more than two years for Hindi cinema to transform after 1991 but the effects were far-reaching. It has been argued that the following were some of the effects of the economic measures upon Hindi film narrative:[46]

1. Hindi cinema did away with the underprivileged as principal subjects of film narrative and began focusing exclusively on the rich—as in *HAHK*.
2. The economic liberalization was interpreted as the state withdrawing from the public space. Since the state vacated film narrative as a participant, the stories became simpler. Films tried to compensate by focusing on spectacle—ritual as in *HAHK*,

and foreign locations as in *Dilwale Dulhania Le Jayenge* (*DDLJ*, 1995) and *Hero No. 1* (1997).

3. The Nation was represented as an abstraction without the state being implicated in film narrative. Allegories of the Nation flourished as different kinds of communities—a happy family in *HAHK*, a school in *Mohabbatein* (2000), the household of a musician-guru in *Hum Dil De Chuke Sanam* (1999), and a cricket team in *Lagaan*.

4. The state withdrawing from its own institutions led to the police being represented as unfettered by the law—as in *Satya* (1999). Gangland wars became a metaphor for unregulated competition, with the police behaving as private agencies.

5. With there being no possibility of social conflict between classes in film narrative, conflict was pushed to the boundaries of the Nation. This registered as 'patriotism' in films like *Border* (1998) and *Lagaan*.

6. The conclusion of the grand narrative of Nehruvian socialism engendered the symptoms of postmodernism and produced pastiche in the cinema of the 1990s—the inclination of films like *Hero No. 1* and *Rangeela* (1995) to be morally blank instead of sententious like the earlier cinema.

Most of the films of the 1990s continue to be melodramas although *Border* and *Satya* may resist the description. One aspect that distinguishes a melodrama in Indian cinema—from a film which is not—is that a melodrama has a strong closure at the level of the family. This requires the support of many other factors but the notion of loyalty usually imparts this strength. A romantic attachment coming to fruition represents a closure but unless it is strengthened by other factors involving loyalty of some sort, it is not strong enough to render the film a 'melodrama'. Genealogy or community is the issue and not family formation through romance as Hollywood might have it.[47] In *Lagaan* the romance is weak but loyalty to the 'community' is a crucial issue and the same is equally true of *Border*. In *Satya* familial bonding is absent but loyalty to a friend becomes a useful substitute.

Globalization and Hindi Cinema

Even as Hindi cinema was responding to the end of socialism, there were far-reaching developments in the social space because of the growth of new economy businesses—especially the IT sector—and its contribution to the global economy. The following are some of the apparent developments which, this enquiry proposes, impacted upon the shape taken by cinema in the new millennium directly or indirectly:

1. The new economy industries which took root in the 1990s were different inasmuch as their business originated abroad rather than within India. This saw Indian professionals travelling overseas as never before and not as tourists as had once been the case.[48]

2. The wage levels in the new economy companies were comparable to that in the West, while the cost of living remained comparatively low. This meant that the employees in new economy businesses had unprecedented spending power. This led to an explosion in consumption and the proliferation of shopping centres and malls in the cities.

3. Because the new businesses were global, an association was made between wealth and working knowledge of the English language which was the key to employment in new economy businesses. The Anglophone Indian, it gradually meant, was the one with the greatest spending power.

4. The development of India became skewed with the concentration of new economy businesses in the metropolitan cities. The proliferation of multiplexes in the cities—because of the new spending power—saw the price of admission in movie houses going up in the cities but remaining the same outside. Mainstream cinema therefore began to target city audiences.

5. With the globalization of Indian business, the Indian from the metropolises came culturally closer to those in the diaspora— closer, in fact, than he or she was to those in small towns only

a few hundred miles away. Because of this factor the cultural perspective of Bollywood was also increasingly shared by South Asians in the diaspora.

6. With the Indian economy becoming more dependent on private enterprise and the economy booming, the corporate sector began to gain more influence in the running of the state than it had.

7. Where mainstream Hindi cinema had been regarded as a pariah by the Indian state when culture was a key consideration, the commercial success of Bollywood globally gave it immense respectability in the government as a revenue earner—when economics became the only consideration.

In the initial phases, globalization had perhaps the same implications for film audiences that modernity had in the 1950s—as a development with glamour even as it held out a threat to the moral fabric of society. The difference was perhaps that unlike modernity, which impacted upon the public culturally, globalization privileged the urban classes economically. It had such an impact upon their spending power that Hindi cinema soon found itself targeting a much narrower constituency, one which was no longer as widely dispersed as before. The biggest blockbusters today are 'multiplex hits' which means that cinema targets a class which has received the benefits of globalization and cannot regard it as a threat any longer. There is also ample evidence that mainstream Hindi films are increasingly addressing Anglophone Indians.[49] While Hindi cinema dealt increasingly with the rich—who may be expected to speak English—the cinema of the 1990s did not appear to address an Anglophone public. One does not, for instance, get the sense that the affluent people in HAHK are Anglophone but this cannot be said of more recent films, as I hope to demonstrate.

The term 'Anglophone' hardly means what it once did because of the rapid ascendancy of English. It does not represent the 'elite' in the same way that it did a few decades ago. A distinction has today been made between English speakers and English users, which is that users only know how to read English words while speakers know how to read English, understand spoken English as well as form their own sentences to converse in English. It may be surmised that there is an ongoing movement of people from user status to speaker status, especially when speaker status is seen to confer distinct career advantages. The proportion will have subsequently increased but according to the 2001 census around 12 per cent of the population was English-speaking but English users were greater in number. 'Anglophone' Hindi cinema makes only a small linguistic demand upon its audience and it may engage a significant section of English users as well. But the important point is that English helps to distinguish between segments of the populace, between those who are attuned to global trends—if in pursuit of careers—and see English as a vehicle for advancement and those who are still 'traditional'.

Melodrama and Personal Aspiration

A characteristic of recent cinema is the arrival of a new motif—personal aspiration. Since the new motif arrived in the global age, a three-way association can justifiably be made between personal aspiration as a desirable virtue, globalization, and knowledge of the English language. Melodrama may therefore be regarded as a form associated with the pre-global in Indian cinema, and it appears to have lost considerable ground within a very short while. The transformation in the shape taken by Hindi cinema in the two decades 1990–2009 can be roughly grasped through an examination of the top four blockbusters of each decade—determined by the 'adjusted gross earnings'[50]—and rearranged chronologically:

> *Hum Aapke Hain Koun..!* (1994)
> *Dilwale Dulhania Le Jayenge* (1995)
> *Raja Hindustani* (1996)
> *Kuch Kuch Hota Hai* (1998)
> *Kabhi Khushi Kabhie Gham...* (2001)
> *Gadar: Ek Prem Katha* (2001)
> *Ghajini* (2008)
> *3 Idiots* (2009)

INTRODUCTION

All these films are romances but, while the first five are family melodramas and *Gadar* is a patriotic anti-Pakistan film set immediately after Partition, the last two are different. *Ghajini* is an action film inspired by Christopher Nolan's *Memento* (2000) and *3 Idiots* is about three friends in an elite educational institution. Both play up urban affluence but unlike *HAHK* which is also about affluent people, they are neither family- nor community-based as the five earlier films are.[51] In *Ghajini* a rich businessman who has a memory defect wreaks vengeance on the gangster who ruined his life and killed his sweetheart. On unpacking the story, recognizing that the 'psychological thriller' aspect is an add-on and the gangster simply a pretext for the action, the film emerges as a love story about an aspiring model and a fabulously wealthy corporate tycoon. The central figure is the model and the touching aspect is her claiming the distant figure of the tycoon for her boyfriend without knowing that the boy she is seeing is the tycoon incognito. The film provides an affirmation that in the world it is depicting, people can aspire to reach above themselves. If *Ghajini* is about people reaching above their own stations, *3 Idiots* is about students who pursue their aspirations instead of 'succumbing to the rat race'. Both films have weak closures and the reason is that in neither film is loyalty the issue thrown into crisis. Hitherto, individual aspiration had not been a key motif in Hindi cinema because it works against the notion of the community and the family. In the key Amitabh Bachchan films featuring the 'Angry Young Man' in which a disadvantaged person rises to wealth and power—*Deewaar, Trishul* (1978), *Muqaddar Ka Sikandar* (1978), and *Agneepath* (1990), family instability drives the protagonist to advance himself but his advancement is not celebrated. Happy endings involve families coming together and the affirmation of natural loyalties; they were never primarily about personal success until now. The Indian 'growth story' has apparently had consequences for mainstream Hindi film and one of these is the sense of a community being absent.

More broadly speaking, blockbusters like *3 Idiots* and *Ghajini* decline to make loyalty the issue. Friendship prevails in *3 Idiots* but loyalty to it is not brought to crisis as a melodrama might have it; they are not 'morally legible' as mainstream Hindi films were. More importantly perhaps, a new grand narrative of enterprise-driven progress emerges after the brief lull in the 1990s when its 'postmodern' phase ruled Hindi cinema. I shall also try to demonstrate that a key element in the new grand narrative is the endorsement of illegality.

The Hindi film may feel closer to the diaspora today but that does not imply the end of the nation-as-community. Films like *Kal Ho Naa Ho* (2003) and *Kabhi Alvida Naa Kehna* (*KANK*, 2007) dealt exclusively with non-residents and *KANK* did not even invoke India but there was the sense of the absent Nation which gave the communities they dealt with their cohesion. This sense was perhaps created by references to the American state themselves being downplayed or absent as in *KANK*.

If the Hindi films of the last few years no longer evoke an inclusive community, they still engage in frequent nationalist rhetoric, although of a different kind; it is their sense of speaking for an inclusive nation while targeting an exclusive audience that makes them political in an unprecedented way.

The Politics of Bollywood

Although the terms 'ideology' and 'politics' are often used to mean the same thing today, it is the 'ideology' of Hindi cinema which has been widely written about rather than its 'politics'. Broadly speaking, ideology is (according to Marxists) related to the superstructure and is constituted largely by unconscious predispositions owing to economic forces of which it is not fully aware. Friedrich Engels described it as 'a false consciousness'. As an illustration, when a film posits a character as 'feminine' it is not depicting a woman who is already feminine. It is, rather, producing the woman as feminine by endowing her with the traits that are ideologically desirable for an ideal femininity in a specific historically created society.[52] While ideological enquiries, which take a magisterial view of actual political developments, may lead to larger understandings[53] which are less sensitive to immediate developments in the political space, Hindi cinema in the new millennium not only has much to say about the political forces at work but also has an agenda which can be associated with the ascendant classes it is addressing—groups which wield influence in policy matters. It can be argued that the following are some aspects of new Hindi cinema which make it explicitly political rather than only broadly ideological:

1. Hindi cinema is exhibiting concern in social matters, for example, *Peepli (Live)* (2010) on rural indebtedness.
2. It has tried to make itself topical— for instance, in dealing with sports when cricket preoccupies the public, as in *Chak De India* (2007) and *Iqbal* (2005), and businessmen as in *Guru* (2007), which was acknowledged as a fictionalized version of business tycoon Dhirubhai Ambani's life.
3. Cross-border terrorism and political issues involving India and Pakistan are now being dealt with explicitly in blockbusters—as in *Veer-Zaara* (2005) and *Fanaa* (2006) instead of allegorically.
4. They are engaging in sharp criticism of the political classes, especially of corruption, for example, *Rang De Basanti* (2006).
5. Film directors and stars are gaining access to the corridors of power and are sharing platforms on issues. For example, the actor Aamir Khan shared a platform on education with visiting US Secretary of State Hilary Clinton after he made a film about educating a disadvantaged child in *Taare Zameen Par* (2007).[54]
6. Mainstream films now appear to have a discernible cultural impact. The film *Lage Raho Munna Bhai* (2006) was apparently so influential in bringing 'Gandhian values' back into vogue that it was later screened at the UN where it was hugely appreciated.[55]
7. Politics and politicians are becoming the subject matter of mainstream films as in *Raajneeti* (2010). Hindi cinema takes a much clear stand on the political class by having politician protagonists.

8. Economic and business issues are now commonly dealt with in mainstream Hindi cinema—as in *Guru*. This can be of interest only to specific sections of the public but the films invoke the Nation as an inclusive community. One finds evidence here of the interests of sections of the public being portrayed as 'national interest'.

Hindi cinema has traditionally not shown a desire to 'intervene' in political issues and even when social injustice has been its theme, its approach has been passive—political and social issues treated as a given. The vocal tendencies of new cinema have seen it being lauded by the media but the political agenda it furthers is hardly as transparent as it might appear. Since the 'India' addressed by Bollywood is asymmetrically constituted, its social concern, likewise, shows the same asymmetric characteristics although this needs deeper investigation. This book is an enquiry into the asymmetric nation constituted by Hindi cinema and the expectation is that understanding the asymmetry will help us understand some of the alignments in India and the political forces which often masquerade as 'opinion'. Needless to add, Hindi cinema's new tendencies reveal themselves gradually after 2000—with the Anglophone Indian emerging only in *Page 3* (2005) and *Rang De Basanti* and, even then, his or her characteristics not in entirety.

The Tenor of the Book

This book about cinema as socio-political evidence is devised as a collection of essays devoted to individual films (or clusters of films) in the new millennium, which are by and large dealt with chronologically. In order to contextualize the new tendencies, frequent references are made to the older cinema from which new cinema diverges. To keep the arguments simple for those not familiar with the older cinema, the number of older films cited will be restricted to a key handful. Also resorted to are frequent references to world cinema, the rationale not only being that many of the films are remakes of Hollywood films but also that in the new millennium the globalization of entertainment has seen Indian cinema becoming acutely aware of what is happening outside. Anglophone audiences responding to Bollywood are also much more aware of world cinema than Hindi film audiences once were.

The films (or groups of films) selected for examination here have all been influential, although in different ways. Apart from bringing out the transformation of the mainstream Hindi film after it became 'Bollywood', it is hoped that the individual essays will provide fresh insights into political developments in India in the past decade. If, as is being argued, mainstream Hindi cinema has been the utterance of a public constituting the Nation, interpreting the utterances can be enormously helpful in understanding the direction in which the Nation is being driven. Most readers may not have seen the films and in order to make the book of interest to them, and also accessible, there is some narration. Since the book is not theory-down but intended to be 'bottom-up', that is, it draws political conclusions from empirical data available in cinema, it has been necessary to cite contemporary views/reports from outside cinema.

This is an enquiry into the transformation of a 'national cinema' and we must also choose the characteristics to study. The features characterizing a national cinema include the mode of production, distribution and exhibition, narrative content or themes, the genres which dominate the cinema, and the dominant film style.[56] Important work has been done on the mode of production in Hindi cinema[57] but if there is enough reason to believe that it is being transformed, the book will not go into it. Some use of data pertaining to exhibition and reception will be made but only to the extent that it is pertinent to the notion of the asymmetric Nation of the new millennium. As regards Hindi cinema's generic or thematic content, the effort is to look for related political discourses across different kinds of narrative. Lastly, since an effort has been made to make each chapter stand on its own as an independent essay (although reading the chapters in chronological order is recommended), some element of repetition is considered necessary to ensure clarity.

Notes

1. For instance, see Ashish Rajadhyaksha, 'The Cinema Effect I and II', in *Indian Cinema in the Time of Celluloid: From Bollywood to the Emergency* (New Delhi: Tulika, 2009), pp. 84–132.

2. The terms 'film' and 'cinema' are used interchangeably here unless I am referring to a particular film—'film' as opposed to a film.

3. This is derived from the ritual view of media communication (as opposed to the 'bullet transmission model') which conceives communication as a process through which a shared culture is created, modified, and transformed. James W. Carey, *Communication as Culture: Essays on Media and Society* (Winchester, MA: Unwin Hyman, 1989), p. 43. The term 'consumer co-author' is used by Michael R. Real, *Exploring Media Culture: A Guide* (Thousand Oaks: Sage, 1996), pp. 268–9.

4. This also follows from Sudhir Kakar's observations made about Indian cinema: 'The prospect of financial gain, like the opportunity for sexual liaison, does wonderful things for increasing the perception of the needs and desires of those who hold the key to these gratifications … [Film-makers] must intuitively appeal to those concerns of the audience which are shared.' Sudhir Kakar, 'The Ties That Bind: Family Relationships in the Mythology of Hindi Cinema', *India International Centre Quarterly Special Issue*, Vol. 8, No. 1, March 1980, p. 13.

5. See M. Madhava Prasad, *Ideology of the Hindi Film: A Historical Construction* (New Delhi: Oxford University Press, 1999), pp. 50–1. Prasad contrasts the relay of meaning in the Hindi popular film to the 'production of meaning' in classical Hollywood cinema. According to his reading, the production of meaning takes place when the raw material in the form of the narrative is made available to the audience to interpret. Indian popular cinema, in contrast, uses the narrative as a vehicle to relay a pre-existent meaning which corresponds to the 'conceptual meaning' in theoretical terminology. See David Bordwell, *Inference and Rhetoric in the Interpretation of Cinema* (Cambridge, MA: Harvard University Press, 1989), pp. 8–9.

6. Arthur C. Danto, 'Deep Interpretation', in *The Philosophical Disenfranchisement of Art* (New York: Columbia University Press, 1986), pp. 51–3.

7. A difficulty with the theory-down approach is that an instance cannot prove a theory right. Also, one of the basic premises of the theory-down approach is that interpretation should be doctrine-driven, but an instance is only a trivial case which neither proves a theory right nor provides security to the interpretation because theory deals with the norm, while interpretation deals with deviation and anomaly. See Noël Carroll, 'Prospects for Film Theory: A Personal Assessment', in David Bordwell and Noël Carroll (eds), *Post-Theory: Reconstructing Film Studies* (Madison: University of Wisconsin Press, 1996), pp. 42–3.

8. See M.K. Raghavendra, *Seduced by the Familiar: Narration and Meaning in Indian Popular Cinema* (New Delhi: Oxford University Press, 2008), pp. 162–5, 239–40, and 302n29.

9. Data courtesy of National Film Development Corporation of India (NFDC). Cited by John A. Lent, *The Asian Film Industry* (London: Christopher Helm, 1990), p. 52.

10. Federation of Indian Chambers of Commerce and Industry (FICCI), *Indian Entertainment Industry: Envisioning for Tomorrow*, March 2001, prepared by Arthur Andersen.

11. *Om Shanti Om* at the Box Office Mojo International. Reported in Wikipedia, www.boxofficeindia.com (accessed on 14 January 2014).

12. Shahrukh Khan to Derek Malcolm in *Vanity Fair Supplement*, 2002, p. 4 and Subhash Ghai in *Vanity Fair Supplement*, 2002, p. 12.

13. Ravi S. Vasudevan, 'The Meanings of "Bollywood"', *Journal of the Moving Image*, http://www.jmionline.org/jmi7_8.htm (accessed on 21 October 2013). A penetrating account of how Hindi cinema was transformed to Bollywood has been written by Ashish Rajadhyaksha. See Ashish Rajadhyaksha, 'The "Bollywoodization" of Indian Cinema: Cultural Nationalism in a Global Arena', *Inter-Asia Cultural Studies*, Vol. 4, No. I, April 2003, pp. 26–39.

14. Just as consumers in some parts of the world might become hostile to Coca-Cola if reminded that it was 'American'.

15. As has been noted, the 'story' was traditionally crucial in Hindi cinema to producers, directors, distributors, and audiences alike. See Ashish Rajadhyaksha, 'Viewership and Democracy in the Cinema', in Ravi S. Vasudevan (ed.), *Making Meaning in Indian Cinema* (New Delhi: Oxford University Press, 2000), p. 276.

16. *Screen*, 3 May 2002, www.screenindia.com/archive.

17. ·For a detailed account, see Roy Arnes, *Third World Film-making and the West* (Berkeley, CA: University of California Press, 1987), pp. 55–7.

18. Ibid., p. 57.

19. For instance, see Sumita S. Chakravarty, *National Identity in Indian Popular Cinema, 1947–1987* (New Delhi: Oxford University Press, 1998) and Prasad, *Ideology of the Hindi Film*.

20. See Lothar Lutze, 'Interview with Raj Khosla', in Lothar Lutze and Beatrix Pfleiderer (eds), *The Hindi Film: Agent and Re-agent of Cultural Change* (Delhi: Manohar, 1985), p. 39. '[The Hindi film] is bringing easy-speaking Hindi and not the difficult Hindi of Doordarshan and Radio ... [to the spectator]. This is a Hindi that anybody can understand. If they can't understand five sentences completely, one sentence, even one word will tell them—yes, this is what he means—the facial expressions along with the words.' Chidananda Das Gupta also has the term 'All-India Film' for mass-produced post–World War II Hindi cinema, which was often duplicated by the regional cinemas.

21. Chakravarty, *National Identity in Indian Popular Cinema*, p. 99.

22. Prasad, *Ideology of the Hindi Film*, p. 33. Hindi cinema was eliminated from the Hindi public sphere; see Francesca Orsini, *The Hindi Public Sphere, 1920–1940: Language and Literature in the Age of Nationalism* (New Delhi: Oxford University Press, 2002). Instead of cinema, the state used radio through Akashvani to construct Hindi language nationalism. See David Lelyveld, 'Talking the National Language: Hindi/Urdu/Hindustani in Indian Broadcasting and Cinema', in Sujata Patel, Jasodhara Bagchi, and Krishna Raj (eds), *Thinking Social Science in India: Essays in Honour of Alice Thorner* (New Delhi: Sage, 2002), pp. 355–66.

23. Prasad, *Ideology of the Hindi Film*, p. 30. Prasad quotes Michael McKeon, *The Origins of the English Novel (1600–1740)* (Baltimore: Johns Hopkins University Press, 1987).

24. Prasad puts in a disclaimer that the feudal family romance 'should not be thought of as being necessarily and completely a bearer of feudal values, even though the overall narrative derives from romances of the feudal era.' Prasad, *Ideology of the Hindi Film*, p. 31. Given this disclaimer, one wonders at the usefulness of the term 'feudal' in the term 'feudal family romance'.

25. The notion of the landowning zamindar seems more popular in south Indian—especially Telugu—cinema. When Hindi films are remade

versions of south Indian films, these 'feudal' figures make their entrance into Hindi cinema. As instances, one could cite Bapu's *Hum Paanch* (1980) which was a remake of a Kannada film and Siddique's *Bodyguard* (2011), which was originally made in Malayalam and then in Tamil.

26. Beatrix Pfleiderer, 'An Empirical Study of Urban and Semi-urban Audience Reactions to Hindi Film', in Lothar Lutze and Beatrix Pfleiderer (eds) *The Hindi Film: Agent and Re-agent of Cultural Change* (New Delhi: Manohar, 1985), p. 89.

27. Raghavendra, *Seduced by the Familiar*, pp. 242–5, 280–1.

28. Ibid., pp. 35–6.

29. Frederic Jameson, 'World Literature in the Age of Multinational Capitalism', in Clayton Koelb and Virgil Lokke (eds), *The Current in Criticism: Essays on the Present and Future in Literary Theory* (West Lafayette, Ind.: Purdue University Press, 1987).

30. It has been noted that groups—even much smaller ones—with common political interests tend to allegorize themselves as families and/or give themselves the moral attributes of a community. See Partha Chatterjee, *The Politics of the Governed: Reflections on Popular Politics in Most of the World* (New York: Columbia University Press, 2004), p. 57.

31. A key work here is Ravi S. Vasudevan, 'Shifting Codes, Dissolving Identities: The Hindi Social Film of the 1950s as Popular Culture', in Ravi S. Vasudevan (ed.), *Making Meaning in Indian Cinema* (New Delhi: Oxford University Press, 2000), pp. 99–121.

32. Peter Brooks, *The Melodramatic Imagination: Balzac, Henry James, Melodrama, and the Mode of Excess* (New York: Columbia University Press, 1985), p. 15.

33. There seems to be an acknowledgement of the difficulty in applying the term 'feudal' in relation to melodrama in other academic enquiries. See Ravi S. Vasudevan, *The Melodramatic Public: Film Form and Spectatorship in Indian Cinema* (Ranikhet: Permanent Black, 2010), pp. 48–9.

34. Ravi S. Vasudevan, 'The Melodramatic Mode and Commercial Hindi Cinema', *Screen*, vol. 30, no. 3, 1989, pp. 29–50.

35. Russian formalist Sergei Balukhatyi's observations as summarized by Daniel Gerould, 'Russian Formalist Theories of Melodrama', *Journal of American Culture*, No. 1, 1978, p. 158.

36. Raghavendra, *Seduced by the Familiar*, pp. 51–5.

37. If affirming the familiar (sentiments sanctioned by tradition) is tantamount to being conservative, belying expectations could have a contrary effect. An expectation that a Hollywood film might belie is the privileging of family values. Another ruse could be the reworking of genre convention as in Robert Altman's films. This should, however, not be taken to mean that belying narrative expectations would itself be radical.

38. Another difficulty with linking Indian popular cinema's methods to Western models arises out of similarities between Indian and Western texts having been noticed earlier outside cinema. Sanskrit drama is seen to resemble some of the works of Elizabethan playwrights. Common to both are plot contrivances like the writing of letters, the introduction of the play within the play, and the restoration of the dead to life. Often cited are the similar devices in Shakespeare's *Romeo and Juliet* and Bhavabhuti's play *Malati-Madhava*, although the latter has a happy ending. These affinities are cited as instances of how similar devices are often invented independently. Arthur A. Macdonell, *A History of Sanskrit Literature* (New Delhi: Munshiram Manoharlal, 1958), pp. 352–3.

39. Chakravarty, *National Identity in Indian Popular Cinema*, p. 99.

40. Raghavendra, *Seduced by the Familiar*, pp. 98–9.

41. As evidence, *Aurat* (1940) was remade as *Mother India* in 1957. In the former film, the husband is wayward and deserts his wife Radha, the heroine. In the second one as well, he deserts his wife but this time it is because he has been crippled and does not want to become a burden. The village moneylender makes sexual advances to Radha in both films but where, in *Aurat*, she is saved by a storm, she thrashes him soundly in *Mother India* because she is made strong by her loyalty to her husband. In *Mother India*, the heroine gains the strength of a goddess partly because of her loyalty to her living husband. See Gayatri Chatterjee, *Mother India* (New Delhi: Penguin, 2002), p. 48. Also see Vijay Mishra, 'The Texts of *Mother India*', in *Bollywood Cinema: Temples of Desire* (London: Routledge, 2002) pp. 70–80.

42. See M.K. Raghavendra, *Bipolar Identity: Region, Nation and the Kannada Language Film* (New Delhi: Oxford University Press, 2011), p. xxvi. When the story is told by a Hindi film, the emphasis changes accordingly. The emphasis in V. Shantaram's *Ayodhya Ka Raja* (1932), which is based on the same story, is more on the king's nobility and the

poverty that he willingly suffers for the sake of dharma rather than on the conduct of his queen and prince.

43. This is not to deny that there was agrarian unrest in this period, which *Mother India* also addresses.

44. Raghavendra, *Seduced by the Familiar*, pp. 195–6.

45. Sudipta Kaviraj, *The Trajectories of the Indian State: Politics and Ideas* (Ranikhet: Permanent Black, 2010), p. 73.

46. Raghavendra, *Seduced by the Familiar*, pp. 236–81.

47. In mainstream Hollywood cinema, love of family, love of father/ruler, and love of country are intertwined concepts and the family also provides a legitimizing metaphor for hierarchical society—father as the head, mother as subservient, and children as totally dependent. Romantic love and the institution of the family are also logically linked, and lovers are transformed into fathers and mothers and the romance necessarily terminates in the founding of the family. See Sylvia Harvey, 'Woman's Place: The Absent Family of Film Noir', in E. Ann Kaplan (ed.), *Women in Film Noir* (London: British Film Institute, 1980), pp. 22–34.

48. Industry data shows an increase of 26 per cent in Indians going abroad in 1993 over 1992, around 16 per cent per annum from 2004 onwards. See *The Indian Outbound Travel Market with Special Insight into Europe as a Destination* (Madrid: World Tourism Organization, 2009), p. 21.

49. A NASSCOM–McKinsey study in 2005 predicted that leisure-spending would be largely driven by the IT-enabled industry. Derek Bose, *Brand Bollywood: A New Global Entertainment Order* (New Delhi: Sage, 2006), p. 16.

50. From www.boxofficeindia.com (accessed on 22 June 2011).

51. *3 Idiots* is set in a college but it is about competition among the students for individual advancement. The three friends are laudable for wanting to do their own things and not for sharing a common purpose. Their loyalty to each other is not especially tested.

52. Mas'ud Zavarzadeh, *Seeing Films Politically* (Albany: SUNY Press, 1991), p. 93.

53. An instance would be to prefer to attend to the ground of history 'conceived in its vastest sense of the sequences of modes of production and the succession and destinies of various human social formations'

rather than in political history and the actual turnover of events. See Prasad, *Ideology of the Hindi Film*, pp. 147–8.

54. See 'Hilary Heaps Praise on Aamir for His Education Campaign', *The Indian Express*, 18 July 2009, http://www.indianexpress.com/news/hillary-heaps-praise-on-aamir-for-his-education-campaign/491123/ (accessed on 6 October 2011).

55. See 'UN All Praise for *Lage Raho Munna Bhai*', *The Times of India*, 11 November 2006, http://articles.timesofindia.indiatimes.com/2006-11-11/us/27786612_1_mahatma-gandhi-satyagraha-vinod-chopra (accessed on 6 October 2011).

56. Jinhee Choi, 'National Cinema: The Very Idea', in Noël Carroll and Jinhee Choi (eds), *Philosophy of Film and Motion Pictures* (Oxford: Blackwell, 2006), p. 316.

57. Prasad, *Ideology of the Hindi Film*, pp. 47–50.

1

The Global and the Pre-modern
Raaz (2002)

The Hindi 'B' Movie

This chapter focuses on the Hindi horror film, the genre which is part of a larger category roughly corresponding to 'B' cinema which includes cheap action films and mythological films like *Jai Santoshi Maa* (1975). But the term 'B film' cannot perhaps be applied in its original sense to Indian cinema where there have never been exhibitions of double features. A 'B film' was originally a low-budget commercial movie that was not an art-house or pornographic film. In its original usage, the term identified a film intended for distribution as the less publicized, bottom half of a double feature.[1] Since, in the Indian context, payment to stars constitutes a significant portion of a film's budget,[2] a 'B' movie is specifically a film with little-known stars. If one were to examine the origins of low-budget 'B' cinema, the career of the actor-wrestler Dara Singh——rather than horror cinema—would be a good starting point. Dara Singh emerged as a star around 1962–3 with the first film in which he acted and not merely wrestled being Babubhai Mistry's *King Kong* (1962). If the association between Dara Singh and the rise of 'B' cinema is conceded, the most useful speculation about their rise attributes it to the economic conditions of film production at the time.[3] According to this hypothesis, there were several reasons for the rise of 'B' cinema. Firstly, there was a sharp rise in film production costs in the 1960s and a chronic paucity of cinema halls. This meant that exhibitors began to make demands for higher rentals. Apparently, film production hit a record low in the early 1960s. There was also a rise in occasional film producers who had never produced films before. Between 1963 and 1965, the contribution of 'occasional' film producers to the number of films produced increased from 46 per cent to 58 per cent.[4] Whereas a mainstream film costs around Rs 7 million, a low budget film could be made for 10 per cent of the amount.[5] Secondly, while Hollywood had provided the main source of imported cinema, the 1960s saw the advent of low-budget European–American co-productions largely from Italy and Japan. Thirdly, by the 1960s the small-scale industrial sector—because of cheap labour—became more profitable than the large-scale sector. This may have led to the emergence of a suburban working population away from the cities in which cinema halls were concentrated. This may have been the time when 'tent' cinemas began to be set up in the suburbs to screen the cheaper films. To these reasons, I would add another because the 'B' films starring Dara Singh are thematically different from mainstream cinema. Apart from *King Kong* being about a wrestler in an imaginary kingdom ruled over by a wicked king, *Rustom-e-Rome* (1964) is about a war between Rome and Babylon in which the Kingdom of Jhama—because it lies between the two states—is accidentally caught. These films bear no resemblance to mainstream cinema of the 1960s in terms of their themes. Since there is no reason why small producers should not have also dealt with the familiar themes of the early 1960s, I propose that the future of the modernist themes of mainstream cinema was clouded in doubt at the time and 'B' films were able to drift back to the pre-modern. India was defeated in the Sino-Indian War in October 1962 and it has been separately demonstrated that mainstream Hindi cinema took a different course after 1962.[6] By and large, the Nation is not inscribed in 'B' cinema because it addresses only target audiences in specific areas and is not pan-national. This may explain how a Dara

Singh film could be set in Rome rather than in an Indian kingdom—as a later-day mainstream film like *Dharam Veer* (1977), which draws its theme from 'B' cinema, does. The proposition offered here is that military defeat also facilitated 'B' cinema in the mid-1960s because the imagined Nation was weakest in the public consciousness immediately after 1962.

The thematic differences between mainstream cinema and 'B' cinema which arose around 1962–3 may have continued when 'B' cinema was found to be viable. A hypothesis explaining its proliferation is that 'B' cinema provided evidence that India could accommodate a Hindi cinema which was not national but addressed only small semi-urban and urban pockets. The precise origins of the Hindi horror film are difficult to locate but mainstream hits such as *Mahal* (1949) and *Bees Saal Baad* (1962), being-nominally ghost stories, could have provided some inspiration for the later films. Still, these two films are not 'fantastic' like the typical horror film; they are better characterized as 'uncanny'.

In defining 'fantasy', Tsvetan Todorov concentrates on the response generated by the 'fantastic' events in the story. In this light, the fantastic must be considered not just one mode but three: 'fantastic', 'uncanny', and 'marvellous'. 'Fantasy' creates a situation in which the reader/audience experiences feelings of hesitation and awe provoked by strange, improbable events. If the implausibility of the events can be explained rationally or psychologically (for example, as a dream or hallucination), then the term 'uncanny' is applied instead of 'fantastic'. In the film series *The Lord of the Rings* (2001–3) and/or the Indian mythological film in which an alternative world or reality is created, the term 'marvellous' is considered most appropriate to describe the work.[7] 'Fantasy' is an epithet applicable to later horror films like those by the Ramsay brothers and not to *Mahal*. If the career of Ramsay brothers is an indication of the trajectory of Hindi horror cinema, the genre may have commenced with *Do Gaz Zameen Ke Neechey* (1972). Horror cinema as represented by their films is generally regarded as catering to small towns and rural India[8] which suggests that it is less national than the mainstream Hindi film.

The Hindi Film and 'Fantasy'

Mainstream Hindi cinema, as will be frequently emphasized in this book, has played the part of a national cinema. As indicated earlier, there are various ways in which the Nation is allegorized in film narrative and an issue particularly brought into crisis by Hindi melodramas after 1947 is that of 'loyalty'. The mainstream Hindi film also asserts that 'loyalty' and 'love' are different emotions and the loved one is, therefore, rarely made an object of loyalty. What happens, usually, is that love comes into conflict with loyalty and loyalty prevails although usually it is resolved that the two emotions need not be in conflict. In a film of the 1960s involving adultery, *Gumrah* (1963), the unfaithful wife returns to her husband out of loyalty, but she married—her widowed brother-in-law—not out of love but because her dead sister's children might be ill-treated by a stepmother; here, it is not the nuclear family which is being valorized. This aspect of the mainstream Hindi film will become important in the context of *Raaz*.

A key characteristic of the Nation in the mainstream Hindi film is that it is 'modern'. If the films after 1947 are frequently set in the city, the city is also an emblem of Nehruvian modernity.[9] The city is not always the chosen locale and there are other motifs associated with modernity. When the farmer is the key motif, modernity can be represented by dams (as in *Mother India*, 1957) or by mechanized farming (as in *Upkar*, 1967). In the later films, doctors, colleges, and industry can also serve as useful emblems of modernity. The Hindi mainstream film was once labelled 'fantasy' but what is important here is that occult elements (for example, 'magic' and rituals associated with it) rarely feature in it. As Ashis Nandy has convincingly argued,[10] the reform movements of the nineteenth and early twentieth centuries consciously tried to remake India in the image of the colonizers and this explains why the mainstream film—since it addresses the postcolonial Nation—eschews the magical elements in which tradition had once been rich. Even mythology was rejected by the mainstream films in their mature years and the kind of mythological films favoured were the 'saint' film (for example, *Sant Tukaram*, 1936) in which the issue addressed was social reform (an offshoot of modernity) rather than the gods and demons of the Puranas. Devotion followed by divine intervention is allowed[11]—as is reincarnation—but these are cornerstones of Hindu belief and are not 'fantastic' just as the miraculous power of faith as in *Ben-Hur* (1959) cannot be termed 'fantastic' when the cinema is from Hollywood. If 'fantasy' still flourishes in regional popular cinema, it is because regional cinema is not 'national' and primarily addresses local identities. The 'B' film, because it includes magical elements in a 'pre-modern' way, lies outside the mainstream and has not addressed the Nation. It is different from mainstream Hindi films like *Mahal* and *Bees Saal Baad*, in which rational explanations are eventually provided for supposedly supernatural occurrences.

Raaz and Its Popularity

The following table compares the all-India collections of *Raaz*— duly adjusted for inflation—with those of other films: two 'B' films of which one is a celebrated horror film from the Ramsay brothers stable and the other is a 'B' movie directed by Vikram Bhatt who also directed *Raaz*. The third (*Devdas*) was the highest-grossing mainstream film of 2002:[12]

Comparative collections of *Raaz*

	Budget (Rs in crore)	Adjusted gross (Rs in crore)
Raaz (2002) (Director: Vikram Bhatt)	4	97.73
Purana Mandir (1984) (Director: Ramsay Brothers)	NA	70.02
Kasoor (2001) (Director: Vikram Bhatt)	5	20.72
Devdas (2002) (Director: Sanjay Leela Bhansali)	50	155.45

From the data provided in the table it is apparent that the box-office receipts of *Raaz* were substantially more than that of celebrated 'B' films with the approximately the same budget and, as a return on investment, many times higher than that of the highest grosser of the same year, that is, 2002, and Vikram Bhatt's earlier 'B' film success. The issue to be examined here is that if a 'B' film, given its low budget, makes nearly as much money as a mainstream film, could there not be something 'mainstream' in its concerns? An examination of *Raaz* will now be appropriate.

The film starts with a group of college students having a picnic in Ooty. One of the girls dies after being attacked under mysterious circumstances outside a bungalow near a forest. It is revealed that she acted as if possessed and attacked her boyfriend before dying. Professor Agni Swaroop, who is an expert in spiritual and paranormal phenomena, is called in and he declares that the girl was killed by an evil spirit which was unwittingly awakened by her.

After the titles, the story turns to Sanjana (Bipasha Basu) and Aditya Dhanraj (Dino Morea) in Mumbai in a business gathering with some overseas partners, where Aditya is too busy to attend to his wife. On her frantic drive home, she hears a voice calling her from within the car and she loses control of the vehicle. After her recovery, Aditya suggests a vacation to work out their problems. He is in the hospitality business and offers Sanjana a trip to any corner of the world but Sanjana chooses Ooty (where their relationship began) to save their failing marriage. In Ooty they stay in the same bungalow in the forest near which the girl was attacked and, soon, Sanjana starts experiencing mysterious, unexplainable happenings. Professor Swaroop is duly called in and his diagnosis is that an evil spirit is present in the house. The two also recover a revolver in the forest which is traced to a military man named Colonel Malik—and it turns out that the firearm was last seen in the possession of the Colonel's deranged daughter Malini who has since then been missing.

In the last part of *Raaz*, Aditya returns to Bombay to meet a delegation from Hong Kong and Sanjana is left alone in Ooty. The evil spirit begins to torment her and it is only after Aditya's return that the truth emerges. During his last visit Aditya was accosted by Malini who took shelter from the rain in their cottage and there she had seduced him. Malini became possessive and, when Aditya asserted that it was his wife Sanjana whom he loved, she took her own life with the pistol. Aditya had buried the corpse in the forest with the help of his servant Robert and thrown the pistol away. Sanjana is deeply hurt by Aditya's admission of infidelity but Professor Swaroop persuades her that unless she acts to save her husband, Malini will try to kill Aditya in order to have him for herself. To cut a long story short, Aditya is injured and is fighting for survival but Sanjana manages to locate Malini's corpse and burn it although Malini's spirit kills Professor Swaroop. Sanjana and Aditya are finally reunited after she is convinced of his love for her.

By and large, most Indian horror films, including those from the Ramsays, place the origins of the monster or ghost in the hoary past but *Raaz* is an exception because the spirit is of a person recently dead. Secondly, there is an attempt to bring the ghost into a global world in which delegations from Hong Kong need attending to. This becomes routine in later cinema—in which people move across the globe and work in places like Singapore or Capetown—but *Raaz* appeared when this had not yet become commonplace. The protagonists of *Raaz* are affluent and have holiday cottages and may be taken to speaking English fluently but, unlike later Hindi films in which people begin speaking in English at the smallest opportunity, they only speak Hindi. In the party sequence involving the overseas clients, for instance, we only see Aditya from a distance and do not hear him speaking a language which can only be English. Sanjana's ire with Aditya for not speaking to her at the party perhaps also carries a hint of the language he is required to employ. This suggests that *Raaz* is not addressing Anglophone audiences as many mainstream Hindi films later do but is targeted at traditional Hindi speakers who might even be uncomfortable with English.[13] The motif of adultery is also significant here because until a year or two after *Raaz*, the issue did not gain currency in Hindi cinema and it can even be argued that it is Aditya's dealings with global business which leave him susceptible to seduction.

But if Aditya is 'sophisticated' because of his overseas dealings, so is Professor Swaroop[14] because of his traditional learning and his library of books. What *Raaz* appears to be doing, therefore, is to suggest the moral implications of globalization which might open Indian men to temptation but also reassure the audience by referring to traditional 'spiritual knowledge' which might offer solutions when situations get out of hand in this way.

I have, earlier in this chapter, invoked the issue of loyalty and observed that 'love' and 'loyalty' are different emotions and directed towards different objects. *Raaz*, to my knowledge, is one of the few Hindi films in which the objects coincide. Loyalty is rarely made an issue in the 'B' film which is why I do not believe that it is 'national' in the manner of the mainstream film and a clue is to be found in the fact that rather than valorizing tradition or the past, it uses aspects of the past to induce horror.[15] This is also accentuated by the special characteristics of the 'B' film actor who has a more ambivalent presence, a factor which needs explanation.

Most Hindi 'B' movies are horror films or cheap thrillers and need to draw suspense out of their narratives, which is not an easy task since Indian popular cinema has traditionally been indifferent to suspense and surprise; what is sought is the essaying of the familiar in its various forms,[16] with melodrama therefore being favoured.[17] Instead of devising a suitable plot structure to conceal the story till the very end,[18] Hindi suspense films rely on withholding one or two key items of information and/or using actors with ambivalent presences—men and women whose countenances do not spell out goodness and innocence. This ambivalence is accentuated when protagonists later shown to have murderous or criminal intent sing songs— when singing announces innocence in the mainstream film. *Raaz* is a horror film but it reverses many of these devices. The film is an adaptation of Robert Zemeckis' *What Lies Beneath* (2000), where the husband is trying to kill the wife, but *Raaz* affirms the wife's constancy when only that will save her husband.[19]

It is significant that the mainstream actors have been allowed to exhibit ambivalent presences only at key moments in Hindi film history and two performances relevant here are those of Dev Anand in Guru Dutt's *Jaal* (1952) and Shahrukh Khan in Abbas–Mustaan's *Baazigar* (1993). The male protagonists in both films act in a dastardly way towards innocent women with the one in *Baazigar* even killing the girl he is due to marry. As argued elsewhere,[20] the ambivalence of these 'anti-heroes' is devised to problematize persisting worries in the public consciousness—about the moral consequences of Nehruvian modernity in *Jaal* and about the likely effects of economic liberalization and the abandonment of Nehruvian socialism upon the nation's moral fabric in *Baazigar*. It is significant that *Raaz* stands at another key moment in Indian economic/social history—the advent of globalization. Aditya's loyalty to Sanjana and her commitment to save him could allegorize global India and tradition's refusal to drift apart. Unlike most 'B' movies, the Nation is apparently inscribed in *Raaz* and this makes it 'mainstream' although it is also 'pre-modern' in its address. The belying of the ambivalence of the characters played by Dino Morea and Bipasha Basu ultimately becomes reassurance.

This book is focused on the creation of the asymmetric Nation in the new millennium and *Raaz* presents evidence that the Hindi film is still addressing a relatively undifferentiated audience in 2002. This is essentially because it deals with people who are wealthy and with knowledge of English but still allows a Hindi-speaking audience to identify with them. When Hindi cinema deals exclusively with the wealthy after 1991–2, it is by no means addressing only the wealthy, which is why care is taken to 'universalize' the problems of the wealthy. The very fact that a businessman and a scholar want their families to be brought together in *HAHK* (1994) indicates that the compulsions of wealth have been 'de-problematized'.[21] *Raaz*, in a comparable way, deals with a class accustomed to travelling abroad routinely and this is indicated by Aditya asking Sanjana to choose the part of the world she would like to travel to and she chooses Ooty—a familiar location in India. When this 'global couple' is accosted by a disembodied spirit, there is a sense of the global Indian still retaining his/her affinity with the pre-modern and this is a unifying characteristic that gradually leaves Hindi cinema.

Notes

1. James Monaco, *How to Read a Film: The Art, Technology, Language, History and Theory of Film and Media* (New York: Oxford University Press, 1981), p. 204.

2. Actual data is hard to come because many of the financial particulars of the film industry are rarely admitted. But there are popular estimates that 40 per cent of a film's budget is paid to the lead star. See Matt Rosenberg, 'Bollywood', http://geography.about.com/od/culturalgeography/a/bollywood.htm (accessed on 20 May 2012).

3. Valentina Vitali, *Hindi Action Cinema: Industries, Narratives, Bodies* (New Delhi: Oxford University Press, 2008), pp. 140–53.

4. Ibid., p. 134.

5. Ibid., p. 152. The author quotes from *Picture Post*, December 1968, pp. 119–21.

6. M.K. Raghavendra, *Seduced by the Familiar: Narration and Meaning in Indian Popular Cinema* (New Delhi: Oxford University Press, 2008), pp. 152–69.

7. Tsvetan Todorov, *The Fantastic: A Structural Approach to a Literary Genre*, translated from French by Richard Howard (Ithaca, NY: Cornell University Press, 1975), pp. 24–40.

8. Ashish Rajadhyaksha and Paul Willemen, *Encyclopedia of Indian Cinema* (New Delhi: Oxford University Press, 1995), p. 177.

9. Sunil Khilnani, *The Idea of India* (New Delhi: Penguin, 1998), p. 61.

10. Ashis Nandy, *The Intimate Enemy: Loss and Recovery of Self under Colonialism* (New Delhi: Oxford University Press, 1983), pp. 20–9.

11. Devotion leading to a happy outcome because of divine intervention. An example would be the family dog empowered by divinity to assist in the resolution of misunderstandings as in *HAHK*. For how devotion is dealt with in mainstream cinema, see Raghavendra, *Seduced by the Familiar*, pp. 63–4.

12. Data found on the website of IBOS, which is a news service intended to provide news focusing on the business of international cinema in various Indian markets: http://ibosnetwork.com/asp/filmbodetails.asp?id=Raaz; http://ibosnetwork.com/asp/filmbodetails.asp?id=Purana+Mandir; http://ibosnetwork.com/asp/filmbodetails.asp?id=Kasoor; and http://ibosnetwork.com/asp/filmbodetails.asp?id=Devdas+%282002%29 (accessed on 23 May 2012).

13. The horror film is generally seen as dealing with the repressed self in terms of the 'other', with the 'other' being the woman, the proletariat, other cultures, ethnic groups, alternate ideologies, or sexual deviations. See Robin Wood, 'An Introduction to the American Horror Film', in Bill Nichols (ed.), *Movies and Methods*, vol. 2 (Calcutta: Seagull, 1993), pp. 199–200. By this token, it can be proposed that the global Indian was in the position of the 'other' to Hindi film audiences in the early years of the new millennium.

14. The prefix 'Professor' also carries a greater sense of traditional knowledge and many Indian magicians call themselves 'Professor'. This is different from the prefix 'Doctor' which denotes Western education and a PhD degree.

15. An example is the Ramsay brothers' production *Purana Mandir* (1984) in which a demon incarcerated 200 years ago by a king is released accidentally by the king's decendants. This aspect of the horror film makes it transgressive in a way that mainstream cinema is not. See M.K. Raghavendra, 'Nation and Transgression: Ideology and the Horror Film in India and Pakistan', *Phalanx: A Quarterly Review for Continuing Debate*, no. 6, July 2011, http://www.phalanx.in/pages/article_i006_nation_and_transgression.html (accessed on 13 January 2013). By the same token, *Raaz* is much less transgressive than *Purana Mandir*.

16. For instance, see Rosie Thomas, 'Indian Cinema: Pleasures and Popularity', *Screen*, vol. 26, nos 3–4, 1985, p. 10.

17. Raghavendra, *Seduced by the Familiar*, pp. 55–8.

18. In the terms coined by the Russian formalists the '*fabula*' corresponds to the story and the '*syuzhet*' to the plot. Where in a whodunit, the fabula is concealed, to be revealed only in the last chapter, a melodrama is highly communicative of fabula information. David Bordwell, *Narration in the Fiction Film* (London: Methuen, 1985), p. 70.

19. This invokes the story of Sati Savitri whose devotion helped bring back her husband from the dead.

20. Raghavendra, *Seduced by the Familiar*, pp. 280–1.

21. In *DDLJ* (1996), similarly, a small-time shopkeeper in London will not allow his daughter to marry a rich businessman's son because she is pledged to a farmer's family in Punjab. The argument here is that there is a deliberate move to assert that wealth does not make one different.

2

The Adulterous Woman

Jism (2003) to *Kabhi Alvida Naa Kehna* (2006)

Hindi Noir

A particular form of thriller which became popular in the Hindi cinema around 2002–5 tells the story of the adulterous/murderous wife. What makes it interesting to the film researcher is the absence of a similar motif in the older melodramas where the woman protagonist was, by and large, an emblem of virtue or fidelity. This kind of film seems to derive from a sub-category in American noir cinema, and one of the better known of the Hindi films—Amit Saxena's *Jism* (2003)—is an evident adaptation of Lawrence Kasdan's *Body Heat* (1981).

Film noir has many characteristics but only one is relevant to my purpose and that is the absence of romantic love and the family.[1] It should be mentioned that in mainstream Hollywood cinema, love of family, love of father/ruler, and love of country are intertwined concepts and the family provides a legitimizing metaphor for a hierarchical society—father as the head, mother as subservient, and children as dependents. Romantic love and the institution of the family are also logically linked and lovers are transformed into fathers and mothers and romance necessarily terminates in the founding of the family.[2] All this is broken by the noir, which, in presenting family relationships as perverted, broken, or impossible, actually founds itself on the absence of the family. The film noir heroine is sexually alluring but treacherous and the husband—if he is present—is not sexually active. In fact, the wheelchair or crutches associated with him (*Double Indemnity*, 1944; *The Lady from Shanghai*, 1947) underscores his impotence. The psychological uncertainty of the male protagonist finds its counterpart in the enigmatic characterization of the female. The narration compels the hero to decide about her nature and instead of winning her, he finds her barring access to his goals or holding him in her power. In the end he may have to kill her and/or die himself to break free.[3] This model features in some of the Hindi noir films.

Since adultery in noir is associated with murder, it is not untoward that noir films displaying the motif should be thrillers, but as already indicated while dealing with *Raaz* in the previous chapter, Indian popular cinema has not favoured the 'thriller' as a mode of storytelling. If it has been indifferent to suspense and surprise,[4] there are certain techniques that go with suspense and surprise. One of them is to build up the spectator's sense of anticipation through tight causal linking but that is rarely seen in Hindi popular cinema. Most Hindi films also depend on orchestrated music, which becomes grandiose at emotional moments. When reflecting upon film convention in general we recognize that the unforeseen and silence go together. The heavier background scores are heard when surprises are unlikely to be sprung, when the expected will transpire.[5] The relative paucity of silence in Hindi cinema also implies that much of what happens is expected and its overtones are familiar. The films do not attempt to shock or surprise us into responses as much as demand our complicity. The use of heavy music at emotional climaxes stresses the familiarity of the respective moments and can be traced to a feature of Hindi cinema's aesthetics which is based on cognition rather than recognition.[6] The attempts at composing detective stories in Hindi popular cinema have been hesitant and rely on withholding items of information from the spectator. The camera eye remains omniscient which is never an advantage for a well-constructed thriller that depends on point-of- view. Still, the emphasis upon presenting the familiar does not mean that every episode in the narrative only fulfils predictions. It is more accurate to say that the emphasis is on 'how things will happen' rather than on 'what will happen next'.[7] Hindi popular films are melodramas although they often have the same violent story content (involving jealousy, passion, revenge, and so on) as the detective story. Melodramas, regardless of how much crime and violence they contain, are different from detective stories/thrillers but the difference needs to be explained.

The Russian formalists gave the name *fabula* (the story) to the imaginary construct we create progressively and retroactively as we interact with the text. The actual arrangement of the fabula in the narrative they called *syuzhet* (the plot). The syuzhet is a blow-by-blow recounting of the story as the film or the piece of fiction would render it. To illustrate the difference, a detective novel would yield a fabula beginning with the planning of the murder and concluding with the criminal being brought to book. The syuzhet (corresponding to the novel as actually written) proceeds by concealing parts of the fabula to create 'suspense' and sharpen the impact of the text upon the reader. In contrast to the detective story, as David Bordwell explains,[8] melodramatic narrative is highly communicative about fabula information. Where the detective story emphasizes the act of unearthing what has already occurred, the melodrama plays down curiosity about the past by withholding little from the spectator and employing the omniscient camera-eye. Noir often uses point-of- view and the narrator (usually in voice-over) is often risking his life or sanity in the story[9] he is telling but Hindi cinema has consistently ignored narrator subjectivity. Given Hindi popular cinema's historical predilections, the emergence of the Hindi noir thriller in the new millennium deserves scrutiny.

The Family

The family gradually began to be eliminated from Hindi cinema in the first decade of the new millennium but when the noir films appeared its presence was still strong, for example, the family-centred super hits like *Kabhi Khushi Kabhie Gham...* (2001) and *Kal Ho Naa Ho* (2003). Since American noir bases itself on the absence of the family, it may be useful to first examine the examples of the traditional portrayal of family in Hindi cinema. Unlike in the American film, the representation of the family in popular cinema does not problematize the changing circumstances of the family. The working woman has come into her own today but cinema leaves the patriarchal family more secure than ever. The Hindu joint family has been breaking up but the joint family of popular cinema thrives as late as 1994 in *HAHK*. Indian popular films also do not attempt to persuade the spectator about family values by centralizing the discourse on household discord and the values are apparently an incontestable 'given'. Filmic texts from India disallow the social analysis usually applied to Hollywood,[10] implying that the imaging of the family in popular cinema is not 'representational' of the historical family. To substantiate the argument, if the 'modern woman' of the 1940s and 1950s (*Andaz*, 1949; *Dhool Ka Phool*, 1959) had made way for portrayals of greater emancipation, for example, if the emancipation of women was cumulative (as in history), such later discourses on family values as in *HAHK* might not have been possible. Popular cinema does not problematize the actual family's transformation because it is the traditional (or, rather, the 'traditional-ideal') Indian family[11] which is the constant unit in narrative construction. If the 'traditional-ideal' family is a constant element, then deviations from 'idealness' are anomalies that offer themselves for interpretation. The modern woman of the 1940s and 1950s was one such deviation and the adulterous relationship in the Hindi noir thriller is another one. What I will attempt, therefore, is to interpret the emergence and meaning of the latter motif. *Raaz* had briefly used the motif but films such as Amit Saxena's *Jism* (2003), Anurag Basu's *Murder* (2004), Abbas–Mustaan's *Aitraaz* (2004), Vikram Bhatt's *Jurm* (2005), and Mohit Suri's *Zeher* (2005), as discussed subsequently, are entirely constructed around it.

Jism

Jism (based on American director Lawrence Kasdan's film *Body Heat*, 1981), is set in Pondicherry and tells of the passionate involvement of a lawyer named Kabir Lal (John Abraham) with Sonia (Bipasha Basu), the wife of a business tycoon named Rohit Khanna. Sonia induces Kabir to kill her husband and the murder is dressed up to look like an accident. But Sonia is also embroiled in a conflict with Rohit's sister for his property and things go wrong because of the tussle. Kabir also learns that Sonia was nurse to Rohit's ailing first wife and married him after her death. The film follows *Body Heat* but concludes with Kabir and Sonia killing each other even while discovering their love. Apart from Sonia's sister-in-law, the film also introduces two other characters—Kabir Lal's friends—one of whom is the police inspector entrusted with the task of investigating Rohit Khanna's death. This policeman is in plain clothes which may be regarded as significant because the representation also recurs in *Zeher*.

If the policeman in uniform has consistently represented the authority of the state, in *C.I.D.* (1956) where a police inspector is charged with murder, the policeman is in plain clothes, as if to establish that the individual and not the state is indicted. The plain-clothes police inspector in *Jism* may therefore be regarded as a moral counterpoint to the hero without the state being brought into the narrative, that is, to treat him only as an investigator and not invoke the authority of the state. The second aspect of the film has to do with its choice of location. Pondicherry in the film (as Goa in *Zeher*) is apparently chosen because it is closest in the popular mind to a foreign locale and it is also filmed in this way. In the actual Pondicherry, the structures invoking its status as a former French colony are restricted to a few streets, with the rest of it like any town in Tamil Nadu but the Pondicherry of the film might be in Seychelles or Reunion or some such island where the policemen wear colonial red hats, not recognizable to Hindi film audiences as India. The film also takes care to keep out street or beach scenes where local people might be conspicuous. The music employed—although in Hindi—is also largely guitar-accompanied unlike standard Hindi film music in which electronic effects and percussion dominate.

If the film attempts to take away both the state and the Nation from the story, I detect another erasure: that of the parental figure, which is also absent in *Raaz*. The parental figure is often the conduit through which the values inculcated by tradition pass into the story. The parental appearance may be fleeting but it is still a useful tool by which the protagonist(s) can be made custodian(s) of these values. Without this presence, the protagonists of *Lagaan* (2001) would exist in an ethical limbo, which is what the milieu of *Jism* is made to seem. Interpreted together with the other aspects discussed earlier, we may say that the milieu in *Jism* is a space from which the Indian state, the Indian Nation, and tradition (three key moral signifiers in popular cinema) have been evicted. I suggest that the film hits upon this strategy to promote the discourse that adulterous conduct is the outcome when the moral presences of the Nation, the state, and tradition are no longer assured. To make the warning more ominous, the film associates adultery with greed. Her love of money induces Sonia to be adulterous and plan the murder of her husband.

Money as the root cause in an adulterous relationship culminating in murder is a typical plot device in noir and James M. Cain's novel *The Postman Always Rings Twice* (1934) is the classic example. But the proliferation of noir films in the new millennium is singular inasmuch as the models they follow are old—even *Body Heat* being twenty-five years old. Why is the adultery/murder thriller from noir being adapted by Indian cinema in the new millennium? It may, of course, be asserted that the theme provides ample scope for sex and violence but that does not explain why this theme rather than any other—offering the same scope—came into such prominence in this period.

The Other Films

Anurag Basu's *Murder* is set in Bangkok and is about the illicit relationship between Simran and Sunny, her college boyfriend. Simran is Sudhir's wife, whom she married after the death of his first wife Sonia. Sonia was Simran's sister and mother to Sudhir's child, now under Simran's care. The film begins with the Thai police arresting Simran who confesses murdering Sunny. After a clandestine affair, Simran had found out that Sunny had another girlfriend. She was disgusted by this and, as an act of self-defence, killed him when he tried to force himself upon her. The film does not end with this confession because the police have also arrested Sudhir who owns up to the murder as well although the corpse is still to be found. However, this confession has several loose threads including an account of a mysterious blackmailer and the missing corpse. The police are eventually not satisfied with their confessions. They locate Sunny's girlfriend (the blackmailer) and it turns out that Sunny is not dead: he was merely injured and then rescued by her. In the last segment of the film, Sunny savagely attacks Simran and the child but he is shot dead by the police. *Murder*, as it can be seen, though constructed differently from *Jism*, also deals with adultery and murder. Also, what it has in common with *Jism* is its visual emphasis upon global lifestyles and in greed being the cause of the criminal's downfall. It is also constructed as a thriller with parts of the story being gradually revealed.

The film *Aitraaz* , based on Barry Levinson's *Disclosure* (1994), is not a thriller in the strict sense but it revolves around a courtroom drama in which the male protagonist fights a case of sexual harassment. Raj and Sonia once had an affair in South Africa and she proposes to continue the relationship although there are spouses now involved. It is significant that unlike *Disclosure*, the film plays up the mystery by concealing parts of the story till the end, like *Jism* and *Murder*. Raj is morally blameless and loves his wife, Priya, but Sonia has all the makings of the noir heroine. An interesting aspect of *Aitraaz* is that it registers a parental presence but this parent is Priya's. Priya is the one person insulated from any kind of moral contamination. She is emphatically Indian, has no global associations, and is instrumental in the exoneration of Raj by the court. In *Jurm* (2005), wealthy businessman Avinash is arrested for murdering his wife and he tells his story, much as in *Murder*.

I have, earlier, made a few remarks about the plain-clothes policeman in *Jism* to play down the 'Indianness' of the space but the other films discussed here have no need for the ploy though they all use the figure of the law enforcer. The policeman in *Murder* is a functionary of the Thai government and the global nature of the space is not affected by his presence. The courtroom in *Aitraaz* is Indian and must be taken to represent Indian state authority but the original relationship between Raj and Sonia is, significantly, contracted away from India's shores: in a global space emptied of the Indian state, the Nation, and tradition. Sonia's adulterous character owes to its having been molded in this space. The same observation can be made about *Jurm* where the noir heroine's character is associated with the global milieu and Kuala Lumpur is where she is domiciled. The plain-clothes policeman is not seen in any of these films but he reappears in *Zeher* where he is the male protagonist implicated in adultery and also suspected of murder. The story of *Zeher* is set in Goa, a place from which most traces of India have been erased. This becomes more apparent if this space (representing the 'global Goa') is placed alongside the one in *The Bourne Supremacy* (2005) in which few European traces remain. The attraction of an Indian location in an American film is its exotic, oriental appeal and it is the 'oriental' side of Goa that gets emphasis.

The 'Global'

Zeher is similar to *Aitraaz* as the male protagonists in both films are saved by their wives from the clutches of the treacherous noir women. The good wives are, in both films, associated with the Indian state because while Priya in *Aitraaz* is a lawyer arguing Raj's case in an Indian court, Sonia in *Zeher* is a senior police officer.[12] Also, the wickedness of the noir women, in both films, is traced to their global associations. Sonia, in *Aitraaz*, owes it to her role as a fashion model for global brands and Anna, in *Zeher*, to her association with the global drug trade.

The 'global' has similarities with the 'modern' of the 1940s and 1950s and the 'West' of later periods in Hindi cinema, but its implications are different. The 'modern' pertained to a way of life and could be seen as 'good', 'bad', or ridiculous (as in comedy). The 'good' modern was, for instance, often represented by the figure of the doctor (*Dil Ek Mandir*, 1963) and the 'bad' by the club dancer and/ or the urban gangster (*Baazi*, 1951). The ridiculous aspect was most famously represented by Johnny Walker in his many roles (*Kaagaz Ke Phool*, 1959). The 'West' was different inasmuch as it was symbolized by white people or tourist locations as in *Sangam*. The 'bad' West was represented earliest in the 1970s by the hippies of *Hare Rama Hare Krishna* (1971) and the smuggler flying idols out of the country in the 1970s. The negative portrayals of the 'West' can be attributed to Indira Gandhi's 'anti-Western' policies and concluded with her electoral defeat in 1977. In the 1990s, the 'West' was once again an invitation to the tourist/consumer (*DDLJ*, 1995 and *Hero No. 1*, 1997).

The foreign milieus in the Hindi noir films are not tourist destinations as in the 1990s. They are global spaces in which Indians live, work, and succeed. The song sequences on European roads with amused white onlookers embarrassed Indian sophisticates but they had the apparent consequence of distinguishing the Indians. The new films shot in Kuala Lumpur or Bangkok do not include such sequences. The films cannot now say, 'We are not like you', to the locals. The songs, if any, are on the soundtrack but the protagonists conduct themselves discreetly like the locals.

The 'global' in new Hindi cinema is more akin to the 'modern' of the 1950s than to the 'Western' of the intervening period because it combines a hint of glamour with more than a touch of the alarming. Like the 'modern', it is an attractive but also uncertain quantity that might influence Indians harmfully—which is perhaps the message of the Hindi noir heroine. Interestingly, film researchers detect the influence of noir in the Hindi films of the 1950s.[13] While this influence has been identified as pertaining largely to the visual codes, there is an aspect that connects directly with the Hindi noir films of the new millennium. Many of the films of the 1940s and 1950s are also nominally structured as thrillers. More importantly, they introduce the unexpected into their narratives in ways involving character ambiguity. Let me cite two examples to illustrate this point. In Guru Dutt's *Baazi*, the unexpected is introduced through the heroine's respectable father secretly being an urban gangster and the owner of a nightclub, an emblem of bad modernity in the 1950s. The agency responsible for the darker side of his dual nature is therefore 'modernity'. Mehboob Khan's *Andaz* (1949) is not a thriller but the behaviour of the heroine, Neeta, makes the male protagonist, Dilip (Dilip Kumar), believe she loves him. Later on, the film introduces the heroine's fiancé, Rajan (Raj Kapoor), and Dilip is unable to come to terms with his presence in her life. My argument is that the heroine's conduct is ambiguous and the agency blamed for this ambiguity is 'modernity'. It is because Neeta is brought up as a 'modern' woman that Dilip misreads her behaviour, resulting in tragedy.

Film researchers are easily convinced that Indian cinema of the 1950s was imitating Hollywood in order to be modern[14] but the thriller format had perhaps another significance. The thrillers of the 1940s and 1950s perhaps illustrated ways of problematizing the uncertainties in the modernization project. If the outcome of modernization was uncertain, the 'modern' could be employed as the entity within the narrative that accounted for a mystery.

What we apparently witness in the Hindi noir thrillers is a replication of tendencies in the 1950s with the 'modern' replaced by the 'global'. The outcome of globalization was as uncertain in the new millennium as the outcome of modernization was in the Nehru era and this is being problematized by the Hindi noir thriller. The characterization of the adulterous woman may owe to

American noir but it addresses apprehensions in the minds of the public about the possible erosion of traditional values when India embraces the 'global' wholeheartedly. The motif of the adulterous and murderous woman can even be read as the resistance of tradition to globalization.

Kabhi Alvida Naa Kehna (KANK) and the End of Hindi Noir

Karan Johar's KANK takes the theme of adultery a step further by actually appearing to endorse it. The film tells a story about a sportsman in New York who, apart from being husband and father, takes up with a married woman. It concludes with two divorces and the lovers deciding to marry and move to Toronto. If this plot is a striking departure from convention, more so than in Jism and the others, there are other anomalies that mitigate the endorsement and these are, specifically, the narrative being deliberately confined to the US—with no acknowledgement of India—and the playing down of the symbols representing tradition, such as, the mangalsutra, the patriotism, and the religious fervor to name a few. Taken together, the anomalies make it *appear* that the space of the narrative has been deliberately emptied of the Indian Nation and tradition to render it suitable for adultery and this runs parallel to the methods adopted by the Hindi noir films.

The motif that still remains recognizable—despite the disguise— is the venerated parent. The father played by Amitabh relishes the company of young women but he treats sex simply as a commodity, having a place in his heart only for his late wife. The mother in Hindi cinema, as often acknowledged, is the site of virtue in the narrative.[15] Hence, the adulterous male protagonist's mother remaining with her daughter-in-law, Rhea, and grandson, rather than going with him carries the same connotations as Ravi saying, 'Mere paas maa hain!' in Deewaar (1975).[16] Only Rhea (Preity Zinta) does not have eyes for anyone but her spouse and she, significantly, is also a mother. This is different from the five thrillers beginning with *Jism*, as discussed earlier, where tradition in the shape of the venerated parent is virtually absent. The difference is perhaps located in the thrillers being a dire warning against the ravages of globalization upon traditional lifestyles within India and *KANK* accepting, quite cheerfully, the possibility that lifestyles might be influenced and even transformed with Indians going global.

Yet, when *KANK* permits the adulterous Dev (Shahrukh Khan) and Maya (Rani Mukherjee) to embark on their own, it does not suggest that the social fabric is under threat in any way. *KANK* is, rather, asserting that the fabric is secure despite the Devs and the Mayas. Apart from Shahrukh Khan and Rani Mukherjee suggesting vulnerability, Dev being disabled—he hobbles through the film—reassures us that he is not the triumphant hero. Where Rhea and the others live in opulence, Dev moves into a bare apartment, the likes of which may not have housed a film hero after 1992. Dev and Maya have little except each other, and that is another anomaly in a cinema where one must be rich to be in a story. If the film is sympathetic to those who break traditional taboos it is also suggesting that they will not be left with very much. *KANK* is perhaps the first Hindi film to accept cultural globalization even while reassuring its constituency that, regardless of the transformations experienced, what is essential to tradition will be carried forward. Given that *KANK* endorses the same socio-cultural phenomena that Hindi noir dramatically opposes, *KANK's* success also marked the conclusion of Hindi noir as a genre and the moment when Hindi film audiences across India were reconciled to the consequences of globalization.

Notes

1. Sylvia Harvey, 'Woman's Place: The Absent Family of Film Noir', in E. Ann Kaplan (ed.), *Women in Film Noir* (London: British Film Institute, 1980), pp. 22–34.
2. Ibid., pp. 22–34.

3. David Bordwell, 'The Classical Hollywood Style', in David Bordwell, Janet Staiger, and Kristin Thompson, *The Classical Hollywood Cinema: Film Style and Mode of Production to 1960* (London: Routledge & Kegan Paul, 1985), p. 76.

4. See Ashis Nandy, 'The Hindi Film: Ideology and First Principles', *India International Centre Quarterly*, vol. 8, no. 1, 1981, pp. 89–96; Rosie Thomas, 'Indian Cinema: Pleasures and Popularity', *Screen*, vol. 26, nos 3–4, 1985, pp. 116–32.

5. 'The characters in a film drama never know what is going to happen to them but the music always knows.' Lawrence Morton, in an interview with George Antheil, *Film Music Notes*, vol. 2, no. 2, November 1942, cited by Bordwell, 'The Classical Hollywood Style', p. 34.

6. Hindi film aesthetics ... is based not on cognition but on recognition. The fan knows what to expect ... Thus the Hindi film is a particular product of 'the aesthetics of identity', which J.M. Lotman (*Die Structur Literarischer Texte*, Munchen, 1972) opposes to the 'aesthetics of opposition'. A typical, also trivial, product of the latter is the detective story, which functions, as a rule, on the basis of the reader's ignorance of "whodunit".

   Lothar Lutze, 'Bharata to Bombay: Change and Continuity in Hindi Film Aesthetics', in Lothar Lutze and Beatrix Pfleiderer (eds), *The Hindi Film: Agent and Re-agent of Cultural Change* (New Delhi: Manohar, 1985), p. 5.

7. Thomas, 'Indian Cinema: Pleasures and Popularity', p. 130.

8. 'The narration will also be quite unrestricted in range, closer to an omniscient survey, so that the film can engender pity, irony, and other "dissociated" emotions.' David Bordwell, *Narration in the Fiction Film* (London: Methuen, 1985), p. 70.

9. This would be more applicable to Roman noir although American film noir also employs it, such as in *Double Indemnity*. See Tsvetan Todorov, *The Poetics of Prose* (Oxford: Blackwell, 1997), pp. 42–52. Also Claire Johnston, 'Double Indemnity', in E. Ann Kaplan (ed.), *Women in Film Noir* (London: British Film Institute, 1980), p. 100.

10. The following passage gives a rudimentary but useful picture of the transformation:

    Hollywood ... had always attempted to reinforce those American values that enjoyed widespread support. Among these were the norms and sentiments that cherished the family, the home, and the healing and nurturing power of love. However, by the 1960s a sizeable segment of the population no longer shared these or other communal feelings. Central to the malaise that enveloped both real- and reel-life characters is disillusionment with the family. In the older formulaic endings of most films, a loving kiss sealed the matrimonial bargain between a man and a woman and seemed to promise to continue to do so till death did them part. Their actual married life was left to the audience's imaginations. However, once Hollywood introduced admirable heroines who would not accept monogamy as a substitute for career and a carefree existence, who refused to bask demurely in the reflected status of their husband's occupation, and who demanded every jot and title that the law and their own individual or collective efforts might obtain, it sounded a little tocsin: the trouble between the sexes was just beginning when the organ played the wedding march ... *Kramer Vs Kramer* and *Ordinary People* seemed to seal the fate of the nuclear family and suggest that the future portends a new ordering of the domestic and occupational verities. The all-male homestead would in future link father and son in the only emotionally sensitized and lovingly nurturant haven in what had otherwise emerged as a heartless world, while the workplace would likely become the scene of a harsh and less than feeling competitive struggle between career driven women and ambitious men, the battleground for a cold war of the sexes'.

Stanford M. Lyman, 'The Road to Anhedonia: Patterns of Emotional Conflict in American Films, 1930–1988', in David D. Franks and Viktor Gelas (eds), *Social Perspectives on Emotion: A Research Annual*, vol. 1 (Greenwich, Conn.: Jai Press, 1992), pp. 179–80.

11. M. Madhava Prasad (*Ideology of the Hindi Film: A Historical Construction* [New Delhi: Oxford University Press, 1999], pp. 30–1), prefers to use the term 'feudal family romance' to designate the Indian domestic melodrama. This seems to imply that the family as portrayed in Hindi cinema has some historical correspondence with the family in feudal times. The issue has been discussed in the Introduction.

12. Significantly, while Siddharth is always in plain clothes, Sonia dons khaki while investigating Anna's 'death'.

13. For instance, see Ravi S. Vasudevan, 'Shifting Codes, Dissolving Identities', in Ravi S. Vasudevan (ed.), *Making Meaning in Indian Cinema* (New Delhi: Oxford University Press, 2000), pp. 109–10.

14. Ibid., pp. 108–9.

15. Ibid., p. 110.

16. In *Deewaar*, the older brother pours scorn on his younger sibling—a policeman—by listing all the things that he himself possesses, such as, a bungalow, a car, and property, and demanding to know what his brother has. The younger son's response is brief: 'I have mother'.

3

'Undivided India'

Gadar: Ek Prem Katha (2001) and Veer-Zaara (2004)

Representing Pakistan

A factor to be noted about Indian nationalism in the late nineteenth century was that it was dominated by Hinduism. This was to such an extent that groups with other religious identities needed to find ways to be 'nationalistic' outside Hinduism.[1] Unlike the Christians, the Muslim minority had 'extra-territorial' loyalties as those brought to the fore during the Khilafat Movement (1919–24). Despite later efforts to make Indian nationalism less apparently 'Hindu', this factor may have contributed to the Partition of India. The tale of the two emergent Nations is, therefore, profoundly influenced by the relationship between the two religions.

The relationship between India and Pakistan has preoccupied the public from time to time after 1947 resulting in its representation in Hindi cinema in various ways. Although it is difficult to ascertain the number of actual representations of Pakistan, the first is perhaps to be found in M.L. Anand's *Lahore* (1949) which is set during the

Partition. Hindi cinema was apparently silent thereafter until Manoj Kumar's *Upkar* (1967) which was made shortly after India's 1965 war with Pakistan. Apart from dealing with the 1965 war explicitly, the film also allegorizes the relationship between the two countries as one between two brothers—the responsible one and his wayward younger stepbrother who demands a division of the family land. Raj Khosla's *Do Raaste* (1969), a slightly later film, also includes the same motif of the younger brother demanding division of family property. That Hindi cinema did not represent Pakistan till so late in the independent nation's history is not unexpected—given its sense of the temporal because it generally declined to deal with historical events until relatively recently.[2] As discussed earlier, Hindi cinema has resorted to allegory to deal with political/historical events but these events usually pertain to the immediate and it is uncertain why the Partition of India should figure as an allegorized event as late as 1967. A plausible explanation is that with Jawaharlal Nehru's daughter, Indira Gandhi, becoming Prime Minister in 1967, the public saw Indian history as getting back on course after a brief interruption[3] and Hindi cinema began to take stock of the independent Nation's history.

After *Upkar*, the next Hindi patriotic film with an anti-Pakistan bias was perhaps Dev Anand's *Prem Pujari* (1970). The film did not succeed though. Pakistan was in turmoil at the time with the East (present Bangladesh) gradually slipping out of its grasp. A war between India and Pakistan took place in 1971 in which India had a decisive victory and Pakistan was dismembered. The 1970s was a period in which Indira Gandhi swung to the left and embarked upon her kind of radical populism; Hindi cinema has, therefore, little use for patriotism after 1971. The 1980s was a period in which there was strife within India, most notably, in Punjab. Pakistan and a patriotic rhetoric was therefore not pertinent to Hindi cinema until the 1990s.

A key conflict in Hindi cinema until the early 1990s pertains to the one between the rich and the poor. It is not that cinema treats the rich with disfavour but that it tends to see the rich as owing something to those less fortunate. The economic liberalization of

1991–2 changed the face of Hindi cinema although it took a year or more for its political meaning to be understood: that India had officially abandoned Nehruvian socialism. The response in films beginning with HAHK (1994) was to remove the poor from among the protagonists in any narrative and accord them the smaller positions, like that of servants in a rich household as in HAHK or to stop problematizing class differences as in many other films like Ram Gopal Verma's Rangeela (1996) in which a successful film actress' love for a common ruffian faces no opposition from anyone. Social conflict within the Nation admitted by the worldview of Nehruvian socialism was now irrelevant. But, as indicated in the Introduction, there are other ruses by which social conflict within the nation can be effectively disclaimed and one of these is to push discord to its borders, in effect to revert back to patriotism. The post-liberalization period is one in which Indian popular cinema became abruptly patriotic although the political conditions needed to support the sentiment did not exist until the end of the decade, that is, when the Kargil episode excited the nation. Needless to say, Hindi cinema in this patriotic period did not specifically distinguish between Pakistan and the British and if the latter are the villains in 1942: A Love Story (1994), Pakistan is the villain in J.P. Dutta's Border (1998) which deals with the 1965 war. Border is a straightforward war film about a battalion of Indian soldiers holding off a much stronger contingent of Pakistani soldiers supported by armour and it treats Pakistan as a military adversary, which is different from the next anti-Pakistan patriotic film, Anil Sharma's Gadar: Ek Prem Katha (2001) which appeared at around the same time as the much milder anti-British patriotic film Lagaan (2001).

Gadar: Ek Prem Katha and Partition

Anil Sharma's Gadar: Ek Prem Katha apparently broke HAHK's seven-year record for gross collections and held its own for five more years.[4] Gadar: Ek Prem Katha is a film set during the time of Partition. Perhaps it is the first mainstream film to have its narrative constructed entirely around the event. The film tells the story of a truck driver, Tara Singh (Sunny Deol), a Jat Sikh who falls in love with a Muslim girl, Sakina (Amisha Patel), belonging to an aristocratic family. The film begins by showing Muslim mobs killing unarmed Sikhs and Hindus in 1947 and Hindus and Sikhs retaliating by killing innocent Muslims. Among those in a Hindu/Sikh mob is Tara Singh, who is enraged by the carnage he sees. At about this time Sakina and her family are fleeing India. Ashraf Ali (Amrish Puri) is a highly placed official who is forced to flee but Sakina is accidentally left behind in the railway station. Tara Singh sees her and decides to protect her and this becomes the reason for a flashback. Tara was a simple lorry driver with ambitions of becoming a singer. While on his travels in a hill station—perhaps Shimla—he ran into some girls from the college which included Sakina. After initially being made fun of, he was encouraged by Sakina to demonstrate his singing skills publicly and thus win respect. Tara has recognized Sakina in the riots and that is why he saves her from his associates.

Sakina is in a state of shock but she comes around because of his ministrations. Tara intends to help her get to Pakistan but she knows nothing about her parents' whereabouts. When he escorts her to the border she changes her mind about going; she is in love with him although they are from different classes and confesses to him. The two get married and have a son.

In the third part of the film, news comes to Sakina that her father Ashraf Ali has become the mayor of Lahore. She gets in touch with her family and everyone is overjoyed. She and Tara decide to visit her family in Lahore with their son. Unfortunately, there is a visa problem for the son and only she can go across. Tara and the child want to go over a few days later. Sakina reaches home and everyone is happy until Sakina's father makes it known that he will not permit her to return to India. He also arranges it so that Tara and their son are denied visas. The plan is to get Sakina married to another man—a person from a rich family. Tara and their son know nothing of this but they manage to cross the border to Lahore. They stay with a Muslim friend who is now living there and manage to make contact with Sakina. When Ashraf Ali's attempts to get Sakina remarried are of no avail and her husband Tara Singh is also at hand, his next ploy is to get Tara Singh converted to Islam at a ceremony where nearly everyone from Lahore is present. Tara Singh has hesitantly consented to the conversion and the ceremony begins. But instead of going through the prescribed procedure Ashraf Ali asks Tara Singh to say, 'Islam *zindabad*!' and 'Pakistan *zindabad*!' He hates it but relents. It is only when Ashraf Ali insists on him saying 'Hindustan *murdabad*!' that he refuses. The rest of the film is full with action sequences as Tara Singh demolishes hordes of Pakistanis—Ashraf Ali's men, the police, and the military. As Tara and his family head for the border, they are stopped and Sakina is injured by her own father. It is in the hospital that Ashraf Ali realizes his mistake and the three are allowed to return to India.

Gadar: Ek Prem Katha is about as rabidly anti-Pakistan as Indian cinema has ever been but there is more to it than merely that. Nominally, the film like several non-mainstream films about Partition is taken up with the theme of 'man's inhumanity to man'. But Partition does not carry the same meaning for Pakistan that it does for India. There has apparently been only one film about Partition coming from Pakistan[5] called *Kartar Singh* (1959). That film is about a Sikh miscreant at the time of Partition who has a change of heart but is killed when he is escorting a Muslim victim of violence across the border. According to a Pakistani critic, the film helps reveal that Hindus and Muslims could have attained freedom without tearing each other apart if the political leadership of the three sides—the British, the Congress, and the Muslim League— had a better perception of the basic reality as it existed for most people in the subcontinent.[6] What this suggests is that Partition was inevitable to Pakistan but the bloodshed might have been avoided. While Partition violence, for Pakistan, signifies the birth pangs of a newly emerging nation, for India, it has tended to mean 'man's inhumanity to man' and this is the dominant exhortation not only of *Gadar: Ek Prem Katha* but also of *Pinjar* (2003), the television series *Tamas* (1987), and Pamela Rooks' *Train to Pakistan* (1998). Yet, none of the others pursue jingoistic nationalism as relentlessly as *Gadar: Ek Prem Katha*, which virtually blames the Muslims for Partition violence.

It is significant that the vision of Partition as 'man's inhumanity to man' has largely ignored violence in Bengal which was nearly as great as the violence in Punjab although it was more sporadic.[7] One reason for the Bengal experience being sidelined is perhaps that its meaning is more complex; there was a clearer association between religion and class, and land went to the poor Muslims in the East[8] when the Hindu landowners were dispossessed. Radical historians in India have attempted to look at Partition through private memories and through personal narratives[9] but both received Indian and Pakistani historical interpretations attempt to give meaning to the events of 1947 by moulding them into a key moment in the realization of the destiny of the respective nation states.

India came out in 1947 as a secular nation which means that—at least in theory—India is on the side of religious tolerance. Pakistan, on the other hand, is an Islamic state. As compared to 'India', 'Pakistan' is a recent term, and so it is also difficult for Pakistan to dispute the notion that it was 'carved out of India' though both nation states came into existence together. It is perhaps these advantages that the Indian state covertly exploits when it promotes texts mourning the violence of Partition through awards and acclaim. It is perhaps also significant that the writer Saadat Hasan Manto, best known for his short fiction exploring the inhumanity of Partition, is better regarded in India than in Pakistan[10] where he lived during the latter part of his life.

The point where *Gadar: Ek Prem Katha* is an ideological 'advance' upon the other films constructed around Partition is when it extends regret towards 'man's inhumanity to man' to also include regret of the existence of Pakistan. The film was made in 2001 when the nationalist political party Bharatiya Janata Party (BJP) had come to power at the centre and the loss of 'Akhand Bharat' (or undivided India) has been constantly regretted by the Hindu Right in India of which the BJP is a part.[11] *Gadar: Ek Prem Katha* uses several devices towards this end and the most explicit one is to have a mentally deficient Pakistani young man—the son of a friend of Sakina's father—who believes that independence has not yet been won, is avowedly anti-British and also has a tendency to hoist the Congress flag—the Indian tricolor but with a spinning wheel at the centre— at inopportune moments. Another strategy is to contrast India and Pakistan in terms of their social composition. It is interesting that when Hindi cinema becomes patriotic after 1991–2, it shifts its focus from the rich to the less-affluent sections. *Lagaan* deals with a village community and Tara Singh's family is a rustic family living off the land. Sakina's father's family, in contrast, lives ostentatiously with attentive servants. The only 'good' Pakistani is Tara Singh's former friend from undivided India who lives in humbler quarters in Lahore with his shrewish wife and five hungry children.[12] Most Hindi films in which rich women marry poor men, male protagonists are allowed access to their wives' riches, such as in, *Yaadon Ki Baraat* (1973) and *Daag* (1973). Here the wife shuns her aristocratic lineage and prefers to share the life of an ordinary citizen with her husband. The ruse of the 'happiness of common people' and contrasting it with the affections of the rich has been used before, such as in, *Bobby* (1973) but that was when Nehruvian socialism was still the creed. Here, it is being used to contrast democratic India with 'feudal' Pakistan. As may be expected, Sakina is also welcomed by Tara Singh's family although she is a Muslim and they are Sikhs. This is in contrast to Sakina's family which insists that her husband should be a Muslim even if she needs to marry again. This is clearly intended to highlight the secular credentials of the Indians. When patriotism is not the sentiment promoted by a Hindi film, one may expect a marriage across religious boundaries to be resisted by both families as in Mani Ratnam's *Bombay* (1995). Lastly, India is always assisted by the film's cinematography—with views of the countryside in which wheat fields are conspicuous—while Pakistan is portrayed through the city, lavish lifestyles, and official ceremonies. India is evidently the more fertile and democratic space. This last strategy is employed once again by a later film, *Veer-Zaara* (2004), which is also about love between an Indian man and a Pakistani woman.

Veer-Zaara: Love and Conquest

Yash Chopra's *Veer-Zaara*, which is set over a long period of time and ends in present India and Pakistan, was a super hit and also the biggest grosser of 2004. The film begins in a Pakistani jail which houses an Indian named Veer Pratap Singh (Shahrukh Khan). A woman human rights lawyer named Samiya Siddiqi (Rani Mukherjee) is entrusted with fighting his case. After she convinces him to tell her everything Veer Pratap Singh's story is related in a flashback. He was a squadron leader with the Indian Air Force, working as a rescue helicopter pilot. The cause of all his troubles was a Pakistani girl.

Zaara Haayat Khan (Preity Zinta) is an independent and sprightly young Pakistani girl travelling to India. She is on her way to Kiratpur with the ashes of her Sikh governess, Bebe. Before dying, Bebe (Zohra Sehgal) had begged Zaara to fulfil her final wish—to take her ashes to the holy Sikh city and scatter them in the Sutlej where her ancestors had their ashes similarly scattered. Zaara decides to carry out Bebe's dying wish but the bus she is travelling in gets involved in an accident and she is saved by Veer Pratap. As luck would have it, Zaara and Veer Pratap are brought together again a little later and he escorts her to Kiratpur and arranges for the ceremony. He then takes her to visit his village where it is assumed by his parents (played by Amitabh Bachchan and Hema Malini) that the girl with him is his fiancée. When they learn that she is a Muslim from Pakistan they exhibit no qualms but persist in matrimonial plans. After a whole day of such pleasantness, Veer Pratap escorts Zaara back to the railway station where her actual fiancé Raza (Manoj Bajpai) is waiting for her. Veer Pratap was not told about Raza and he is shocked but he collects himself to wish them goodbye.

In Pakistan, Zaara realizes that it is Veer Pratap whom she loves but also that it is her duty to keep her family's honour and marry her fiancé, a wedding that will further her father's political career. But

Zaara cannot simply forget Veer and finally tells her mother that she has fallen in love with him. Zaara's maid and confidante Shabbo calls Veer and tells him how miserable Zaara is without him; she dares him to come and take Zaara away. Veer who had told Zaara that he would give up his life for her, quits the Indian Air Force and goes to Pakistan to bring her back with him to India. Zaara's mother, Mariam Hayaat Khan (Kirron Kher), however, begs him to leave Zaara alone as her father Jahangir Hayaat Khan (Boman Irani) is a high-profile politician whose reputation will be ruined if news gets out that his daughter is in love with an Indian. Veer respects this request and decides to leave for India but Raza, who is outraged by the shame Zaara has brought to him, frames Veer and has him wrongly imprisoned on charges of being an Indian spy with another identity. Veer spends twenty-two years in prison until Saamiya Siddiqi courageously defends him.

Since Veer is thought to have been killed in a bus accident no one is searching for him from India and his true identity is impossible to prove. But Saamiya thinks it will be helpful to travel to India and find someone who can identify him. She proceeds to his village to find that both his parents are now dead. A village school is being run there and in-charge is a woman who Saamiya recognizes as Zaara Haayat Khan and the whole story comes out. Zaara did not marry Raza but decided to return to India. Her parents are now dead. Imagining Veer to be dead, she has been carrying on the good work started by his parents. Zaara returns to Pakistan to give evidence in the case and Veer Pratap is acquitted. He and Zaara return to India with Saamiya keeping them company. Everything ends well as we learn that Raza has now left Pakistan and has settled abroad.

As may be gathered, *Veer-Zaara* has several aspects in common with *Gadar: Ek Prem Katha* although it does not exult in anti-Pakistan rhetoric like the latter film. The most obvious aspect is the motif of the woman coming from an aristocratic family and the man being more rooted to the soil. The second aspect pertains to the woman abandoning her aristocratic lineage to live more simply in India in harmony with the land and its people. The third pertains to India being portrayed as a well-knit, tolerant, and democratic community, while Pakistan is constituted as a rigidly religious hierarchical society with little commerce between the classes. When Zaara abandons Pakistan and comes over to India to run a school—without even the justification of Veer Pratap (believed dead) being in India—the film is virtually asserting that such 'meaningful action' which is natural in India is difficult in Pakistan. Also significant is Saamiya's conduct which indicates that she is comfortable in Indian society where human rights as well as women are respected. The director Yash Chopra also uses an old strategy from Deewaar[13] when the prisoner Veer Pratap Singh has accidentally been given the number 786. Saamiya convinces the jailor that it must be a miracle for a Hindu to get a number so dear to Allah and Veer could, in fact, have been 'chosen'.

Underneath all this is the strategy making an Indian man marry a Pakistani girl and the two coming to live in India. This carries echoes of 'carrying off of a bride' or eloping which is familiar to Indians from mythology. One helpful story may be the one in which the Rajput King Prithviraj Chauhan eloped with the daughter of his arch-enemy Jaichand, the King of Kannauj,[14] in the twelfth century. There is an element of conquest in this kind of elopement and Prithviraj Chauhan's élan is still celebrated. Jaichand has often the status of a villain because it is alleged that he betrayed Prithviraj Chauhan to the Muslim invader Muhammad Ghori. The archetypal elopement which this medieval story recalls may be the one involving Krishna and Rukmini. In any case, in most Hindu–Muslim romances in mainstream Hindi cinema involving an elopement, the man is Hindu and the woman Muslim—whether Bombay (1995) or the two films dealt with here. With the gender equality demanded by the modern romance, this interpretation of the inter-religious romance as conquest may be resisted but romance in Hindi popular cinema has rarely been 'modern' in this sense. This suggests that underneath the rhetoric of 'love' in both Gadar: Ek Prem Katha and Veer-Zaara, what is being dealt with is an Indian/Hindu conquest although there is some mitigation in Zaara primarily choosing social action in India rather than Veer.

Both films analysed in this chapter are mainstream films which also makes them more conservative in their political discourses than Partition films made outside the mainstream like Chandra Prakash Dwivedi's Pinjar (2003) in which a Sikh woman forced into marriage with a Muslim chooses to remain behind in Pakistan.[15] Significantly, however, the two films are also less generous than a mainstream film about Partition made in 1949, that is, M.L. Anand's Lahore. In that film, a Hindu woman and a Muslim woman who are married against their wishes in Pakistan and India, respectively, are repatriated to their own countries. The observation is that Lahore provides evidence that—regardless of Partition trauma being fresh in the minds of the audience—mainstream cinema was less inimical to Pakistan in 1949 than in the new millennium. Judging from the way in which Veer-Zaara contrasts India and Pakistan as political spaces, India's professed tolerance may have aided in distancing Pakistan because of the discourse around religious intolerance and 'man's inhumanity to man' around Partition promoted in India. The Indian public was perhaps not as persuaded about Pakistan being an 'intolerant space' in 1949 as it was in 2004.

This reading of Veer-Zaara, it must be acknowledged, is different from the one given by other film scholars,[16] some of whom have seen the border-crossing in the film as radical although they see the film favourably largely in relation to Gadar: Ek Prem Katha and The Hero (2003), the latter being another jingoistic anti-Pakistan Hindi film appearing in the same time period. Pakistani writers have also commented favourably on Veer-Zaara[17] although with some reservations, and once again in contrast to the examples of jingoism just cited.

Since Hindi cinema has traditionally been a pan-Indian cinema it has set its own limits at the boundaries of the Nation. This is evidently not to suggest that it restricts its camera to India but that even when much of it is set abroad, its subject is India and the Indian community. Before the advent of globalization, Hindi cinema did not need to contend with a social interface with the rest of the world but with Indians working abroad becoming a common experience it has had to rethink its narrative strategies—especially with regard to its portrayal of monogamous heterosexuality. As discussed earlier while dealing with the adulterous woman in the Hindi cinema, the male character played by Amitabh Bachchan, in *KANK* (2006), is casual in his relationships with American women but in the film care is taken to see that none of these relationships is lasting and termed as 'love'. It is virtually inconceivable in a mainstream Hindi film that an Indian man should indulge in monogamous heterosexuality or enter into a relationship which leads to matrimony with someone from outside the Nation.[18] *Rang De Basanti* (2006) does not allow its British heroine to marry the man she loves although he returns her love. This tendency has been equally true of relationships between Indians and Pakistanis. Randhir Kapoor's *Henna* (1991) provides evidence of it. In this film, the woman protagonist, a Kashmiri from Pakistan, dies trying to save the Indian man[19] whom she loves—for the Indian woman he is due to marry. This drawing of the national boundary being a constant in Hindi cinema, the question of why the two Indo-Pakistan romances dealt with in this chapter are allowed to come to fruition arises.

The years in which the two films were made, India was ruled by the BJP which, as already indicated in this chapter, has generally played up to the dream of 'Akhand Bharat' or an undivided India allegedly undermined by the Congress in 1947. Both films may have sensed the upsurge in the 'Akhand Bharat' sentiment in this period of BJP rule; they show India as a morally superior space in which democracy and tolerance naturally flourish without the impediments placed upon them as in Pakistan. As already suggested, *Gadar: Ek Prem Katha*, is more aggressively Hindu-nationalistic of the two which *Veer-Zaara* is not. When huge crowds assemble in Lahore to witness Tara Singh's conversion to Islam it acknowledges that Pakistan is not simply a space ruled by a rogue aristocracy but that there is a Pakistani public which might participate willingly in such events. The film may not be sympathetic to this public but there is still an acknowledgement that Pakistan is a legitimate nation populated by people who *chose it. Veer-Zaara* is markedly different. The film came out when India's economic fortunes were on the rise and the national mood was upbeat. Sensing this, the BJP embarked upon the 'India Shining' campaign but lost the national elections the same year.[20] *Veer-Zaara* displays much of this optimism and when Zara, Shabbo, and Saamiya look up to India as a moral beacon, it also casts doubt on the viability of Pakistan as a democratic proposition; Raza moving abroad also suggests this. As already indicated, both films are about India/Hindu 'conquests' but *Veer-Zaara* is a conquest of a different kind because it also suggests that Pakistani women like Zaara must come to India to live meaningful lives. The optimistic India it portrays is perhaps the 'undivided India' that Pakistan missed.

Notes

1. M.S.S. Pandian describes how a Tamil Christian attempted to Indianize Christianity in the early twentieth century as a result. See M.S.S. Pandian, 'Nation as Nostalgia: Ambiguous Spiritual Journeys of Vengal Chakkarai', *Economic and Political Weekly*, vol. 38, nos 51/52, 27 December 2003, pp. 5357–64.

2. See M.K. Raghavendra, 'Structure and Form in Indian Popular Film Narrative', in Vinay Lal and Ashis Nandy (eds), *Fingerprinting Popular Culture: The Mythic and the Iconic in Indian Cinema* (New Delhi: Oxford University Press, 2006), pp. 24–46.

3. This is not to say that while Jawaharlal Nehru was viewed favourably, the period in which Lal Bahadur Shastri ruled was regretted. *Upkar*, in fact, eulogizes Shastri and treats Nehru with veiled derision. It shows a road populated by beggars and names it 'Nehru Road'.

4. This is after adjusting for inflation. The information is taken from the website of IBOS Network, 'Box Office Decade in Review: 2001— Gadar, K3G, Lagaan', 31 December 2009, http://www.ibosnetwork. com/newsmanager/templates/template1.aspx?a=21924&z=7 (accessed on 13 June 2012).

5. See Rahul Kapoor, 'Film-makers Refused to Portray Partition', *Real Bollywood*, 1 November 2006, which reports a talk by film scholar, Ira Bhaskar, http://www.realbollywood.com/news/2006/11/film-makers-refused-to-portray-partition.html (accessed on 14 June 2012).

6. Mushtaq Gazdar, *Pakistani Cinema 1947–1997* (Karachi: Oxford University Press, 1997), p. 81. Meghna Guhathakurta, 'Families, Displacement', in Ghislaine Glasson Deschaumes and Rada Ivekovic (eds), *Divided Countries, Separated Cities: The Modern Legacy of Partition* (New Delhi: Oxford University Press, 2003), pp. 96–105.

7. Guhathakurta, 'Families, Displacement.'

8. See Meenakshi Shedde, 'In East Pakistan, Partition Was Seen as a Good Thing', *DNA*, 7 July 2006. Shedde talks to film scholar Moinak Biswas who says,

> But in East Pakistan, many of the Hindus were landowners. And according to scholars like Partha Chatterjee, with Partition, there was expropriation of land by the tillers, leading to an agrarian revolution. The Bangladeshi poet Al Mahmood even says, 'Partition was a good thing.' It is mainly the Hindus who were traumatized and so don't want to talk about it. But for a generation of poor Muslim tillers, it was an escape from a life spent behind the plough.

9. For instance, Gyanendra Pandey, *Remembering Partition: Violence, Nationalism and History in India* (Cambridge: Cambridge University Press, 2001).

10. For instance, see Mohammed Hanif, 'Our Case against Manto', *Herald* (Beta)-*Dawn*, 10 May 2012, http://herald.dawn.com/2012/05/10/our-case-against-manto-2.html (accessed on 13 June 2012).

11. For instance, see Stuart Corbridge, 'Cartographies of Loathing and Desire: The Bharatiya Janata Party, the Bomb, and the Political Spaces of Hindu Nationalism', in Yale H. Ferguson and R.J. Barry Jones (eds), *Political Space: Frontiers of Change and Governance in a Globalizing World* (New York: State University of New York Press, Albany, 2002), pp. 151–72.

12. The threat of Muslims outnumbering Hindus because of their indifference to birth control is a threat perpetually held out by the Hindu right-wing.

13. The protagonist, Vijay, is a coolie with the same number in *Deewaar* and the arm-band with the number becomes his lucky charm even when he is no longer a coolie.

14. This refers to the epic medieval poem *Prithvirajaraso* by Chand Bardai. See Romila Thapar, *A History of India*, vol. 1 (Harmondsworth: Penguin, 1966), pp. 235–6.

15. See M.K. Raghavendra, 'The Reinterpretation of Historical Trauma: Three Films about Partition', in Sukalpa Bhattacharjee and C. Joshua Thomas (eds), *Society, Representation and Textuality: The Critical Interface* (Delhi: Sage, 2013), pp. 233–6.
16. Rajinder Dudrah, 'Borders and Border Crossings in *Main Hoon Na* and *Veer-Zaara*', in Meenakshi Bharat and Nirmal Kumar (eds), *Filming the Line of Control: Indo-Pak Relationships through the Cinematic Lens* (New Delhi: Routledge, 2008), pp. 53–4.
17. Arshad Amanullah and Aijaz Gul, 'Cinema in Pakistan: History, Present Scenario and Future Prospects', in Meenakshi Bharat and Nirmal Kumar (eds), *Filming the Line of Control: Indo-Pak Relationships through the Cinematic Lens* (New Delhi: Routledge, 2008), pp 184.
18. This is consistent with some predictions of globalization pundits. For instance, see Mike Featherstone, 'Localism, Globalism, Cultural Identity', in Rob Wilson and Wimal Dissanayake (eds), *Global Local: Cultural Production and the Transnational Imaginary* (Durham: Duke University Press, 1996), p. 60.

    ... The result of the increasing intensity of contact and communication between the nation-states and other agencies is to produce a clashing of cultures, which can lead to heightened attempts to draw boundaries between the self and the others. From this perspective ... the changes taking place as a result of the current phase of intensified globalization can be understood as reactions which seek to discover particularity, localism, and difference ....

19. *Henna* demarcates Pakistani Kashmir as 'Kashmir' by making the populace ethnic 'Kashmiris' but shows Indian Kashmir simply as 'India' by giving the characters Indian names not found commonly in Kashmir.
20. A useful account of the election can be found in an interview in *The Hindu*. See 'A Campaign that Lost Sheen', an interview with Ronald B. Inden by Prasun Sonwalkar, *The Hindu Magazine*, Sunday, 3 October 2004, http://www.hindu.com/mag/2004/10/03/stories/2004100300160200.htm (accessed on 18 June 2012).

4

The Youth Film as Dissent

Rang De Basanti (2006) and the Political Class

The Anglophone Indian and the Youth Film

It has been widely noticed by critics that Hindi cinema after 1992 privileges the affluent as the worthiest of subjects. This has also been broadly true of the films discussed in this book so far. Although these films are about people who might be well versed in the English language one rarely gets the sense that the people inhabiting them are 'Anglophone'. While they may speak English there one does not get the sense from the films that English would be the language they are most comfortable with. In fact, even *Jism* and its associates employ elaborate Hindi which is not peppered by English phrases—although they are living global lifestyles. The earliest Hindi film in which one gets the sense of 'Anglophone' subjects in this sense is Rakeysh Omprakash Mehra's *Rang De Basanti* (2006), which is probably also the first explicitly political of the new films. Characters, when surprised, casually exclaim 'shit' regardless of whom they are addressing; one character even addresses a porter carrying her luggage as 'sweetheart' as a gesture of familiarity—something unimaginable in the earlier Hindi cinema. The film includes extended segments in which only English is heard. This is not to say that the characters in the film come from the same class: while the protagonist Daljit Singh or DJ (Aamir Khan) is a Sikh whose mother runs a *dhaba*, the most affluent of them Karan Singhania (Siddharth) is the son of a successful businessman who lives in a bungalow with an enormous driveway. Another is a young Muslim named Aslam (Kunal Kapoor) who lives in a dilapidated dwelling in an ancient part of the city while a fourth is a Brahmin named Lakshman Pandey, a grass-roots worker for a Hindu nationalist organization. They belong to different social categories but the film conveys the sense that they belong to a homogeneous group best termed 'urban youth' with attitudes inculcated in them by Western-style liberal education, largely in English. This is emphasized at the conclusion of the film when a number of young people are interviewed by a television channel about the happenings and most of the interviewees reply in English. This last factor provides a clue about the film's address because the interviewees are placed in the position of the film's audience and also asked to judge. The film is, therefore, primarily addressing Anglophone youth from metropolitan cities although this does not mean that Anglophone youth constitute its only audience.

If there have been youth films in Hindi before *Rang De Basanti* they were largely romances involving young people. There may be some deliberate stereotyping pointing to youth as self-absorbed and disconnected from social life[1] but youth films still employ the qualities of their subjects as a way of raising social issues.[2] But if this indicates a political role for youth films, Hindi cinema has generally avoided explicit political engagement. For instance, two key youth films *Bobby* (1973) and *Qayamat Se Qayamat Tak* (1988) are only about young people whose marital plans are opposed by their families. Although the youth represented in Hindi cinema have been described by film researchers as 'typically pliable and deferential towards elders',[3] these films allow for rebellion inasmuch as the youth refuse to bow down to family demands and are even prepared to give up their lives. But the key issue is generational conflict and this is as true of *Rang De*

Basanti, which is perhaps a first in Hindi cinema for pushing romance to the background and becoming deliberately political. Two of its male protagonists have conflicts with their fathers and Lakshman Pandey comes into conflict with a father figure in his Hindu nationalist political party. But before proceeding to examine how its Anglophone and genre characteristics tie up with its political slant, we may first examine the film and its success.

Rang De Basanti and Its Public

Rang De Basanti was a runaway hit but its success was much greater in the metropolitan cities (and with non-residents) than in the hinterland or semi-urban areas. The following table will give the reader an idea of how its collections were distributed across India by comparing it with two other films dealt with earlier in this book:[4]

Rang De Basanti: Distribution of collections

	Mumbai (Rs in crore)	Bihar (Rs in crore)	All India (Rs in crore)
Rang De Basanti (2006)	30.50	NA	71.00
Gadar: Ek Prem Katha (2001)	31.25	7.85	130.25
Raaz (2002)	NA	1.45	37.00

We may presume that where data is not available the film has performed unremarkably. If Mumbai and Bihar are taken to represent the metropolitan centres and the semi-urban centres, respectively,[5] it can be seen that *Rang De Basanti*'s collections are predominantly from the metropolitan areas. *Gadar: Ek Prem Katha* has done very well almost evenly across India, while *Raaz* has done best in the rural/semi-urban and urban centres.

Rang De Basanti begins with an English girl Sue (Alice Patten) being inspired by her grandfather's journal to make a film about Bhagat Singh and his comrades in India, who courageously embraced death for the nationalist cause. Before going on to describe the rest of the film, I should perhaps say a few words about its portrayal of the British. The British, in Indian patriotic cinema of the new millennium, have come a long way since *1942: A Love Story*—in which the wicked Englishman is hanged—and the strategy in the film is to have a well-meaning representative (as also in *Mangal Pandey*, 2005) admiring the Indian nationalists even as he performs his duty as servant of the Raj. In *Rang De Basanti*, the British play two different roles through Sue and her grandfather, a jailor in British India. Implicated in colonialism and its excesses but unwilling, the grandfather is still the objective participant who records 'the truth' and whose account therefore justifies the veneration heaped upon the Indian Nation. British officers did maintain journals but the grandfather's is uncharacteristically euphoric in the endorsement of the Indian cause and therefore serves *Rang De Basanti*'s patriotism rather than history.[6]

Returning to *Rang De Basanti*, Sue is met at Delhi airport by Sonia (Soha Ali Khan) and, through her, meets the male protagonists of the film. There are four of them initially—DJ, Karan whose father is actually an arms contractor, Aslam, and Sukhi (Sharman Joshi). Another friend of Sonia's—who later is engaged to her—is Ajay Rathod (Madhavan), a flight lieutenant in the Indian Air Force. Sue now busies herself looking for a cast to play the revolutionaries and it is some time before she realizes that Sonia's friends are tailor-made for the roles. The four are, however, a happy-go-lucky lot and hardly fit to play revolutionaries. To make matters worse, they have an adversary in Lakshman Pandey (Atul Kulkarni), an ardent Hindu nationalist who disapproves of their flippant ways. Still, the indomitable Sue persuades the protagonists to play parts in her film and infuses them with the idealism of those they will be playing. She still needs someone to play the key role of Ram Prasad Bismil and it is Lakshman Pandey who demonstrates that he has the spirit.

The film cleverly shows the progressive transformation of the young protagonists when it alternates between the film Sue is going to make (in which the protagonists play their parts) and the present of which they themselves are a part. This strategy also helps the film to assert that one can be as radically patriotic today as the young revolutionaries were in their time and show that the protagonists are no less laudable for what they eventually do. To cut a long story short, a moral crisis occurs when Ajay Rathod's MiG aircraft crashes and there is little doubt that the 'faulty Russian spares' are responsible for the debacle but the defence minister insists on Ajay's incompetence, bringing discredit to the dead boy. The protagonists stage a protest but Ajay's mother (Waheeda Rehman) is assaulted so badly that she goes into a coma. The young protagonists now decide that the only way out is to assassinate the defence minister. They shoot him dead and also announce their motives on All India Radio. But the foe is implacable and black-cat commandoes are dispatched to liquidate them. The five die heroically but not before they reveal that one of them—Karan Singhania—has just killed his own father, the arms contractor implicated in the MiG scandal. Sue, who has not participated in the assassination, is in deep distress at the death of her five idealist friends but the struggle will nonetheless continue. This is manifested in interviews conducted by a private television channel of youth from their generation who are vehement for the struggle to continue.

The Global West

The most obvious innovation of the film, it is apparent, is in its enlistment of Sue to an Indian nationalist cause. The 'West' has been represented often in mainstream Indian cinema through white characters, although not always with approval. For instance, in the years when Prime Minister Indira Gandhi was leaning towards the Soviet Bloc, the white smuggler in Hindi films shown as attempting to fly temple idols out of the country tended to symbolize the 'West'.[7] If Sue's grandfather was still a colonialist, Sue herself bears no relationship to the race of colonizers. She is perhaps from the global West and, by making her an agent of Indian nationalism, the film suggests that nationalism and globalism are not incompatible. This finds correspondence in the prediction of globalization scholars[8] who felt that rather than leading to a unified 'global state', the result of the increasing intensity of contact and communication between the nation states and other agencies would be to heighten attempts to draw boundaries between the home country and the others. By this token, Sue's love for the male protagonist remaining unconsummated is an articulation of the inviolability of the national boundary.

Considering that even *Lagaan* (2001) sniggered at the West/ Britain, *Rang De Basanti*'s attitude is unexpected. But a clue is perhaps to be found in some of the other aspects of the film already remarked upon. By 2006, when the film was made, young English-speaking youth had become an economic force to contend with in India because of the new economy businesses (largely, information technology and information technology enabled services) and 90 per cent of them worked in seven metropolitan cities.[9] Most of these people were keyed into global businesses and foreign travel had become commonplace. Globalization, therefore, resulted in young Indians from the cities viewing the West and Britain with less hostility than before, being even inclined to entertain the notion of the colonial Englishman sympathetic to Indian nationalism. In this information are explanations for the film's sympathies, its targeted audience, and its choice of protagonists. But what still needs to be understood is its political discourse.

The 'Community' and Politics

In dealing with the group of protagonists, a key aspect has not been touched upon which is that the group has all the makings of the 'community' familiar to us from Hindi cinema. The film tries, for instance, to give representation to all religious and economic categories within the group. As with other Hindi film communities in which there is an enemy outside (for example, in *Lagaan*), there is a member of the community who has to ultimately make a decision to stay with the community. In *Lagaan*, it must be recollected that the headman joins the community at the end. The issue of 'loyalty' to the dead Ajay Rathod is also invoked by *Rang De Basanti*. Since the community has been a constant way of allegorizing the Nation, how are we to regard this aspect of *Rang De Basanti*? Since the film offers us the parallel story of the young revolutionaries of the 1920s by way of comparison, we could say that the community allegorizes the 'Nation' gradually becoming self-aware. The defence minister and the arms contractor may be taken to represent the 'enemy outside'—like the British. The fact that the group allegorizing the Nation is composed entirely of urban Indians with knowledge of English makes us uncomfortable but the justification may be given that if *Mother India* (1957) can represent the Nation through a single village, could not a group of students from Delhi University be an equally legitimate way of representing it? This is an important question and I propose to examine it later in the chapter.

Rang De Basanti was called 'reformist' and even 'revolutionary' and compared to V. Shantaram's *Duniya Na Mane* (1937) and Bimal Roy's *Do Bigha Zamin*.[10] One reason for its being read as revolutionary by the mainstream media may have been its intense look at national heroes like Bhagat Singh and Chandra Shekhar Azad and also the strategy by which ordinary people are shown to gain stature as political beings. This last strategy is perhaps even a first for Hindi cinema which has tended to 'essentialize' individuals,[11] identifying qualities as intrinsic to them. The strategy is necessitated by another one—the comparison between two political situations, the colonial one in the 1920s and that in contemporary India. It is superfluous to emphasize that the situations are not comparable and the Indian state in the new millennium has hardly acted 'tyrannically' against the class of urban youth portrayed in *Rang De Basanti*. The weakness of the Indian state has, in fact, been an overt signification in later Hindi cinema as will become evident in the subsequent chapters. What *Rang De Basanti* does is, therefore, to feed a political fantasy to the class it is addressing, and the principal issue around which this is constructed is that of 'corruption'.

The film, it can be said broadly, is about corruption although it describes its actual thrust inadequately. What needs more attention is the deliberate location of this 'corruption' in the political class. The figure of the corrupt politician is not new to Hindi cinema and we recall films like Ram Gopal Verma's *Satya* (1999) in which the protagonist liquidates the political boss. Still, *Rang De Basanti* makes a significant departure from this convention inasmuch as the politician's *personal* acts play no part in the narrative action (as they do in *Satya*). The politician in *Rang De Basanti* is not culpable for any individual wrong doing but he is still guilty because he acts the way politicians are believed to. If the politician is made the 'villain' of the film on such grounds, it is apparently not defence minister Shastri who is indicted but his entire class. The 'reform' proposed by the film then appears the elimination of the elected political class because this class is directly responsible for the ills plaguing the Nation. What more convenient emblem for the Nation is there besides the military and what handier way of representing 'national ills' than its betrayal by politics?

Taken literally, the 'reform' proposed by *Rang De Basanti* seems absurd but a closer look at it is necessary as the message can also be read symbolically/covertly. Ever since the liberalization measures of 1991–2, the state has been withdrawing from the spheres where it was actively engaged. Functions like power and water distribution, and public health, once entirely within the ambit of its activities, have been moving progressively into the private domain and there is clamour from the industry for more private participation. Complete withdrawal by the state implies the 'removal' of politics from the public space because politics is (in a sense) the means by which the state is made accountable to the public. The liquidation of the politician in *Rang De Basanti* may then simply be a dramatic (and allegorical) way of representing this 'removal'. It is also significant that a private television channel[12] is a beacon of hope in the milieu in which the protagonists struggle and it is this channel which reports on the violence, reveals the nexus between the defence minister and the arms dealer, and interviews the young people towards the conclusion.

At this point, it will be pertinent to examine why a group of young Anglophones as the 'community' allegorizing the Nation is difficult to accept even when the representation of the Nation by a group of non-resident Indians (NRIs) in New York in *KANK* (2006) presents no such difficulty. Upon examining the two films, it is revealed that while the 'community' in *KANK* is self-contained, that is, not positing a Nation outside itself, the one in *Rang De Basanti* has the actual Nation and real political issues outside—the single issue in it is most vehemently 'corrupt politicians'. Politics in India is a contaminated realm, it must be admitted, but it is still the only means by which democracy can be inclusive. This has not received much attention but every act of withdrawal by the state is also a step by which the electorate is made to relinquish its claims upon politics. The remark may be contested but the middle classes from the metropolises are those with the least use for politics, which is why they are notoriously indifferent to elections.[13] Officialdom is more accessible to them; the English press and the television channels give them more than their due[14] and this means their grievances get (relatively) easy redress—even as the rest must rely upon the political class for their representation. Also, the middle class is accustomed to easing its way by paying bribes. (*Rang De Basanti* acknowledges this propensity to bribe when, in an early part of the film, DJ and his friends are involved in a public scuffle with their adversaries and the former slips an annoyed police officer some money in order to pacify him.) The remaining classes, on the other hand, generally have little recourse to these avenues and depend on their elected representatives and patronage—usually based on religion/caste/group affinities.[15] Since politicians are elected representatives of the public they are also playing roles elsewhere and, regardless of the corrupt practices they are perceived to engage in, their presence is useful, though perhaps not to the Anglophone class from the metropolitan cities. Considering this, the doubtful aspect of the 'nation' allegorized by a cosmopolitan 'community' of youth from the metropolis is that it is an exclusive Nation. It has no use for the elected politicians upon whom most of the actual Nation's less privileged public depends.

The sense of the film trying to constitute the Nation out of a minority group brings us to a fundamental schism present in the polity: the contrary pulls from those who favour laissez-faire policies to 'support growth' and those who favour 'populism'. We have seen how Hindi cinema changed direction after the official conclusion of Nehruvian socialism in 1991–2 but it is as though Nehruvian socialism as a sentiment was not yet completely dead. The indifference of the middle classes towards elections suggests that it is the less-privileged class whose voting is decisive in the electoral process. This implies that the populist pull is likely to gain strength as national elections approach and lose strength when they are over.[16] Since the most vocal classes are in the metropolitan areas and associated with industry—as employees, vendors, and investors—their favouring of free enterprise may be expected. *Rang De Basanti* appeared when the national elections of 2009 were a long way off and this class had a powerful voice. It can be argued that its brand of patriotism is the voice of a vocal urban class associated with industry. *Rang De Basanti* privileging a private television channel as a purveyor of truth substantiates this.[17] While it is not within the scope of this enquiry to take sides politically, from the viewpoint adopted in this book, the film emerges as an expression of patriotism towards an asymmetric nation.

Notes

1. See Susannah R. Stern, 'Self-Absorbed, Dangerous and Disengaged: What Popular Films Tell Us about Teenagers', *Mass Communication and Society*, vol. 8, no. 1, 2005, pp. 23–38.
2. For instance, the influence of the counterculture movement on *The Graduate* (1967) is self-evident. Jean-Luc Godard's *La Chinoise* (1967) virtually anticipated Paris of 1968. Youth films and teen films from Hollywood are generally regarded as having appeared when the industry faced challenges and the importance of young audiences were revealed by research, such as in the 1940s. See Steve Neele, *Genre and Hollywood* (London: Routledge, 2000), p. 119. There has been little dependable research in India on audience segmentation and my proposition here is that youth films feed on political situations in which generational conflict is signified.

3. See Jyotika Virdi, *The Cinematic ImagiNation: Indian Popular Films as Social History* (Delhi: Permanent Black, 2003), p. 187.

4. See Box Office India, http://www.boxofficeindia.com (accessed on 21 June 2012).

5. The data available allows for only the following territories apparently identified in British India: Mumbai, Delhi/Uttar Pradesh, East Punjab, West Bengal, Bihar, C.P. Berar, C.I., Nizam's Hyderabad, Mysore, and others. C.P. Berar may be taken to comprise parts of present-day Maharashtra, parts of Madhya Pradesh, and Chhattisgarh. 'C.I.' is constituted by parts of Madhya Pradesh.

6. Contrary to the grandfather's journal, such 'objective' accounts, under the guise of reflecting upon personal experiences, actually furthered the colonial discourse. See Ranajit Guha, 'The Prose of Counter-Insurgency', in Ranajit Guha and Gayatri Chakravorty Spivak (eds), *Selected Subaltern Studies* (New York: Oxford University Press, 1988), pp. 45–86.

7. Beatrix Pfleiderer, 'An Emprical Study of Urban and Semi-urban Audience Reaction to Hindi Films,' in Lothar Lutze and Beatrix Pfleiderer (eds), *The Hindi Film: Agent and Re-agent of Cultural Change* (Delhi: Manohar, 1985), p. 127. Apart from the crackdown on smuggling in the period and the enactment of a special law (Conservation of Foreign Exchange and Prevention of Smuggling Activities Act [COFEPOSA], 1974), Pfleiderer suggests that smuggling is associated with 'Western behaviour' because smugglers cross the boundaries between East and West.

8. Mike Featherstone, 'Localism, Globalism, Cultural Identity', in Rob Wilson and Wimal Dissanayake (eds), *Global Local: Cultural Production and the Transnational Imaginary* (Durham: Duke University Press, 1996), p. 60.

9. To give the reader an idea, the turnover of the information technology (IT) industry which was around USD 12 billion in 1999–2000 increased to around USD 37 billion by 2005–6. The increase in the number of employees and the total salaries paid to these employees may roughly be proportional considering that the growth of the IT sector revenues has been linear. Since the total number employed in the country—directly and indirectly—is estimated at 11.7 million people in 2012, the total number employed in 2006 could have been about 6 million people in the seven cities. See http://www.nasscom.in/indian-itbpo-industry (accessed on 22 June 2012).

10. Subhash K. Jha, 'The ABC of Revolutionary Films', *Deccan Herald*, 26 February 2006.

11. See M.K. Raghavendra, *Seduced by the Familiar: Narration and Meaning in Indian Popular Cinema* (New Delhi: Oxford University Press, 2008), pp. 45–9.

12. The channel mentioned in the film is NDTV and the same channel is acknowledged in the credits.

13. This has been commented upon both in the mainstream press and blogs. According to estimates, only 30–35 per cent of educated Indians vote in elections. See http://www.bharatvotes.org/middle.html (accessed on 23 June 2012). For an example of deliberations in the press, see 'E-voting the Answer to Electoral Apathy', *The Statesman*, 23 June 2012, http://thestatesman.net/index.php?option=com_content&view=article&id=3 52839&catid=39&Itemid=66 (accessed on 23 June 2012).

14. This is widely recognized. For instance, see the report on the President of India asking the media to shed its urban bias: 'Shed Urban Bias, Focus on Rural Areas, Kalam tells Media', *Zee News*, 16 November 16 2006, http://zeenews.india.com/news/nation/shed-urban-bias-focus-on-rural-areas-kalam-tells-media_336074.html (accessed on 24 June 2012).

15. A helpful enquiry into the role of patronage in India's elections is to be found in Kanchan Chandra, *Why Ethnic Parties Succeed: Patronage and Ethnic Headcounts in India* (New York: Cambridge University Press, 2004).

16. The tardiness in economic reforms, when elections approach, is a constant subject in the press. For instance, the fallout of chief economic advisor to Government of India Kaushik Basu's remark that major economic reforms were unlikely before the next election in 2014. See 'Kaushik Basu Clarifies Stand on Economic Reforms, Says He Was Misquoted', *The Economic Times*, 20 April 2012, http://economictimes. indiatimes.com/news/politics/nation/kaushik-basu-clarifies-stand-on-economic-reforms-says-he-was-misquoted/articleshow/12752261.cms (accessed on 14 May 2012).

17. The 'truthfulness' of the media came under a cloud through the 'Radia Tapes' episode in 2010 when it was found to be actively involved in political lobbying. For instance, see Priscilla Jebaraj, 'The Spotlight Is on the Media Now', *The Hindu*, 24 November 2010, opinion page, http://www.thehindu.com/opinion/lead/article907823.ece (accessed on 24 June 2012).

5

The Agony Aunt and the Small Illegality

Munna Bhai M.B.B.S. (2003) and
Lage Raho Munna Bhai (2006)

Comedy and Hierarchy

Comedy has not represented a genre in Hindi cinema although most films provide comic relief within a narrative in which romance and/or action dominates. If 'comedy' in mainstream Hindi cinema is acknowledged, the most appropriate term to describe it would be 'romantic comedy' because the films are about the overcoming of minor obstacles in the path of love. Romantic comedies from Hollywood (for example, *Bridget Jones' Diary*, 2001) sometimes derive from a popular formula in pulp romance. In stories that work by this formula, an intelligent woman is overwhelmed by the love of an intelligent, tender, and good-humoured man who is transformed in the course of their relationship from an 'emotional pre-literate' to someone who can care and with the capacity to nurture.[1] This has been understood as a fantasy about reciprocation, the wish that men bestow upon women the care and attention that women are expected to bestow as mothers. Romance is thus a way in which women can vicariously experience the emotional succour which they are expected to provide to others without hope of reciprocation in their everyday lives.[2] An 'emotional pre-literate' as a lover can afford opportunity for humour but this formula is truer for straightforward romances. As has been argued about romantic fiction,[3] narratives of this kind promise a secure world, one in which even when there is subordination, the woman is also allowed to achieve a sort of power through stability. These formulae are widespread and recognizable in many of Hollywood's most enduring classics (*My Fair Lady*, 1964; *The Sound of Music*, 1965). Since the explanations for the success of the formula are psychoanalytical, one would expect the formula to be universally popular. Contrarily, however, romantic comedies in Hindi cinema do not favour either of these models. In Hindi film romances and romantic comedies there is no transformation of the man to make him fit for love because both lovers are 'loveable'. Secondly, there is no doubt in the minds of the audience that the hero and heroine are meant only for each other. As in the case of melodrama, audiences are not meant to follow the emotional trajectories of the characters onscreen, but another reason could be that love is less between free agents than a social transaction in which the respective hierarchical positions of the two need to be respected.

Two romantic comedies, *Munna Bhai M.B.B.S.* and *Lage Raho Munna Bhai*, captured the public imagination in the new millennium. They share a plot device common to a significantly large proportion of comedies in India. This comic device involves an innocuous violation of hierarchy: usually a lowly placed person pretends to belong to a higher station or a distinguished person is mistaken for someone lower. In Mehboob Khan's *Andaz* (1949), the comic relief is provided by a clown, named Professor Devdas Dharamdas Trivedi (also known as D.D.T.),[4] who is pretending to be a scholar. In Hrishikesh Mukherjee's celebrated *Chupke Chupke* (1975), a newly wedded professor of botany plays a joke on his wife's family by pretending to be a chauffeur. Two of Hollywood's biggest comedy hits in India worked by the same formula: *Come September* (1961) and *Irma La Douce* (1963). In the latter film, which was remade in Hindi as *Manoranjan* (1974), a Paris police constable impersonates an English aristocrat for the sake of love. In the two romantic comedies discussed here a hoodlum impersonates a learned man or a professional for the sake of winning a loved one who is not averse to him to begin with.

It is significant that a poor man pretending to be rich or vice versa is not often the stuff of Hindi comedy and what counts is station rather than wealth—whether it is denoted by learning or by pedigree. While the violations of hierarchy in Hindi comedy are inevitably innocuous, more serious violations get the opposite effect and are often the material of high drama or tragedy. In *Raja Harishchandra* (1913), a king is reduced to becoming the keeper of the cremation ground. In the countless versions of *Devdas*, the zamindar's son, through a life of dissipation, finds himself a vagrant on the streets, to be cared for only by a prostitute. In Raj Kapoor's *Awaara* (1951), the judge's wife is cast out by her husband because he wrongly suspects her child to be someone else's. Drama results from the son growing up resenting his exclusion from respectable society. In *Trishul* (1978), the deprived protagonist played by Amitabh Bachchan grows up aggrieved at not being acknowledged by his businessman father. With the privileging of affluence in film narrative after 1992[5] and rich protagonists being a basic condition that stories are unwilling to violate, the dramatic motif has all but disappeared; innocuous violations of hierarchy in comedy continue.

The popularity of hierarchical violations as the first cause in any drama, whether comic or dramatic, may be attributed to Indian society being traditionally constituted with hierarchy as the guiding notion. As distinct from other systems, hierarchical status (as denoted by caste) is separate from the status imposed by the exercise of power; the politico-economic aspects are secondary in relation to the ideology of caste.[6] Hierarchy in society is, therefore, not something which has arisen through practice but a *constituting ideological principle*. This means that hierarchical stability within the social structure finds itself enshrined. As may be expected, this notion influences literary and film narrative immensely. Hence, the stories in most of the films cited are set in motion when hierarchical stability is disturbed[7] and resolved when this stability is restored. This narrative model is followed by the two films being examined in this chapter.

The Films

In Rajkumar Hirani's *Munna Bhai M.B.B.S.*, Murli Prasad Sharma (Sanjay Dutt), nicknamed Munna Bhai, is a *bhai* or *goonda*: an extortionist and criminal involved in *dadagiri* (strong-arm methods). Since his father wished him to become a medical doctor, he creates an enterprise named Sri Hari Prasad Sharma Charitable Hospital (named after his father) which comes alive abruptly whenever his father (Sunil Dutt) and mother (Rohini Hattangadi) visit him in Mumbai. One year, however, Munna's plan goes awry when his father meets an old acquaintance, Dr Asthana (Boman Irani), and the two older men decide to marry Munna off to Asthana's daughter Chinki (Gracy Singh). At this point, the truth about Munna is revealed. Munna's father and mother, aghast and heartbroken that their son is a hoodlum and not a physician, leave for their village. Munna decides that the only way to redemption after the humiliation suffered by his family at the hands of Dr Asthana is to become a doctor. He decides to go to a medical college to obtain a graduate medical degree (MBBS). Dr Asthana is Dean at the medical college in Mumbai that he enrolls in.

The first part of *Munna Bhai M.B.B.S.* is a comedy but the film has a change of heart in its later phase. Chinki is actually a doctor (Dr Suman) and works in the same hospital. She chooses to keep her relationship with Asthana secret and Munna finds himself falling in love with her. Although Munna is hopeless at his studies, he brings life to the hospital and gives even the dying the will to live through his ministrations. At the end of the film, Munna abandons his course but he and Dr Suman start a clinic named Sri Hari Prasad Sharma Charitable Hospital with Dr Asthana, who has been conclusively proved wrong in his assessment of Munna, also assisting.

It is apparent that the motif of the small time hoodlum who pretends to be a doctor fits the pattern described earlier. In order to keep the violation of hierarchy innocuous enough to make the film a comedy, Munna Bhai is given a Brahmin surname and a respectable family background. If he had been any less, his relationship with Chinki/Dr Suman could not have been brought to fruition without problematizing the differences in their hierarchical status. Problematizing it would necessarily have cast doubt on the film's claims to being a comedy. The sequel to *Munna Bhai M.B.B.S.* is really the focus of this essay. *Lage Raho Munna Bhai* has two characters from the earlier film—Munna Bhai and his assistant Circuit (Arshad Warsi)—but Indian popular cinema cannot really accommodate sequels.[8] The film, essentially, is depending on the Munna Bhai brand for its success without it having any other links to *Munna Bhai M.B.B.S.* except the formula of the hoodlum-turned-respected-professional. As in the earlier film, its comedy also makes way for the sententious. Making its sententiousness more exceptional is that it uses Gandhi as the pivot—both parodying the notion of Gandhian idealism and campaigning for it.

When the second story begins, Munna is in love with the voice of Jhanvi (Vidya Balan), a radio jockey. He devises a plan to meet her when she announces a contest featuring the life and beliefs of Mahatma Gandhi set for 2 October, Gandhi Jayanti, a national holiday celebrating the birth of Gandhi. Circuit helps Munna win the contest by kidnapping and then bribing a group of professors. As the winner, Munna is granted an interview with Jhanvi wherein he presents himself as a professor of history and a Gandhi scholar. Jhanvi subsequently asks Munna to present a lecture on Gandhi to a group of senior citizens who live in a home she runs called the 'Second Innings House'. In order to prepare for his speech, Munna engages in a period of intense study at a Gandhi institute. For three days and nights (and without food or sleep), Munna reads about the life and teachings of Gandhi.

It is during this period in a library dedicated to the Father of the Nation that Mahatma Gandhi, addressed by his nickname 'Bapu', appears as an apparition and offers help and advice to Munna. He encourages Munna to tell the truth about himself to Jhanvi although Munna does not initially go along. Gandhi appears each time Munna sings 'Raghupati Raghava Raja Ram'. With Gandhi's help, Munna impresses Jhanvi and begins to lead a new kind of life based upon Gandhism (with an emphasis upon non-violence and truth). Munna starts to co-host a radio show with Jhanvi (and Gandhi's apparition), instructing his audiences to follow Gandhi in their everyday lives, the single panacea for all problems being the complete shunning of violence and falsehood, regardless of the cost.

The film has a subplot involving an unscrupulous businessman named Lucky Singh (Boman Irani) who acquires Second Innings House and enlists Circuit to demolish it. After an interlude of 'satyagraha' by Munna and the senior citizens, Lucky Singh yields and the house is recovered although Munna helps him with his daughter's marriage as well. Meanwhile, Munna has also informed Jhanvi that he is not a professor of history but a hoodlum. As in the earlier film, the girl (after some token hesitation) accepts Munna and the tale ends happily.

The Reception

Perhaps, as interesting as the content of Lage Raho Munna Bhai is the reception it received in India, where it was widely taken as a signal to a return to Gandhian values renamed 'Gandhigiri', the film remaining under media/public gaze for quite a while.[9] The film was presented as a moral breakthrough in public life with Gandhi's descendants endorsing the film's version of Gandhism.[10] Indian critics reporting on international responses were convinced that the film was universally inspiring though often without enough evidence:

> Eight months after its theatrical release, the inspiring story of Munna and his experiments with truth continues to touch people's hearts. At the Cannes film festival, where Lage Raho Munnabhai is included in the Cinema of the World section, the film's screening on Saturday

drew a packed house of mostly French students. Lining up in long queues to catch the film that had been strongly recommended in festival reviews, not one person who entered the screening left before the end of the two-hours-thirty-minutes film which was screened with French subtitles.[11]

Also, while writers of Indian origin abroad seemed to go overboard in their praise of the film, the critical responses of non-Indian writers in the international media was more muted, suggesting that the moral/philosophical implications of the film were not quite as 'universal' as Indian writers believed it to be. The difference in tone between non-Indian and Indian writers reporting in the international media is conspicuous. Here is a report from the *International Herald Tribune*, Asia Pacific:

The Gandhi National Museum in Delhi has two memorable exhibits. The first is a glass case containing a couple of Mahatma Gandhi's teeth, an ivory toothpick (used occasionally by Gandhiji) alongside his dentures ... The second is a quote from the Mahatma painted on a large signboard by the entrance to the museum, which describes the India of his dreams.

'I shall work for an India in which the poorest shall feel that it is their country, in whose making they have an effective voice; an India in which there shall be no high class and no low class of people; an India in which all communities shall live in perfect harmony,' he wrote in September 1931.

There would be no room in such an India for the 'curse of untouchability or the curse of intoxicating drinks and drugs. Women will enjoy the same rights as men.'

It is an accurate summary of what India today is not.

... This exercise in lip service was forgotten swiftly—the real excitement was a Bollywood film released on the same day, which has rapidly become the unexpected box-office hit of the year.

The film, 'Lage Raho Munnabhai'... follows the trials of an engaging Mumbai gangster who tries to pass himself off as a professor of Gandhian studies to win the heart of a radio talk show host. A specter of Gandhi, invisible to everyone but him, starts to haunt him, persuading him to abandon his life of crime and adopt a Gandhian existence. Soon the thug is preaching the message of nonviolence to his bewildered criminal associates.

With its big Bollywood soundtrack and dance routines, the movie brings Gandhi firmly into the mainstream and theaters have been packed for the past three weeks.[12]

Here is a writer of Indian origin in *The Boston Globe*:

Gandhi's sudden popularity among all ages and cultures in India brings to an end a long period in which his fame and influence had faded. While Hollywood holds a similar significance in people's lives as Mumbai-based Bollywood, the most popular branch of the Indian film industry, and has more money, resources, and global reach, it has not been able to create the same kind of response as Bollywood was able to generate for a historical figure.

Until August, when a comedy with Gandhi as a central figure was released all over India, most of the people who spoke about Gandhi and his values were alive when he was shot in 1948. Now, all generations have re-embraced the father, or 'Bapu,' of the nation.

In the movie, titled 'Lage Raho Munna Bhai,' gangster Munna Bhai meets Gandhi and instead of indulging in his usual 'dadagiri,' meaning bullying, he endorses Gandhi's teachings of non-violence and battles with his enemy by giving him flowers, rather than punches.[13]

If Indians in the diaspora responded overwhelmingly in favour of the film, *Lage Raho Munna Bhai*'s success was also predominantly an urban phenomenon with 'B' and 'C' centres contributing little to the collections.[14] If one compares the film's overseas success with that of *Krrish* (2006), a film released at about the same time, also an urban success but with its collections more widely dispersed across India, while around 17 per cent of *Krrish*'s gross collections came from overseas, nearly 20 per cent of *Lage Raho Munna Bhai*'s collections came from abroad.[15] If this is considered alongside the responses from the English language press and writers of Indian origin in the international media, one senses that urban audiences of the kind targeted by *Lage Raho Munna Bhai* have more attitudes in common with Indians in the diaspora than with Indians in small-town/rural India. On the basis of this information it can be argued that the wave of 'Gandhigiri' unleashed by the film was an urban phenomenon and largely confined to middle-class Indians from the metropolitan cities and the diaspora. The sense in some of the reporting on the film is of 'Gandhigiri' being a moral/philosophical export to the rest of the world. The Prime Minister, after a private screening, also declared that the film 'captures Bapu's message about the power of truth and humanism'.[16] But the crowning glory was perhaps the film being screened at the United Nations (UN).[17] Considering all this hype around *Lage Raho Munna Bhai* it may be useful to examine the episodes in the film incorporating the film's 'Gandhian message', that is, the way in which Gandhi's apparition intervenes in the protagonist's life. 'Gandhigiri' appears to be the way the urban middle-classes—and their cousins in the diaspora—understand Gandhian philosophy and the film may help us with clues as to what Gandhism means to the public which is frequently given to invoking the Father of the Nation, especially on ceremonial occasions.

'Gandhigiri'

If the responses to *Lage Raho Munna Bhai* suggest that it has a radical political viewpoint to offer, the actual film belies these expectations. The story of the film revolves around Munna Bhai, who is a hoodlum, passing himself off as a professor of history in order to win his loved one's heart. We know from comic literature and film comedy that,[18] where matters of the heart are concerned, such deceit is permissible but the film, while using the situation for humour, moves on to sententiousness when it judges Munna Bhai as a person fit for reform.

'Honesty is best' Bapu tells him but it is significant that the Father of the Nation has no advice to offer Munna Bhai on his criminal way of life—kidnapping and extortion. In fact, when Circuit empties Second Innings House of the belongings of its inhabitants, he does not do so on his own initiative but in partnership with Munna Bhai. 'Dadagiri' continues to be their vocation although Circuit was tricked into picking this house, that is the one occupied by Jhanvi's friends. After Munna Bhai has been transformed through Bapu's moral intervention, there is no indication that he has found another way of life for himself. This is in contrast to *Munna Bhai M.B.B.S.* in which the protagonist takes up a new life.[19]

If one looks at the miracles wrought by Bapu through the instrument of Munna Bhai, one is struck by their innocuousness. Bapu's primary achievement is to go into partnership with Munna Bhai as an agony aunt tendering personal advices of various sorts. An apartment owner manages to get his neighbour not to spit on his wall though a 'Gandhian' strategy. A pensioner who has to pay a bribe to a government official manages to avoid it. This episode—in which the pensioner disrobes and offers his clothes to the official by way of a bribe—apparently had a profound impact upon audiences although the import of the sequence is not that paying bribes is illegal. Although Second Innings House is restored to its inhabitants, Munna Bhai himself apparently remains a hoodlum. We are not told whether the crooked businessman Lucky Singh is transformed in a morally significant way although he is besotted with Gandhi. A key difficulty with the 'Gandhigiri' in *Lage Raho Munna Bhai* is that the film is silent about whether people living on the margins of legality—from Munna Bhai to Lucky Singh—are persuaded to become legit after their encounter with Bapu.

Since Gandhi is invoked so stridently in reviews of the film, we should perhaps recall that Gandhi's strategies were intended to be employed against an implacable state and *satyagraha* was not an approach recommended by an agony aunt to get over middle-class troubles of a private nature. But judging from the reception of the film, the state and the (urban middle-class) public are unanimous about Gandhigiri being best understood as an everyday strategy and not as a political tool, a device for personal solutions in a milieu in which all ways of life (legal and illegal) are admissible. A consensus has perhaps emerged that since Gandhi's message can only be understood in this innocuous way, social life is essentially not transformable.

Discussions about Gandhi in the public space tend to focus on his personal life about which he was very forthcoming and this may be used to explain the approach of the film. But even of his personal life, Gandhi revealed those aspects which did him little credit to be revealed, that is, as a way of cleansing himself. 'Coming clean' as a way of preempting discovery is not 'Gandhian' especially when it is to gain—or not to lose—something one wants dearly. The Gandhian turn in *Lage Raho Munnabhai* is acceptable as comedy which often parodies high ideals in this way, but one is struck by the effortless way in which the film then becomes sententious. In effect, *Lage Raho Munnabhai* is erasing the difference between parodying Gandhism and advocating it as a moral force—which will give the reader some sense of the cynicism with which Gandhian rhetoric is employed in India today.

My earlier argument pertaining to the link between the comedy model to which the Munna Bhai films belong and hierarchy did not perhaps place enough emphasis on the curious stasis that this points to, the sense that social hierarchy is inviolable—although Gandhism tried to work against traditional Indian hierarchy even while trying not to decry what was 'Indian'. But hegemonic urban middle-class control over Gandhi's teachings may have gradually transformed it.[20] Gandhi's actual teachings may not be pertinent here but if the action it can initiate in the public space is restricted to 'Gandhigiri', I would like to propose that Gandhism in its accepted avatar has become socially inconsequential.

Lage Raho Munna Bhai is hardly the moral watershed it is held out to be but its most significant aspect is not that it 'trivializes Gandhi' but the easy way in which it overlooks everyday illegalities while holding out its message of 'truth and non-violence'.

If there is one 'truth' that the film provides evidence of, it is the ubiquity of illegality in the lives of the urban middle-class. As already acknowledged by the sequence in *Rang De Basanti* involving DJ and the policeman, one stays out of trouble by resorting to bribery and it is difficult to imagine a life without small illegalities. Judging from *Lage Raho Munna Bhai*'s tacit approval of everyday illegality (by making the hoodlum 'loveable'), employing goons to settle disputes is something that even respectable people have begun to consider as a useful solution.

Lage Raho Munnabhai appeared in the same year as *Rang De Basanti*; both were successes (although *Lage Raho Munna Bhai* was more successful) and apparently addressed the same kind of audience. This being the case, it is interesting to compare the discourses in the two films. If one bears in mind that Gandhi is the political icon constantly invoked as the gold standard from which Indian politics has moved away, the comparison becomes sharper. While the reformist *Rang De Basanti* advocates heroic honesty and idealism in public life, the Gandhian exercise *Lage Raho Munnabhai* employs the rhetoric of Gandhian honesty cynically by invoking it even while implying nonchalantly that benefiting by small deceits and illegalities in a world which tolerates them is legitimate. Any kind of 'reform' in India should inevitably contend with the ubiquity of the small illegality which, as we shall see, becomes larger and larger as we move onwards in the new millennium.

Notes

1. The 'ideal romance' was identified based on a survey of women readers in a place called Smithton. See Janice Radway, *Reading the Romance: Women, Patriarchy and Popular Literature* (London: Verso, 1987), p. 42–8.
2. Ibid.
3. Rosalind Coward, *Female Desire: Women's Sexuality Today* (London: Paladin, 1984), p. 196.
4. Ravi S. Vasudevan, *The Melodramatic Public: Film Form and Spectatorship in Indian Cinema* (Ranikhet: Permanent Black, 2010), p. 124. Vasudevan argues that assigning a Brahmin surname to this charlatan is a way of lampooning the parasitical features of upper-caste status claims. My own conclusions are more modest. The Brahmin caste being the priestly caste and associated with learning, the Brahmin surname works in the same way as the 'professor' prefix for a clown—as deliberately incongruous.

5. See M.K. Raghavendra, *Seduced by the Familiar: Narration and Meaning in Indian Popular Cinema* (New Delhi: Oxford University Press, 2008), pp. 247–54.

6. Louis Dumont, *Homo Hierarchicus: The Caste System and Its Implications,* (New Delhi: Oxford University Press, 1998), pp. 36–9.

7. Hollywood screenplay-writing manuals have long insisted on a formula and the archetypal plot consists of an undisturbed stage, a disturbance, a struggle for the elimination of the disturbance, and its actual elimination. See David Bordwell, *Narration in the Fiction Film* (London: Methuen, 1985), p. 157. Whereas the disturbance in films from Hollywood pertains to the motivated individual, Hindi films see the disturbance as done to stable hierarchy. The resolution, conversely, pertains to true hierarchy being eventually acknowledged by everyone.

8. See Raghavendra, *Seduced by the Familiar*, p. 35.

9. For instance, see Harjeet Kaur Allagh, 'Bole tho ... Gandhigiri', *The Hindu, Metroplus,* Vijayawada, 31 January 2009, http://www.hinduonnet.com/thehindu/thscrip/print.pl?file=2009013153790300.htm&date=2009/01/31/&prd=mp& (accessed on 27 October 2011) and Shastri Ramachandaran, 'Jollygood Bollywood: Munnabhai Rescues Mahatma', *The Tribune*, 23 September 2006, http://www.tribuneindia.com/2006/20060923/edit.htm#4 (accessed on 27 October 2011).

10. Mahatma Gandhi's great grandson, Tushar Gandhi, was proud of the film, which he says has introduced the new generation to Bapu and his ideology and also did justice to Gandhi's philosophy. See Subhash K. Jha, '"I'm Pleased with Hirani's Gandhigiri," Says Gandhi's Grandson', www.monsterandcritics.com, 19 March 2007, http://www.webindia123.com/movie/interview/march2007/in200307.htm (accessed on 28 March 2014).

11. Rajeev Masand, 'Lage Raho ... Is Hot at Cannes', http://ibnlive.in.com/news/lage-raho--is-hot-at-cannes/40958-8.html (accessed on 1 November 2011). One wonders how the critic could be certain that not one person in the audience left before the film ended.

12. Amelia Gentleman, 'Does Urbanized India Have Room for Gandhi?' *International Herald Tribune*, Asia Pacific, 20 September 2006, http://www.nytimes.com/2006/09/20/world/asia/20iht-letter.2880999.html (accessed on 29 October 2011).

13. Swati Gauri Sharma, 'How Gandhi Got His Mojo Back', www.boston.com, 13 October 2006. This is how this piece ends: 'What

America needs is a film that encourages people to take up Gandhigiri, Kinggiri, or Kennedygiri. If it worked for Bollywood, it could work for Hollywood', http://www.boston.com/news/globe/editorial_opinion/oped/articles/2006/10/13/how_gandhi_got_his_mojo_back/ (accessed on 27 October 2011).

14. 'B' and 'C' centres correspond to small towns and semi-urban centres. While precise data is difficult to come by, Mumbai territory contributed · over 46 per cent to the films collections, while in the case of *Gadar: Ek Prem Katha*, which was had more widespread success, Mumbai territory contributed just over 24 per cent. *Lage Raho Munna Bhai* does not even feature as a hit in territories like Rajasthan and Bihar. See www.boxofficeindia.com.

15. See www.boxofficeindia.com. The complete URLs include: http://wayback.archive.org/web/20131020213049/http://boxofficeindia.com/showProd.php?itemCat=212&catName=MjAwNg, http://wayback.archive.org/web/20131204132438/http://www.boxofficeindia.com/showProd.php?itemCat=308&catName=TGlmZXRpbWU, http://wayback.archive.org/web/20131020213049/http://boxofficeindia.com/showProd.php?itemCat=212&catName=MjAwNg, and http://www.rediff.com/movies/2006/sep/07ajp1.htm?q=tp (accessed on 28 March 2014).

16. See 'Manmohan Watches Munnabhai', *The Hindu*, 26 October 2006, http://www.hinduonnet.com/thehindu/thscrip/print.pl?file=2006102615091100.htm&date=2006/10/26/&prd=th& (accessed on 28 March 2014). The prime minister had, the article reports, also praised the film on his visit to South Africa at around the same time.

17. See 'UN All Praise for *Lage Raho Munna Bhai*', 11 November 2006, http://articles.timesofindia.indiatimes.com/2006-11-11/us/27786612_1_mahatma-gandhi-satyagraha-vinod-chopra (accessed on 1 November 2011).

18. Some stories of P.G. Wodehouse use the ploy and this may account for the writer's continuing popularity in India. A film in which this is used is Billy Wilder's *Some Like It Hot* (1959).

19. Although this has not been explored, the difference between the two films may point to a change of attitudes between 2003 and 2006.

20. 'After independence, the nation-state ignored Gandhi's politics for a ritual celebration of his life and death.' Sudipta Kaviraj, *The Trajectories of the Indian State: Politics and Ideas* (Ranikhet: Permanent Black, 2010), p. 68.

6

Thieves Like Us

Enterprise in *Bunty Aur Babli* (2005), *Dhoom 2* (2006), and *Guru* (2007)

The Petty Criminal

The motif of the criminal as protagonist is a fairly old one in Hindi cinema. One of the earliest of such roles was essayed by Dev Anand in Guru Dutt's *Jaal* (1952). Dev Anand often played chameleon-like figures given to a lack of scruples—a smuggler in Portuguese India in *Jaal*, a black-market operator in cinema tickets in *Kala Bazaar* (1960), and a tourist guide who casually forges a signature to help himself in *Guide* (1965). In each of these films, the protagonist subsequently redeems himself through remorse or some act of contrition. The 'Angry Young Man' films starring Amitabh Bachchan in the 1970s and 1980s[1] represented another kind of figure given to a life of illegality and the motivation offered were the injuries done to him by society. Leaving aside the figure of the urban gangster around 2000 (chiefly in films like *Satya*, *Vaastav*, and *Company*) the remaining kind of petty criminal—the one most relevant to my purpose—is the one also from the 1970s and equated by film theorists with the dispossessed.[2] One of these is found in *Zanjeer* (1973) as Sher Khan, who owns a gambling den, although this kind of criminal figures more prominently in Ramesh Sippy's *Sholay* (1975) in the shape of the two protagonists Jai and Veeru. As in *Zanjeer*, they are enlisted by a police officer to fight a larger evil, this time a dacoit named Gabbar Singh. This motif of the small criminal ridding the Nation of a larger evil also occurs in *Yaadon Ki Baraat* (1973) although in this film he is not enlisted by a policeman. Considering the interpretation given to him as the marginalized or dispossessed, the petty criminal enlisted by the state to fight a larger evil can be understood as the redefining of legality to admit the marginalized into the mainstream of social life; it can be argued that this finds a parallel in Indira Gandhi's moves towards a socially committed judiciary in the 1970s.[3] This chapter discusses three films in which people on the fringes of legality are similarly 'enlisted' or treated indulgently by the state because of their usefulness to the Nation.

Bunty Aur Babli: Crime as Entrepreneurship

Bunty Aur Babli directed by Shaad Ali is, uncharacteristically for a film of the period, about two people from a small town in north India. It is, however, not about communities in the small town but about personal aspiration which, as indicated earlier, is a new motif. Rakesh Trivedi (Abhishek Bachchan) comes from a small village named Fursatganj. His father is a ticket collector in the railways, and wants him to follow his footsteps. Rakesh, however, dreams big; he is not willing to enter government employment and wear a 'shabby black coat'. He has a business plan and is convinced he will make it big one day, become a Tata, a Birla, or an Ambani. Vimmi Saluja (Rani Mukerji) is from a Punjabi family in another small village; she spends hours watching films, studying supermodels, and dreams of becoming Miss India one day. She is not willing to marry 'Surinder' who her father and mother want her to marry and who is expected to be a good husband. Unable to bear the pressure from their respective families, both leave home separately to seek their fortunes.

Although the film is set in small towns and gives us a vivid portrayal of the small-town milieu which is not without some affection, its scorn for government employment in which the exercise of power is not a given (as in the railways) is more in tune with attitudes in the metropolises.[4] Rakesh gets in touch with a finance company in which the manager is appreciative of his scheme but turns it down while quietly appropriating the information it provides. Meanwhile, Vimmi finds herself turned out of the entry round of the Miss India beauty contest with jeers. As luck will have it both of them meet accidentally at the railway station and decide to travel to Kanpur— he to contact the higher bosses of the finance company and she to try to get back into the the beauty contest. Not only is neither of them successful but Rakesh finds that his ideas have been stolen by the manager, who is now comfortably lodged nearby in an expensive hotel. This becomes cause for them to devise a plot to cheat the manager of the money which should rightly belong to Rakesh. They are successful and this leads to their taking on the identities of 'Bunty' and 'Babli' and embarking upon a successful career as con artists across north India.

Bunty Aur Babli is actually a caper film, of which there has perhaps been no other in Hindi cinema. The closest to it, as already suggested, are some sections from *Sholay* although that film also includes other segments which are from different genres. *Bunty Aur Babli*'s approach to the crimes is clearly celebratory and comic. It does this largely by casting comedy stars and actors who have a history of playing movie villains as the duo's victims.[5] This helps to justify Bunty and Babli's doings as some form of enterprise. Also important is the fact that it celebrates their lavish lifestyles after they come into wealth in this way. It is significant that while it endorses this kind of cavalier attitude with regard to their financial adventures, Babli's virtue is not compromised. In fact, when someone at a pageant enrolment hints at sexual favours from her, she soundly slaps him. Although they are constantly in each other's company and stay together they are not physically intimate until they are married. Although Babli frequently breaks into tears thinking of her family, even this is played as comedy. Rarely during their capers, for instance, are their anxious families given attention. When the parents are shown, it is always perfunctorily and never with the sense that the two belong to a community which deserves their loyalty. Getting emphasis is only their desire to reach above their stations financially. This celebratory approach reaches its summit when the companions dupe the 'richest man in the world'—played once again by a comic personality—to whom they lease out the Taj Mahal to get married in. Vimi impersonates a minister named Phoolsakhi who resembles Mayawati,[6] a political figure unloved by the upwardly mobile classes from the metropolises and a figure of disdain for the English-language press. Eventually, they become renowned for their deeds and *Bunty Aur Babli* even gloats at their tricking the world's richest man: the watchmen at the Taj have a hearty laugh when Bunty and Babli's involvement in the caper becomes known. Newspaper reports paint them as admired because of their help to the poor—although the film includes no episode which brings out their altruism. None of Bunty and Babli's trickery emerges as clever; it is incredible that people should be taken in but the film insists that there should be no obstacles in their path—almost as though their enterprising spirits deserved encouragement. All this, it must be noted, is very different from Hindi cinema's traditional approach. If it was morally sententious until quite recently, here it is celebrating the confidence artist, who is presented as a hero worth emulating in the new age.

Eventually, however, the law in the shape of a senior police officer named Dasharath Singh (Amitabh Bachchan) gets on Rakesh and Vimi's track. The film plays a rather doubtful trick here. At their first meeting in a bar, when neither the policeman nor the con artists know who the other is, Rakesh and Dasharath Singh become intimate under the influence of drink. The conversation invokes—fleetingly—the off-screen relationship between the actors Abhishek and Amitabh Bachchan as son to father as if to reassure us that there is no threat from the policeman. This proves 'prophetic' because Dasharath Singh does catch up with them—when they have become parents, abandoned crime, and are returning to their own small town.

The policeman decides that the 'law must stop crime but not destroy lives' and the two are let off. As an epilogue, Dasharath Singh returns to visit them some time later and recruits them 'to clean up society'. What this signifies is uncertain but the last frame shows them in some foreign metropolis putting on dark glasses and giving fake IDs. Perhaps this points to their usefulness as entrepreneurs of a certain kind in a global set-up.[7]

In the Introduction, I dealt with the notion of 'aspiration' which had become a characteristic motif in some of the new cinema and no film illustrates this better than Bunty Aur Babli. It is not untoward for cinema to take a cheerful look at crime and be on the side of the criminal and an illustration of this is The Sting (1973) or Ocean's Eleven (2001) in which care is always taken to spell out that the victim is either an unsavoury sort—usually a criminal himself—or an impersonal institution like a bank or a casino.[8] In the Hindi film, Chori Mera Kaam (1975), the small criminals assist in the apprehension of an important gangster. It is the challenge or the adventure that is given emphasis in the caper/heist film and not the entrepreneurial qualities of the protagonists because the detailing largely goes into the execution aspect. While Bunty Aur Babli pays no attention to the adventure aspect, it does not delineate those who deserve to be relieved of their money from those who do not, it is celebrating entrepreneurship without making such moral distinctions. It is significant that Dasharath Singh is always in plain clothes even as his colleagues wear uniforms. As indicated, while dealing with the adulterous woman, this can be understood as a way of playing down the aspect of the policeman representing the state. It paves the way for individual choice on the part of the policeman—to let the criminals off —something which might not have been possible if the policeman had been uniformed. This decision is subsequently justified when Dasharath Singh finds a use for them globally.

What makes us uncomfortable about Bunty Aur Babli is the approval it bestows upon deceit when it clearly frowns on several other things—the life of an employee (especially one with no potential for financial advancement), communities in the small town, and politicians with mass base. When Vimi tells Dasharath Singh after she has renounced crime that she is sick of making mango pickle, it is also making the life without financial ambition seem ignoble. This viewpoint is made more problematic when it goes along with an approval of the laxity of the law. Two other films dealt with in this chapter have virtually the same viewpoint to offer and both include the indulgent state as a key motif.

Dhoom 2: Global Enterprise

Sanjay Gadhvi's Dhoom 2, which was an enormous financial success, begins on a train in the desert on which is travelling the Queen of England with her retinue, her grandchildren, and the crown jewels. Even as she is playing with her children, a figure descends from a helicopter onto the train, gets inside, and makes off with the crown jewels after impersonating her and defeating all her guards in combat on the roof of the train. This man is an international thief who leaves behind a calling card marked 'A' after every successful heist. Dhoom 2 is about an assistant commissioner of police, Jai Dixit (Abhishek Bachchan), and his efforts at catching this master thief Mr A (Hritik Roshan). The romantic attachment in the film is between Mr A and Sunehri (Aishwarya Rai), a woman thief who admires Mr A but is also an undercover agent for the police. Sunehri finally shoots Mr A dead to save him from being arrested but this turns out to be a fake killing and Jai Dixit tracks them down and finds them running a restaurant in Jamaica, having renounced crime. But the assistant commissioner magnanimously lets them go and returns to Mumbai.

Dhoom 2 is a global-age replica of Bunty Aur Babli and travels everywhere from the Namib Desert to Mumbai to Rio just as the earlier film traverses the small towns of north India. Thieving is the natural logic of globalization, the film appears to say. The British crown jewels is an important motif because the Kohinoor diamond which graces them is popularly believed to be Indian property and the implicit moral justification in the heist is that the British stole the diamond from India. (Bunty Aur Babli, similarly, needed an initial moral push and used the manager of the financial company who cheats Rakesh in this way.) Thievery being the natural way of globalization reminds us of the mysterious epilogue in *Bunty Aur Babli* as the general sense in *Dhoom 2* is that the state is proud of someone as enterprising as Mr A although he is breaking the law.[9] In order to prepare the public for the film dealing with a new morality appropriate to the times, it puts in a teaser—the assistant commissioner having a former classmate Shonali (Bipasha Basu) with whom he is on friendly terms and the term 'affair' is used to describe their relationship. But the relationship is shown to be strictly above board with Shonali being only a committed professional. Using Bipasha Basu is deliberate because she played the adulterous woman in *Jism*.

Both films dealt with so far have taken up a motif discussed in relation to *Sholay* and *Zanjeer*—the state enlisting a small criminal to fight a larger evil. In both *Bunty Aur Babli* and *Dhoom 2* the larger 'evil' may be equated with globalization where Indian 'entrepreneurs' are required to show their mettle. There may not be any overt indication here that globalization is 'evil' but it is still a challenge which till recently—as in *Jism*—had threatening implications. Although the criminal protagonists of *Dhoom 2* are not 'enlisted', Mr A, in recovering the British crown jewels has already demonstrated his usefulness in the globalized world. He has already 'served the Nation' and the indulgence of the state acknowledges it. The motif of a prized artefact stolen by the colonialists being recovered is a common theme in postcolonial cinemas[10] but in *Dhoom 2* the thief does not makeover the artefact—as though private ownership by an Indian is equal to the Nation having custody of it.[11]

Dhoom 2, one of the biggest hits of the decade, had more widespread success than *Bunty Aur Babli* and enjoyed blockbuster status in every territory except Bihar and Mysore.[12] Many of the lines in the film are spoken in English and some songs have whole verses in the English language.[13] Its widespread success is difficult to explain in the terms I have chosen in the earlier chapters. Why is this success not like that of *Bunty Aur Babli*, that is, confined to one or more cities? Perhaps other aspects like spectacle and music contributed because *Dhoom 2* is almost frenzied in its showcasing of global hotspots and its dancing. The remaining film to be discussed in this chapter—*Guru*—was a success abroad among NRIs and was even reviewed in the *TIME* magazine.[14]

Guru: Shareholder as Public

The three films discussed in this chapter are not alike generically which makes their comparable discourses more striking. While *Bunty Aur Babli* is close to a caper film, *Dhoom 2* is impossible to categorize and is best understood as a new sub-genre within action.[15] *Guru* is a biopic which is not a popular genre in Hindi cinema. While the two films discussed earlier had directors who were virtually unknown, *Guru* is directed by Mani Ratnam who has made his reputation in Bollywood with a kind of political cinema. Basically, Mani Ratnam's films (in Hindi and Tamil) are not the normal kind of 'fantasies' but seize upon subjects which have the potential for controversy and proceed to deal with them realistically (although with songs and dances) but in an uncontroversial way. Some of the subjects dealt with by Mani Ratnam are Kashmiri separatism in *Roja* (1992), the Bombay riots in *Bombay* (1995), and the falling out and the resultant political tussle between M. Karunanidhi and M.G. Ramachandran within the Dravida Munnettra Kazhagam (DMK) Party in *Iruvar* (1997), which was made only in Tamil. Many of his films have been studied by film academics and theorists and the consensus among them is that they echo the dominant ideology of their times.[16] *Guru* is based on the life of polyester tycoon, Dhirubhai Ambani, and has all the characteristics of an authorized biography although it is nominally fiction. Since my interest is only in how it fits a pattern seen in the fiction cinema of the period, I will not go into how true it is to fact but will treat it as a piece of fiction.

Considering that *Guru* is a 'biopic', it is strange to find it faithfully echoing many of the plot devices of *Bunty Aur Babli*. It features a young man and a young woman, both of whom want to leave home and meet accidentally on a train. It is emphasizes the young man's resourcefulness and his qualities as an entrepreneur. It blames the system for not allowing a young man with initiative to come up by fair means. The young man is phenomenally successful and founds a company but skirts legality. He is finally apprehended by the state for these illegalities but treated indulgently. The film ends with the protagonist dreaming of going global and making his company one of the world's largest, producing goods of the best quality.

Rather than go into the story minutely—which is episodic—it may be more useful to simply understand how the illegalities indulged in by Gurukant Desai (Abhishek Bachchan) are treated. Those initiatives of Gurukant which are not illegal—like his dealing with the aristocratic Azad Contractor who controls the textile trade—are used to demonstrate his acumen but his illegal doings are shown differently—as 'happenings in his company'. One illegality is Gurukant's company, Shakti Corporation, claiming exports falsely in order to entitle itself to higher import quotas. Another illegality is the importation of machinery in the guise of spares and setting up an entire plant line which is not licenced. Gurukant's tested method in getting away with all this is to show great servility towards those exercising authority although this is offered to the audience as tact, amiability, and humility.

Central to Guru, however, are a few personal relationships used to demonstrate the male protagonist's great personal warmth. Especially important is the love play and playful banter between Guru and his wife Sujata (Aishwarya Rai), who is shown to have great love and loyalty for her husband, which is well deserved. The second is the key conflict between Guru and an implacable newspaper magnate, Manik Dasgupta (Mithun Chakraborty), to whom Guru is initially 'almost a son'. Guru has a strong friendship with this man's granddaughter, Meenu (Vidya Balan), who is slowly dying of some incurable ailment. Meenu's husband Shyam (Madhavan) is an intrepid journalist working for Manik Dasgupta who has a hand in exposing Shakti Corporation's illegal doings despite his personal regard for Guru. What is offered here is a covert assertion that in a milieu in which powerful persons might know each other personally and even share in the other's private grief, personal relationships are not impediments to justice being pursued, that the guilty will be judged and punished.

As the people intent on punishing Gurukant close in on him, the protagonist has a stroke and is incapacitated. This becomes the moment when a notice is served on him to be present at an official hearing in which he will be judged. Guru is unwell and the film uses the opportunity not only to demonstrate his courage in the face of adversity but also to present him as a 'visionary'. There is no doubt in the minds of those judging him that he has been involved in serious illegalities and Gurukant Desai offers no credible defence except a 'namaste'. At the crucial moment, however, he makes a speech in which he expounds upon the ephemeral nature of today's laws which can be undone tomorrow. He invokes Mahatma Gandhi who was jailed by the British but who is now the Father of the Nation. Gurukant Desai, modestly, denies that he is Mahatma Gandhi but the film offers him to us as someone who saw the 'licence raj', the huge number of government controls in force as counterproductive and therefore broke laws in the same way that Gandhi broke British laws. This plea is incredible but what comes across is that those judging him have no reply to the personal anecdotes describing the hostile circumstances in which he set up business; they actually believe that they constitute a defence (conveyed through reaction shots registering their sympathy). Gurukant is also portrayed as a man of the people because he speaks no English while the bureaucrats who judge him speak little Hindi. When they finally pronounce judgement, Gurukant is found guilty on some of the counts and despite his being liable to be jailed along with his wife, as the film suggested, he is only made to pay a nominal fine.

To portray Gurukant Desai as a true 'man of the people', the film shows shareholder meetings of Shakti Corporation in which he addresses the 'Shakti family'. There are several of them and they grow larger each time. There is an effort to present the fraternity of Shakti shareholders as 'the public'. This makes it seem that he is actually a rebel working against the law on behalf of a 'public'. The fact that many of the economic controls were subsequently done away with (from 1991 onwards) is taken as an indication that he was 'ahead of his times'. It is significant that business academics have seen this as a legitimate response and the film as presenting the 'triumph of capitalism over socialism'[17] but this is a dubious conclusion. Making money for oneself (and one's shareholders) by breaking the law is hardly equal to questioning the political philosophy underlying the law. By the standards of business ethics the businessman who is allowed to break the law without being penalized also enjoys an unfair advantage over his competitors. But if one accepts a body of shareholders as 'the public' and disregards inconvenient aspects like unfair trade practices, it is easy to be persuaded that a devious law breaker is a selfless radical.

An episode in the film which is hastened through is difficult to comprehend unless one already has some sense of what it is about. At one moment, Guru is brought face to face with a high-ranking political functionary whom we see only from behind. He tells the protagonist that a licence that he is asking for is impossible to be granted because it is against the law. In response Gurukant tells this man that he only came to meet him because 'whatever was left with him by Chachaji (or Uncle) is too heavy for him to bear and that he should be relieved of the burden'. The result of this information is that Gurukant Desai gets his licence immediately. This sequence evidently pertains to illegal political funds held by Gurukant Desai and the man we see from behind is a political heir of someone just dead. Gurukant, here, is portrayed as someone in the confidence of the political class. *Guru* and the high-ranking politician in this segment may be deemed to be illustrating the same businessman-politician nexus seen in *Rang De Basanti*—one which the earlier film felt was reason enough for assassinations. But here, Gurukant Desai is made a visionary and a patriot. A significant factor is that the same public apparently upholds the viewpoints of both films.[18]

I began this chapter by going into the portrayal of the thief in Hindi cinema which serves as a basis for the other portrayals in the three films just examined. The earlier films, it must be noted, did not celebrate 'enterprise' but simply made out a case for the inclusion of the criminal within the social mainstream. The discourse in the films pertained to the criminal also being that of the Nation. Never did the earlier films celebrate illegality as enterprise as blatantly as the three films do. Where *Lage Raho Munnabhai* merely saw illegality as inescapable these films see it as attractive. This is exceptional as even a relatively recent enquiry into Hindi cinema describes Hindi's cinema's dependence on *dharmic* codes.[19] In the terms of this enquiry, it is not the man-in-the-world but the renouncer who is of greater interest to Bombay cinema. The three films examined in this chapter provide evidence that an iconoclastic view of traditional belief may be much more pertinent today—that it is worldly[20] rather than other-worldly. Given these factors, what do the three films just discussed say about audience perceptions in the new millennium?

For much of Hindi cinema's history, it fiercely upheld moral values traditionally considered sacred and this was assisted by Nehruvian socialism being the official political creed. With Nehruvian socialism being abandoned, it is—at least among the socially ascendant classes of the cities—as though ethics other than those values directed towards material advancement is irrelevant. The state, which was once a moral agent in Hindi films of the 1950s,[21] is now only seen as an instrument to facilitate this advancement. With the advent of globalization, there is a perception that a state which is indulgent towards the law breaker will make Indian enterprise globally effective and competitive. This suggests implicit approval on the part of the audiences of the films—predominantly those from the ascendant urban classes—of the weakening state because its laxity makes it 'enterprise-friendly'.

Notes

1. These films have been widely written about but they had a lesser-known precursor in O.P. Ralhan's *Phool Aur Pathar* (1966) which also employs many of the same motifs.

2. Characterized as 'the criminalized but essentially-honest proletariat'. See M. Madhava Prasad, *Ideology of the Hindi Film: A Historical Constitution* (New Delhi: Oxford University Press, 2008), pp. 142–4.

3. M.K. Raghavendra, *Seduced by the Familiar: Narration and Meaning in Indian Popular Cinema* (New Delhi: Oxford University Press, 2008), pp. 182–3.

4. The film had insignificant collections in Bihar, Rajasthan, and Central India territories. It did not do well in Mumbai but was a super-hit in Delhi/Uttar Pradesh. Since Uttar Pradesh would have been similar in characteristics to Bihar, Delhi may have been the territory in which it did best. This suggests that the film was not a success in the semi-urban areas despite it being about two people from small towns. See http://www.boxofficeindia.com/showProd.php?itemCat=111&catName=RE VMSEkvVVA= (accessed on 24 June 2012).

5. For instance, two actors seen in such roles in the film are Ravi Baswani, who is known for key comic roles in films like *Chashme Buddoor* (1981) and the cult comedy *Jaane Bhi Do Yaaro* (1983) and Ranjit, who has played villains for decades.

6. She is probably a combination of Mayawati and the 'bandit queen', Phoolan Devi, who was a member of parliament until she was assassinated. Both of them are women from backward castes or Dalit backgrounds whose constituencies are far away from the metropolitan cities.

7. The film is seen to belong to a category of films which has brought about huge changes in social relationships in towns. The 'usefulness' of Bunty and Babli is not simply transforming the values in their milieu but is perhaps more far-reaching. Janaki Abraham, 'Veiling and the Production of Gender and Space in a Town in North India: A Critique of the Public/Private Dichotomy', *Indian Journal of Gender Studies*, vol. 17, no. 2, June 2010, pp. 191–222.

8. Usually a caper film is a film in which a group of people undertake a single daring act like a robbery. See Ron Wilson, 'The Left-handed Form of Human Endeavor: The Crime Films of the 1990s', in Wheeler Winston Dixon (ed.), *Film Genre 2000: New Critical Essays* (Albany, NY: State University of New York Press, 2000), p. 154. Obviously, none of the Hindi films correspond to this model. They are closer to sections of Arthur Penn's film *Bonnie and Clyde* (1967).

9. Jai Dixit turns down a suggestion to shoot Mr A. 'We want to stop crime, not kill people,' he tells his colleague. This clearly carries echoes of *Bunty Aur Babli* as does his being always in civilian clothes and his indulgence towards the thieves at the end. Abhishek Bachchan who plays Jai Dixit also played Bunty in *Bunty Aur Babli* in which the policeman 'wants to stop crime but not destroy lives'.

10. An instance is the Nigerian film *The Mask* (1980), directed by Eddie Ugboma, in which Major Obi (Agent 009) is sent on a mission to recover the mask of Queen Adesua of Benin from the British Museum. See Mbye Babucar Cham, 'Film Production in West Africa', in John D.H. Downing (ed.), *Film and Politics in the Third World* (New York: Praeger, 1987), pp 19–31.

11. Indian liquor baron Vijay Mallya bought Tipu Sultan's sword in London in 2004. It was made clear that the sword belonged to him. K. Satyamurty, 'Tipu's Sword Is Mallya's', *The Hindu*, National Section, 8 April 2004, http://www.hindu.com/2004/04/08/stories/2004040805881200.htm (accessed on 13 October 2013).

12. See www.boxofficeindia.com (accessed on 26 June 2012).

13. Aysha Iqbal Viswamohan, 'English in Filmsongs from India: An Overview', *English Today*, vol. 27, no. 3, September 2011, pp. 21–4.

14. Richard Corliss, 'Bollywood's New Guru', *TIME*, 16 January 2007, http://www.time.com/time/arts/article/0,8599,1578636-3,00.html (accessed on 25 June 2012).

15. See Rachel Dwyer, 'Bollywood Bourgeois', *India International Centre Quarterly*, vol. 33, nos 3/4, 'India 60', Winter 2006–Spring 2007, pp. 222–31.

16. See Tejaswini Niranjana, 'Integrating Whose Nation? Tourists and Terrorists in *Roja*', *Economic and Political Weekly*, vol. 24, no. 3, 15 January 1994, pp. 79–82 and Ravi S. Vasudevan, 'Bombay and Its Public', in Rachel Dwyer and Christopher Pinney (eds), *Pleasure and the Nation: The History, Politics and Consumption of Popular Culture in India* (New Delhi: Oxford University Press, 2001), pp. 186–211.

17. Tejas A. Desai, 'Contemporary Lessons in Economic Philosophy Drawn from Two Recent Indian Films', WP No. 2009-04-02, Indian Institute of Ahmedabad, April 2009, p. 4 available at http://iimahd. iimahd.ernet.in/assets/snippets/workingpaperpdf/2009-04-02Desai.pdf (accessed on 29 June 2012).

18. One way of ascertaining this is the responses of the same influential film critic to the two films. Well-known television film critic Rajeev Masand is equally approving of both viewpoints in 'Masand's Verdict' on IBN Live, http://ibnlive.in.com/news/masands-verdict-rang-de-basanti/4473-8-p0.html and http://ibnlive.in.com/news/masands-verdict-thumbs-up-for-guru/top/31056-8.html (accessed on 29 June 2012).

19. Vijay Mishra, *Bollywood Cinema: Temples of Desire* (London: Routledge, 2002), pp. 4–6.

20. Nirad C. Chaudhuri, *Hinduism: A Religion to Live By* (New York: Oxford University Press, 1979), pp. 15–16.

21. Raghavendra, *Seduced by the Familiar*, pp. 129–32.

7

The 'Hyperreal' and the Narrowing Nation

Om Shanti Om (2007)

Films about Showbiz

The motif of showbiz is not a familiar one in Hindi cinema although all Hindi films are 'musicals' but it is a key motif in the Hollywood musical: *42nd Street* (1933), *Top Hat* (1935), *Singin' in the Rain* (1952), *The Band Wagon* (1953), *Funny Girl* (1968), *Cabaret* (1972), and *All That Jazz* (1979), to name a handful. An explanation is that Hollywood cinema is broadly realistic (or 'mimetic' in Aristotelian terms), while Hindi cinema is not. Since showbiz abounds in hyperbole like the musical itself, it is a subject comfortable with hyperbolical depiction. Hindi cinema, as argued elsewhere, has followed traditional Indian dramaturgy in holding itself up not as mimesis but as 'truer than the real'.[1] This means that cinema is employed to relay a pre-existent meaning recognizable from tradition,[2] usually with strong emphasis. Since all depictions in Hindi cinema consequently tend towards hyperbole, showbiz enjoys no natural advantages as a subject.

Although there have been a few earlier showbiz-related films like *Kala Bazaar* (1960), in which the protagonist sells movie tickets in the black-market, and *Teesri Kasam* (1966), where a *nautanki* dancer is being escorted by a young rustic from town to town, the only Hindi film which can be compared to *Om Shanti Om*—which is the focus of this chapter—is Ramgopal Verma's *Rangeela* (1996) which provides as detailed a rendering of the film industry as any. But before we make the comparison it may be helpful to describe *Om Shanti Om* first.

Om Shanti Om: Brand as Message

Farah Khan's *Om Shanti Om* is a tale of reincarnation and its first half is about a young person's obsession with the film industry. Om Prakash Makhija (Shahrukh Khan) is a young man smitten by a film star named Shanti (Deepika Padukone). Om lives a middle-class existence with his mother (Kirron Kher) and works as a junior artist and saves Shanti's life during a filming sequence involving fire. Shanti is drawn to him but he accidentally learns that she is secretly married to a powerful producer named Mukesh Mehra and also pregnant. But Mukesh Mehra is in financial trouble and intends to marry the financier's daughter. He therefore kills Shanti in cold blood on a film studio set by setting it on fire. Om tries to rescue her but is also beaten up by his henchmen. Om is not gravely wounded but he is hit by the car of another film star Rajesh Kapoor and dies in hospital. At that time Rajesh Kapoor's wife is giving birth to a son at the same hospital and he is reborn as Rajesh Kapoor's son, Om Kapoor.

When the second half begins it is thirty years later and Om Kapoor (Shahrukh Khan) is already a leading film hero. A mad old woman (Om Prakash's mother) imagines she is Om Kapoor's mother and tries to meet him. Due to this and by accidentally being on the burnt down film set as well as meeting Mukesh Mehra, Om Kapoor recollects his past life. He is reunited with the old woman and Om Prakash's friend, Pappu Master (Shreyas Talpade). The three plot vengeance against Mukesh Mehra and they are ably assisted by a Shanti look-alike named Sandhya (Deepika Padukone). The story of Om Prakash and Shanti is reworked as a story to be given to film by Mukesh Mehra and the producer is lured to the burnt-down set where Shanti was murdered. Before they can extract vengeance, however, Shanti's ghost appears and kills Mukesh Mehra. The film is amusing and the highpoint is Om Prakash pretending to be a south Indian film hero for Shanti's benefit and battling a stuffed toy tiger. Those who have not seen the film may find this description of the film inadequate because the film is not really contained in its story—unlike most other Hindi films[3]—but depends on a carefully maintained attitude which I intend to explore here.

The motif of reincarnation appears to be central to *Om Shanti Om* but this deserves a second look. Reincarnation is a corner stone of Hindu belief but Hindi films dealing with the notion appear to lack faith in it as a philosophical proposition[4] and use it entirely as a narrative ploy to achieve other ends. In virtually every film dealing with reincarnation, for example, *Madhumati* (1956), *Mahal* (1949), and *Karan Arjun* (1995), the reincarnated person is born with the same countenance as the one who departed and the film usually involves a double role. Since the relationship between the mother and son in any film is an important one, the reincarnated man (also true for *Om Shanti Om*) has no mother and this enables him to bond with the dead person's mother as a son. The key strategy is never to make the relationships constituting the two lives enter into conflict. This is very different from Hollywood films which also work with the notion of reincarnation, such as Robert Wise's *Audrey Rose* (1977), but have enough faith in its 'truth' not to use it *only* as a narrative ploy because the relationships clash.

To understand the central thrust of *Om Shanti Om*—which hardly revolves around reincarnation—it may be compared to Ramgopal Varma's *Rangeela* (1996) because it is about a young person's obsession with the film industry. The protagonists of both films are middle-class persons who rise to stardom and the way the star-struck person is represented in the two films is important. In *Rangeela*, the girl is played by Urmila Matondkar, who was not a star. *Rangeela* is actually a realistic portrayal of a young girl entering the film industry, with film-land and its parties presented as satire. It, however, includes a film called 'Rangeela' inside it and this extravagant fantasy and the realistic part of the film combine as pastiche, that is, a medley of film styles. The film-within-the-film functions as blank parody[5] and the 'post modern' aspects of the film have been discussed elsewhere.[6] But rather than becoming a pretext to celebrate film industry glamour, the film-within-the-film is almost dreamlike in its conception. Also pertinent is the overall sense to be got—reinforced by the film's satirical aspect—that the viewpoint from which the film industry is scrutinized is not from within the industry but from the outside and it is the middle-class heroine's personal life that we are invited to identify with. As has been noted, the factor that distinguishes the heroine is not her ambition but her cinephilia, which she shares with the layabout whom she chooses over her leading man.[7]

Om Prakash in Farah Khan's film, in contrast, cannot be accepted as a middle-class youth. Shahrukh Khan plays him in exactly the same way that he plays Om Kapoor the film hero, and it is evident that both characters are only turns being done by a leading entertainer. There is also little doubt that this is deliberate and not a failure of performance because of the amusing spoof of south Indian film histrionics arranged by Om Prakash for Shanti's benefit—which involves so many people and so much hardware that that it could hardly have been put together by a junior artist. If Shahrukh Khan in Om Prakash's role is hardly convincing as a middle-class youth desperate about his film career, this is not a failing on the part of the actor as he has demonstrated his ability in films like *Rab Ne Bana Di Jodi* (2008) to shed his star charisma when required to do so. Secondly, he always displays more charisma as Om Prakash than the leading lady Shanti whom he is besotted with and upstages her in every other sequence. Deepika Padukone who plays Shanti was not a leading star and this may account for it but the choice of a then minor female actor suggests that it was intended. Thirdly, the 'middle-class' associates from Om Prakash's life move smoothly into his life as Om Kapoor as though they were meant to share it. Om Prakash's mother does not take her moral role as 'mother' with the customary solemnity and even clowns around when Om Prakash returns as Om Kapoor and makes histrionic demands upon her as part of the conspiracy to fool Mukesh Mehra. That she has spent thirty years without a son to care for her has not affected her. Not only is Pappu Master placed in the reassuring role of a surrogate son, but there is suggestion that she has been well looked after by Rajesh Kapoor, Om Kapoor's father.

If reincarnation is only a narrative device, the next obvious question pertains to the purpose the device is serving. It is significant here that the second part—with Shanti's look-alike Sandhya—does not culminate in a romance. In fact, each embrace between the two concludes with Om planting a chaste kiss upon Sandhya's forehead as if to be clear about the relationship. Considering that Sandhya's is also an incredible appearance which the film offers perfunctorily and without justification,[8] it can be argued that the film is only interested in Om Prakash's aspirations being fulfilled, that is, his ascendancy to star status. But since Om Prakash himself is less a character inhabiting a story than Shahrukh Khan doing a turn, the fiction in the film gets less emphasis than its male star—who becomes its 'message'. It can perhaps even be described as a kind of mythical 'biography'.

The second half of the film also includes a Filmfare Awards ceremony in which Om Kapoor is chosen as the best actor. This ceremony shows various other film stars appearing as themselves—Feroz Khan, Abhishek Bachchan, Rekha, Chunky Pandey, Govinda, Salman Khan, Hritik Roshan—and behaving in accordance with their public images often cultivated outside cinema.[9] This suggests that if the discourse of the film is 'Shahrukh Khan', it is not an exclusive one because most of known Bollywood is included in it. I propose that 'reincarnation' is deliberately chosen as a theme because it has no social dimensions which might have distracted the public from responding to 'Shahrukh Khan and Bollywood' as the film's sole message. It is interesting at this point to examine the role of the villain, Mukesh Mehra. Every significant villain in Hindi film stories points in some way to a social category: the politician in *Rang De Basanti*, the heroine's father as the mayor of Lahore in *Gadar: Ek Prem Katha*, and the unscrupulous builder in *Lage Raho Munnabhai*. The villain can be associated with a key social issue tackled in each of the films. But Mukesh Mehra is singular inasmuch as he represents no discernible social category, and his wicked dealings are of an entirely personal nature as if to downplay *Om Shanti Om*'s social meaning. The small role for the female lead in Om Kapoor's life perhaps also points to a wish on the part of the film-maker not to confuse the audience and prevent it from receiving the brand message through the distraction of a romance.

As already indicated in the Introduction, there is a current view that 'Bollywood' can be defined more inclusively than only through films. It can be understood as the ensemble of interests that govern the contemporary entertainment industry.[10] Even though the film is perhaps the key element, other entertainment and consumer sectors such as television, music, advertising, and fashion not only draw upon but also constitute 'Bollywood' in some way. I will argue that this wider reach/implication of Bollywood deeply influences the meaning of a film today. Unlike in *Rangeela* in which the stars— Urmila Matondkar and Aamir Khan—submitted to the narrative, in *Om Shanti Om* the star persona of Shahrukh Khan cannibalizes the role of Om Makhija/Kapoor. Because of this factor, I suggest that there is a collapse of the fiction; what the actors provide is not so much role-essaying as entertainment in various forms with mimicry perhaps being the primary component. Where *Rangeela* has a message pertaining to not losing one's moorings despite success, *Om Shanti Om* has no such social message but replaces it with one pertaining to its brands 'Shahrukh Khan' and 'Bollywood'. To the question of why this message was relayed in this specific period, one can say that Shahrukh Khan's fan base outside the diaspora had been growing since 2005 and had reached such a pitch by 2010 that the University of Vienna organized a three-day seminar entitled 'Shahrukh Khan and Global Bollywood'. The welcome message from the Austrian President, Heinz Fischer, at the inauguration acknowledged the fact that 'this new avatar called Bollywood' had crossed over to non–South Asian audiences.[11] *Om Shanti Om* appears to have been made only to take advantage of the larger meaning/reach of Bollywood.

The Brand and the Nation

After 1947, the commercial cinemas of India were not favored by the state and especially targeted for their 'derivative nature', being inspired by the sensationalist aspects of Hollywood cinema, their orientation towards melodrama and action rather than psychological and social realism. While national institutions were formed to protect, preserve, and develop art, literature, music, and theatre, the political elite considered commercial cinema to be an inadequate space in which a culture of citizenship could be nurtured.[12] Hence popular Hindi cinema, which had been suturing cultural differences before 1947 helped imagine the Nation in the ways already described—despite the state, which gave it little encouragement. Hindi cinema's low self-esteem is not only evidenced in the pronouncements of various film-makers[13] but also in the films themselves. In Hrishikesh Mukherjee's *Guddi* (1971), a film from 'middle cinema' about a girl who develops an obsession for film star Dharmendra, a visit to a film studio is organized to demonstrate that film stars—even those who play villains—are good people. *Rangeela* is close behind when the heroine is wooed by her leading man but she chooses her penniless boyfriend. The boyfriend's lower status is not problematized (for example, through family disapproval) but there is a sense that career success is secondary and loyalty to one's past commitments primary. The film, in fact, makes us initially believe that it is her leading man whom she loves but springs a surprise at the end as though the film was abruptly recalling older (pre-1991) virtues.

Om Shanti Om does not treat Bollywood as a 'community' allegorizing the Nation—as might have happened—but as an assemblage to be admired and envied by those outside. Om Prakash's view of it may even be taken to represent the view expected from the public. The film, as is evident, marks a new era in the film industry's depiction of itself because its tone is so self-congratulatory. The transformation of Hindi cinema's self-image owed to the fact that it was now no longer treated as a pariah. Two international events in London in 1982 and 2002 showed how Bollywood was admitted publicly as a constituent of 'Indian culture'. The one in 1982 was a 'Festival of India' which went along with similar festivals from before in showcasing India's cultural heritage; occupying centre stage was a polished stone *Yakshi* from the third century BC. The event in 2002 was the 'Indian Summer' described in the Introduction in which Bollywood was the principal exhibit.[14]

With most cinemas in the world succumbing to the onslaught of Hollywood but Hindi cinema holding its own locally and even gaining internationally, there was widespread cultural acceptance accorded to Bollywood. The Indian state did not fall behind either. While it will be difficult to say when approval of Bollywood by the state became manifest, one indication may be got from national awards like the Padma Shri and the Padma Bhushan. The way in which the Nation chooses to bestow awards and honours upon its citizens is a useful way to understand the priorities of the state at any given moment. Among film stars with an image for social concern, Raj Kapoor received a Padma Bhushan when he was 49, while Aamir Khan got the same award when he was 45. Raj Kapoor, incidentally, did not get the Padma Shri, while Aamir Khan received one when he was 38. Film stars Dilip Kumar, Dev Anand, and Dharmendra were not honoured during their active careers although all of them received the Padma Bhushan in the new millennium. In contrast, Shahrukh Khan received the Padma Shri in 2005 when he was at the height of his success. It would appear that past icons were rewarded only when the film industry attained the respectability it has after 2000. Hence, it would not be incorrect to say that Bollywood has been acknowledged by the state because of its global success as a business model. But while successful businesses have, by and large, only economic significance, Bollywood is associated directly with cultural artefacts which have shaped the idea of India.

The Transformation of Fiction

Om Shanti Om perhaps represents the extreme case of the brand becoming the content but there are other indications that the meaning of Hindi popular cinema in its new avatar could well be dominated by its brand image. What this means is that considerations outside cinema dominate films and, in a sense, subvert the fiction. Here are some ways in which this process may be carried forward:

1. The visibility of children or siblings of well-known stars on television long before their films actually arrive and prepare the ground for their acceptance.
2. Publicized off-screen relationships becoming an influencing factor in the writing of screenplays.
3. Roles played by actors in films paralleling relationships in real life, for example, Amitabh Bachchan playing Abhishek Bachchan's father in *KANK*. When the policeman played by Amitabh lets off the criminal played by Abhishek in *Bunty Aur Babli*, it is easily read as a justification of nepotism.
4. Deliberate placement of product brands within each film.
5. Film costumes gradually making way for designer wear.
6. Personalities cultivated in commercials informing the fiction and references to them being made in the films.
7. Characters in films being given the names of film stars.
8. Film magazines devoted to cinema dying out but Bollywood news (friendships, enmities, associations, relationships) and film news (releases, successes, flops, collections, and so on) becoming general news in the media, especially on television news channels.
9. There are also elaborate fictions made about stars in advertisements which are intended to tell the public what the stars are 'really' like.

Shahrukh Khan in *Om Shanti Om* may be emblematic of what is happening to the fiction in Hindi cinema but the same is increasingly true of other performers like Aamir Khan, Akshay Kumar, and Hritik Roshan, whose performances are redolent of the commercials in which they appear. A factor also to be taken into account here are the muscular bodies cultivated by the stars which do not inform the fiction in the films. Where Sylvester Stallone or Arnold Schwarzenegger star in films in which their physiques are justified—the roles of boxer or robot being their best known ones, respectively—Bollywood films do not take the trouble to justify the physiques cultivated by the actors and this means that the spectator is made aware that it is the physique of the star rather than that of a fictional character that is being exhibited. The star persona of an actor was once also used to represent social types: the working class hero represented by Dharmendra, the angry marginalized represented by Amitabh Bachchan, the city slicker by Dev Anand, or the impulsive and ebullient rustic by Dilip Kumar. It can be argued that if Shahrukh Khan's star persona in *Om Shanti Om* represents no social type, neither does it represent the actor as an individual. It is perhaps describable as a simulacrum, a copy which has apparently no corresponding original. Indian popular cinema was often regarded as escapist and a 'collective daydream'[15] but these are perhaps not terms that sit comfortably on a film like *Om Shanti Om*. The 'escapism' of Hindi cinema and its sententiousness, both pointed to an 'ideal' of some sort. As I have indicated, both owe to the understanding (shared by traditional poetics/dramaturgy in India) that whatever literature and performance represent should be 'truer than the real'. Or, seen from an external perspective, it was a tidied-up copy of what is real in the world. It is because the world of *Om Shanti Om* is part of a collapsed fiction that it is not a tidied-up copy but closer to a 'hyperreal'.[16] While a film like *Rangeela* still performs its instructive role through its discourse on loyalty, *Om Shanti Om* cannot be described in this way.

It is difficult to say in what direction Bollywood will take Indian cinema but the aspect of greatest importance is perhaps that it may disengage Hindi cinema from the Nation. It can also be argued that while the Hindi popular film once exercised influence on behalf of

India (partly in the Third World),[17] Bollywood could soon be an advertisement only for itself. The international response to Danny Boyle's *Slumdog Millionaire* (2009) provides us with some additional clues here. Upon release, and in the several months leading up to the awards ceremony, the term 'Bollywood' was repeatedly used in association with the film. For example, a piece in the *New York Times* suggested that the most remarkable thing about the film was that, despite the director's strenuous denials, it could well be a Bollywood film. A *Village Voice* reviewer asserted that Bollywood actually met Hollywood in Danny Boyle's film. What is significant here is that far from presenting a picture of India that Indian cinema once did in the Third World, *Slumdog Millionaire* presents the kind of prejudiced picture[18] that the newspapers in the West once painted of India's social reality, one that is hardly likely to propagate 'Indian values' to non-Indian audience. Despite this fact, *Slumdog Millionaire* was widely celebrated in India because of the contribution of Bollywood artists like A.R. Rahman and Anil Kapoor to its success. Since the ascendance of Bollywood personalities through *Slumdog Millionaire* is seen as more important than India's portrayal in the film, it can be argued that the response to the film points the way to Bollywood becoming detached from its role with regard to the Nation but being endorsed by a once unsympathetic state. Theoretically, therefore, Bollywood could become independent of India (if it is not so already) because of going global—the way Coca-Cola exists independent of the US. This, ironically, is the moment when the Indian state has begun to acknowledge it most fervently. Even if *Om Shanti Om*'s perspective has not been imitated after 2007, the film could point the way to the systematic construction of a persuasive 'hyperreality'[19]—endorsed by the state—in which the public participates vicariously.

The political focus of this book is largely around how the Nation imagined by Hindi cinema has become narrower and more exclusive in the new millennium and the film is also of significance here. Symptoms of the narrowing Nation have been discovered in various representations, such as, the summary treatment of the political class in *Rang De Basanti*, Mahatma Gandhi reduced to an agony aunt advising on middle-class anxieties[20] in *Lage Raho Munna Bhai*, and a body of shareholders assuming the status of the public in *Guru*. Another motif which also becomes increasingly common is that of 'friendships' between people from rightly antagonistic social categories, such as the thieves, the sympathetic policeman, and the press baron's ailing daughter looked after by the industrialist whose dealings he is investigating. This feature points to a charmed 'elite circle' within the influential classes being regarded as legitimate by the films and passing scrutiny by the audience. I propose that the discourse in *Guru* is accepted because the public which should be alarmed at the implications of such a 'friendship' is invited to participate vicariously in the lives of highly placed people, who are brought closer and rendered 'human'. *Om Shanti Om* may not appear to fit the pattern but there is an aspect of the film which points to the same inclination.

There are nominally two worlds in *Om Shanti Om*'s fiction— the real one and the one designated Bollywood—and the two are kept apart, the people inhabiting the first one participating vicariously in the second. When Om Prakash secretly watches the last confrontation between Shanti and Mukesh Mehra (perhaps the only scene in which Shahrukh Khan drops his star persona), this is the sense conveyed. Immense wealth and influence are shown to be naturally associated with Bollywood personalities and this is not only because Om Kapoor has a lavish lifestyle and a public following. The killing of Om Prakash by Rajesh Kapoor in a traffic accident is a key event glossed over by the film and its implications need to be examined. Om is reborn as Rajesh Kapoor's son but I have already demonstrated how spurious the motif of reincarnation is and we need to look further. The fact is that without the reincarnation we would be made uncomfortable by Om Prakash's death at the hands of Rajesh Kapoor without the latter being called to account. Perhaps, understanding this, the film hints at Rajesh Kapoor ensuring that Om Prakash's mother is well looked after. But the issue is also whether his killing of Om Prakash should not have naturally involved the law. Does the film's refusal to examine this aspect not point covertly to the influence of the 'elite circle' being routinely used to subvert the state—and this being widely accepted? This is a significant motif because Bollywood actor Salman Khan was involved in a drunken driving incident in 2002 in which several pavement dwellers were killed but, by all appearances, the criminal suit of manslaughter against the actor is quietly put aside or in hibernation.[21] The success of *Om Shanti Om* suggests that Bollywood audiences take this as legitimate. If in the three films about indulgent law, as discussed in the last chapter, Hindi cinema endorses the emergence of an elite circle outside the processes of the state, the arguments just offered with regard to *Om Shanti Om* point to Bollywood making a claim for a place within that circle.

Notes

1. Eliot Deutsch, 'Reflections on Some Aspects of the Theory of Rasa', in Rachel M. Van Baumer and James R. Brandon (eds), *Sanskrit Drama in Performance* (Delhi: Motilal Banarasidas, 1993), p. 217. Also see, M.K. Raghavendra, *Seduced by the Familiar: Narration and Meaning in Indian Popular Cinema* (New Delhi: Oxford University Press, 2008), pp. 51–5.
2. M. Madhava Prasad, *Ideology of the Hindi Film: A Historical Construction* (New Delhi: Oxford University Press, 1999), pp. 50–1.
3. The 'story' is central in mainstream Indian cinema to producers, distributors, and audiences alike. The dissection by audiences of what they have seen concentrates overwhelmingly on this aspect, which is not only a component of film but somehow seen to contain the entire film-going experience. See Ashish Rajadhyaksha, 'Viewership and Democracy in the Cinema', in Ravi S. Vasudevan (ed.), *Making Meaning in Indian Cinema* (New Delhi: Oxford University Press, 2000), p. 276.
4. To cite a known iconoclast on the significance of reincarnation in Hinduism, Nirad C. Chaudhuri sees the religion as worldly and reincarnation not proposed seriously enough by it. According to him the notion of reincarnation is because Hindus love the world so much that they have invented a system by which they will never leave it.

Nirad C. Chaudhuri, *Hinduism: A Religion to Live By* (New York: Oxford University Press, 1979), pp. 15–16.

5. See Frederic Jameson, 'Postmodernism and Consumer Society', in E. Ann Kaplan (ed.), *Postmodernism and Its Discontents* (London: Verso, 1988), p. 16.

6. Raghavendra, *Seduced by the Familiar*, pp. 265–6.

7. Lalitha Gopalan, *Cinema of Interruptions: Action Genres in Contemporary Indian Cinema* (New Delhi: Oxford University Press, 2002), pp. 2–3.

8. Sandhya cannot be Shanti's ghost because that would disallow the actual ghost. Mukesh Mehra accepts her likeness to Shanti blandly as though look-alikes are a common phenomenon.

9. Indian film magazines are hardly about films. For a detailed examination of how they function, see Rachel Dwyer, 'Shooting Stars: The Indian Film Magazine *Stardust*', in Rachel Dwyer and Christopher Pinney (eds), *Pleasure and the Nation: The History, Politics and Consumption of Public Culture in India* (New Delhi: Oxford University Press, 2001), pp. 247–85.

10. Ashish Rajadhyaksha, 'The "Bollywoodization" of Indian Cinema: Cultural Nationalism in a Global Arena', in *Inter-Asia Cultural Studies*, vol. 4, no. 1, April 2003, special issue on 'Cinema, Culture Industry and Political Societies', pp. 25–39.

11. Kamala Ganesh, 'The Phenomenon of Bollywood in Europe', *The Hindu*, Opinion, 9 October 2010, http://www.thehindu.com/opinion/op-ed/article820213.ece (accessed on 6 July 2012).

12. Ravi S. Vasudevan, 'An Imperfect Public: Cinema and Citizenship in the Third World', in *Sarai Reader 1: The Public Domain* (Delhi: Sarai, The New Media Initiative, 2001), p. 60.

13. For instance, S.S. Vasan blames low taste on the part of the public for low standards in film artistry. S.S. Vasan cited in R.M. Roy (ed.), *Sangeet Natak Akademi Film Seminar Report* (New Delhi: Sangeet Natak Akademi, 1956), pp. 29–30.

14. Ashish Rajadhyaksha, *India Cinema in the Time of Celluloid: From Bollywood to the Emergency* (New Delhi: Tulika, 2009), pp. 134–5.

15. The writer to first use this phrase was, perhaps, Sudhir Kakar in *Intimate Relations: Exploring Indian Sexuality* (New Delhi: Penguin, 1989).

16. This formulation takes its cue from Jean Baudrillard, 'Simulacra and Simulations', in *Selected Writings* (Stanford, CA: Stanford University

Press, 1988), pp. 166–184. 'Simulation ... is the generation by models of a real without origin or reality: a hyperreal.'

17. Madhu Kishwar, 'The Idea of India', *Manushi*, no. 139, posted in June 2004, http://www.indiatogether.org/manushi/issue139/idea.htm posted June 2004 (accessed on 2 December 2009).

18. For a useful review, see Mathew Schneeberger, 'Is *Slumdog Millionaire* Worth the Praise?', *Rediff Movies*, 30 January 2009, http://www.rediff.com/movies/2009/jan/29is-slumdog-worth-it.htm (accessed on 8 July 2012).

19. A feature which has become ubiquitous in the media is Bollywood represented as a 'celebration'—people in bright costumes singing and dancing incessantly—without there being a context or cause. This clearly does not invoke an 'ideal' of any sort because there is no narrative but it does promote identification by the viewer.

20. Mahatma Gandhi is the Father of the Nation but this suggests that the 'nation' his concerns pertain to is a narrower one—one which relies on his personal beliefs but eschews his political agenda.

21. Even the media has stopped reporting on the manslaughter indictment. This post from 2007 is apparently the latest on the subject on the web, http://www.showbizspy.com/article/53176/salman-khan-released-from-prison.html (accessed on 8 July 2012).

8

The Reservations of Middle-class Concern

Page 3 (2005), *Corporate* (2006), *Traffic Signal* (2007), and *Fashion* (2008)

Madhur Bhandarkar and 'Middle' Cinema

The earlier chapters in this book have not focused on film-makers because their emphasis has been on motifs and political biases and, very often, films which are not superficially of the same themes exhibit the same motifs. Madhur Bhandarkar is an exception among the recent film-makers as he has hit upon a design which no other Indian film-maker appears to use—the shape of the exposé. The categorization prevalent in Hindi cinema in the 1970s—mainstream, middle, and art cinema—are perhaps no longer valid today. Middle cinema was once entirely different—thematically—from mainstream cinema[1] and the origin of middle cinema in the 1970s has been written about by scholars,[2] but the situation prevailing then no longer holds. Where film-makers like Shyam Benegal and Hrishikesh Mukherjee hardly moved from the 'middle' path into the mainstream, the rise of the multiplex and Anglophone Indian in the cities—and the mainstream film predominantly addressing the same audiences—has seen film-makers beginning with small budgets but moving into the mainstream and the distinction gradually becoming only a matter of the budget. Examples are film-makers like Vishal Bhardwaj who began with two Shakespeare adaptations (*Maqbool*, 2003 and *Omkara*, 2006) and later made *Kaminey* (2009). Madhur Bhandarkar is different from even this group because his films remain, in terms of approach, the same but he has begun to work with larger budgets as the following data indicates:[3]

Madhur Bhandarkar's film budgets: A comparison

	Budget (Rs in crore)	Gross Receipts (Rs in crore)
Page 3 (2005)	3.00	15.59
Corporate (2006)	4.00	16.60
Traffic Signal (2007)	4.00	12.12
Fashion (2008)	22.00	41.75

Middle cinema of the 1970s was broadly of two kinds: one, films which could be categorized as 'healthy family entertainment', that is, light comedies and love stories with fleshed out middle-class characters instead of 'heroes' and 'heroines', such as films by Basu Chatterjee (*Sara Akash*, 1969; *Rajnigandha*, 1974) and two, the socially conscious cinema of Shyam Benegal (*Ankur*, 1974), Govind Nihalani (*Aakrosh*, 1980), and so on. Directors like Hrishikesh Mukherjee made both kinds of films, for example, *Chupke Chupke* (1975) and *Namak Haram* (1973). Madhur Bhandarkar's films may be socially conscious but they are so in a different way. His *Corporate*, for instance, can be compared to Benegal's *Kalyug* (1981) but he emphasizes the glamour as Shyam Benegal did not and also introduces an element of sleaze. Madhur Bhandarkar is not a 'mainstream' film-maker but his films are still symptomatic of the processes set in motion after the economic reforms of 1991, and their implications complement my postulation about mainstream Hindi cinema in the new millennium.

Page 3: Helplessness and Justice

Page 3, which is about commercialization of Indian journalism in the past decade or so, takes its title from the part of the English language newspaper which deals with the social life of celebrities. Madhavi Sharma (Konkona Sen Sharma) comes to Bombay and becomes a reporter. She is required to cover parties in which the city's rich socialize. The film is episodic and describes in some detail the pretence and hypocrisy of the city's rich and famous people. Madhavi shares a flat with an air hostess Pearl Sequiera, who is trying to land herself a rich husband and an aspiring actress Gayatri Sachdeva who begins to share the room with them later. Gayatri wants to act in an art film and gets to meet a 'socially committed' film-maker named Charu Mohanty, who promptly tries to extract sexual favors from her. Other characters are a film star, Rohit Kumar, an assistant commissioner of police who coaches film stars in the use of firearms on shoots, several people who are into publishing, entertainment, and business, and an industrialist Romesh Thapar, whose wife Anjali runs (honestly and sincerely) a home for abandoned children. Gayatri becomes pregnant by Rohit Kumar who refuses to come to her assistance and she has to go in for an abortion after attempting suicide. Madhavi is desperate to get out of celebrity reporting and finds a mentor in crime reporter Vinayak Mane (Atul Kulkarni). A policeman she grows to respect is inspector Arun Bhonsle. She witnesses a drug bust in which a dealer wanted by the police is arrested. When the pusher tries to bribe Bhonsle as he is being driven away, the inspector throws him out of the jeep and kills him. Vinayak Mane, who is witness to the episode, assures Bhonsle that this will not be reported, that some things can be dealt with only in this way. There is obviously an approval for extra-judicial killings here[4] and, judging from the fact that it is the Anglophone public as the target audience for *Page 3*,[5] this approval is coming from roughly the same public which also endorsed the indulgent law in *Bunty Aur Babli* and *Guru*. The dealer in *Page 3* is an individual apparently from a working-class background and the film is unequivocal about which class of criminal deserves liquidation.[6]

Much of *Page 3* takes the shape of satirical anecdotes including small talk between working-class characters—usually drivers waiting while parties are in progress and commenting acerbically upon celebrity life. Madhavi discovers her boyfriend with his male lover in his apartment and this leads to some unpleasantness. But the film still needs to create a moral crisis for Madhavi so it can get on with its climax and resolution. Anjali Thapar kills herself one day and the reason is not known. Madhavi is now in the crime beat and one day, when she is with Vinayak Mane and Bhonsle, news comes in that some twenty-odd poor children have been brought to Bombay in a child-running racket. Most of the children are rescued but ten of them are still found missing. Acting on a tip, and much against Bhonsle's better judgment, the raid of a bungalow in an up-market area is organized. The industrialist Romesh Thapar and his friends are caught with the children.[7] But Thapar brings in high-level influence and not only does he get away but Madhavi is also stopped from working on this story. It is subsequently learnt that Anjali Thapar killed herself because her husband was abusing the children from her own children's home. In any case, Madhavi loses her job for trying to publish an exposé of a big advertiser and has to return to a 'Page 3' beat on another newspaper. At a celebrity party, a few days later, she meets Gayatri who acknowledges having entered into an arrangement with film-maker Charu Mohanty.

The primary method of the film, evidently, is to deal with, simultaneously, two sides of society: the privileged with their lavish lifestyles and the hidden underbelly. This book is devoted primarily to the asymmetric Nation and *Page 3* is about a similar asymmetry—one that is found in contemporary journalism. But the film itself appears 'asymmetric' and the principal reason is that it makes those without privilege live outside the periphery, as it were. There is certainly no effort on the part of the film to present the privileged as a self-contained 'community' and a principal charge against them is that they are self-obsessed, and indifferent to the rest of the Nation. Still, when drivers and security men—who will have pressing concerns of their own—are preoccupied with their masters, the purpose may be social commentary but it also suggests that the less privileged live only vicariously.

Another characteristic of the film which merits deeper scrutiny is its pessimistic ending. If one looks at the socially concerned middle cinema of the 1970s, such as Benegal's *Ankur* and *Nishant* and Govind Nihalani's *Aakrosh*, these much more powerful films, which although pessimistic, display hope.[8] *Ankur*, for instance, tries to see revolutionary spirit in a young boy who has just flung a stone at the zamindar's window and the lawyer in *Aakrosh* vows to defend the tribal accused of murder. If one examines the state of the characters at the end of *Page 3*, in contrast, Madhavi's story has been destroyed and she has lost her job as a crime reporter, Gayatri has submitted to a man she detests in order to further her career, the honest cop Bhonsle has allowed a child molester to get away because of pressure from above, and Romesh Thapar is gloating at being let off. A significant aspect of this is that while *Page 3* is less bleak in tone than a film like *Aakrosh*, it still concludes more pessimistically.

Looking at *Ankur* and *Aakrosh*, one finds that the key issue is justice, that is, whether the marginalized can hope to combat injustice when they cannot make themselves heard. *Aakrosh* appeals to the liberal and concerned middle class to enable the oppressed, while *Ankur* predicts the anger of the marginalized to eventually ignite society. *Page 3*, in contrast, is not voicing a demand for justice. 'Justice' is usually a plea from the victim and none of the protagonists in *Page 3* are 'victims' as much as frustrated liberals, that is, people seeking to pursue vocations without fear or favor. There is, for instance, no plea made on behalf of the abused children. Each of those thwarted in the film suffers, instead, at the hands of enterprise—to which no appeal can be made. Madhavi's story is stopped and she is sacked because of a corporate advertiser; Gayatri submits to a successful film-maker because she needs to be cast in his film;[9] Bhonsle loses out at the crucial moment because of the influence of industrialist Romesh Thapar.[10] None of these liberal professionals is cast in the heroic mould as were their equivalents in the middle cinema of the 1970s and 1980s, such as the lawyer in *Aakrosh* and the journalist in Romesh Sharma's *New Delhi Times* (1985). If those in the earlier films unearthed and exposed monstrous acts or conspiracies, those in *Page 3* do not. The film may be pessimistic but its remonstrations are too minor. I would like to argue that the protests for justice in the earlier films, the sense of outrage they tried to generate, were essentially directed at the state: from what authority other than the state could one demand justice? *Page 3* comes after the large-scale withdrawal of the state from areas in which it had authority and made way for market forces and enterprise. The characters are up against enterprise but acknowledge that they are implicated in a condition which is irremediable, that is, increasing dominance of the market over the state since the economic reforms are irreversible.[11] The film concludes pessimistically because there is no authority to which one might appeal. At the same time, its disquiet is feeble because there is also no prospect of redress. There is a curious inconsistency involved here. It is not that the film does not admit to miscarriages of justice because the issues of the extra-judicial killing and the abused children would be serious on any forum, but it still desists from protesting. It is helpless against enterprise—which is the oppressive centre of its world—but will not protest on behalf of the genuine victims because they are outside the periphery. I would like to argue that, unwittingly, *Page 3* points to a recognition that the authority of the state is too weak to respond to appeals for justice, while enterprise, which has usurped its power, is committed to maintaining the asymmetry which subverts its justice. When functionaries of the state act, it is in contravention of the law and against a class not empowered by enterprise.

Corporate: A New Object of Loyalty

Corporate revolves around the struggle for market control between two industrialists, the Sehgal Group of Industries owned by Vinay Sehgal (Rajat Kapoor) and the Marwah Group owned by Dharmesh Marwah (Raj Babbar). The two groups are traditional rivals in the food products business. Nishigandha Dasgupta a.k.a. Nishi (Bipasha

Basu) is vice-president of the Sehgal Group, while Vinay Sehgal's brother-in-law Ritesh (Kay Kay Menon) joins in later as senior vice-president. Ritesh and Nishi have a long-standing relationship which now resumes.

There are several issues over which the two groups are fighting. The Sehgal Group has just attracted a foreign investor which has strengthened it but the Marwah Group has local political support. Politicians are themselves divided because the Sehgal Group has central government support but, for the moment, the Marwah Group is triumphant. But the latter has an Achilles heel in its philandering chief executive officer (CEO), Pervez, who is attracted to Nishi. When Nishi learns that the Marwah Group is planning a new soft drink launch, she arranges to meet Pervez 'accidentally' in Delhi, and hints at sexual favours at their next meeting in Bombay. Pervez is so overcome that he offers her a job at twice the salary immediately, which she agrees to consider. Nishi, however, also secretly arranges a prostitute for Pervez and this gives her the opportunity to steal the plans for the new mint-based soft drink from Pervez's laptop.

Corporate is inclined towards sleaze but the factor that needs examination is how Nishi, despite such sordid personal conduct, can be placed at the film's moral centre along with Ritesh. There is never any doubt that she is only playing along with Pervez and that his doubling her salary does not tempt her. An academic research paper examining the film might describe Nishi as embodying the 'gullible corporate employee' taken advantage of by her employer[12] but Nishi is, in fact, shown to be extremely wily. Her actions on behalf of the company—even when they are morally suspect—are wholehearted and selfless. This seemingly inconsistent conduct needs deeper investigation although a justification is offered, which is, her love for Ritesh.

The Sehgal Group now launches a new mint-based soft drink ahead of their rivals but it is discovered that the water source in contaminated by pesticide. Since postponing the launch would be difficult, Vinay Sehgal coldly bribes his way through the crisis and the new drink is launched—against the advice of Ritesh and Nishi.

Nishi is promoted and this causes jealousy; a top executive defects to the other side and reveals facts pertaining to the insecticide contamination. The Sehgal Group is in the dock but Vinay Sehgal prevails upon Ritesh to persuade Nishi to take the blame—with the understanding that she will be rescued in a few months. But after Nishi agrees and confesses, the Sehgal Group reaches an understanding with their rivals and so there is now no relief for Nishi, who is in jail and pregnant with Ritesh's child. When Ritesh learns that Nishi has been betrayed, he threatens his brother-in-law with exposure but is killed immediately—he falls from his high-rise apartment. The pregnant Nishi has to fight her battle alone now.

The question to be asked at this point is why Nishi fulfils every demand made upon her selflessly even though they are unethical. It would, for instance, have been appropriate for her to be monetarily compensated for her sacrifice but the issue is never brought up even by Ritesh when being sounded by Vinay Sehgal. It is as if bringing money into the scheme would somehow lessen Nishi's virtues. It is significant that feeding the public a soft drink laced with pesticide is less a moral issue than 'standing by the company'. I propose that what makes Nishi 'noble' is, once again, the notion of 'loyalty'. But the question here is which entity deserves this loyalty in *Corporate*. That Ritesh is the object of loyalty sounds unconvincing because Nishi could have moved to another corporate—although not to their rivals—without love being compromised. Navin, the CEO of the Sehgal Group, is shown to do this in the film when the soft drink containing the pesticide is launched and he is not judged harshly. Vinay Sehgal cannot obviously be the object of loyalty either but there is a clue in a conversation in which it is suggested that exposure of the company through a pesticide scandal will hurt investors badly. 'Shareholder wealth' will be depleted and that becomes the pivot of a key moral dilemma. The implicit sense here is that rather than the Sehgal Group being equated with the promoter Vinay Sehgal, it is being equated with the body of minority shareholders who take the place of the 'public'—as also in *Guru*. I would like to argue that investors in a company cannot be given the privileges of the public since they are specifically in the business of making or losing money with the attendant risks. People who innocently consume soft drinks laced with pesticide, perhaps, have more legitimate claims to being considered the 'public'.

Corporate is not restricting its concern to the workings of the corporate sector because Bhandarkar uses the same motif in *Page 3*—working-class characters like drivers and security guards providing asides on the action. Here again we get a sense of the lower echelons in the social hierarchy participating vicariously in the lives of the rich and powerful. Overall, there is only a single hierarchy—although not a 'community'—and one in which the top echelons are corrupt. One sees a parallel between the way *Corporate* views the corporate sector and *Rang De Basanti* views the Nation: as led by self-serving people but still deserving one's loyalty. This elevation of the corporate sector to an object of loyalty comparable to the Nation is possible only because the audience it addresses are implicated in the sector's workings—just as all Indians are implicated in that of the Nation—as employees, vendors, and investors and the sentiment therefore touches a chord.

There is apparently a movement in Bhandarkar's position between *Page 3* and *Corporate*. In the earlier film he saw enterprise as powerful and threatening but its position of overwhelming power as being inescapable. Here he is regarding it as an object of loyalty like the Nation. The Nation has a public and a company has its shareholders to which it must fulfil its promise, is the argument offered. Madhur Bhandarkar's 'bipolar' response towards enterprise both as a threat and a promise reaches its apogee in *Traffic Signal*.

Traffic Signal: Responsibility and Philanthropy

After dealing with the rich and the powerful in two films Madhur Bhandarkar moved down the social hierarchy to make a film about the vendors, beggars, prostitutes, and vagrants who make their living around a traffic signal in Mumbai (formerly Bombay). At the centre of the film is Silsila (Kunal Khemu), the 'manager' of the signal. He pursued various trades at the signal before becoming the manager. Silsila is a humane manager, sensitive and caring but cold-blooded when it comes to delivery. Silsila reports to a mid-level don, Jaffar, who in turn reports to the big boss Haji bhai jaan. The film is crowded with details pertaining to the way of life of those it is dealing with. Noorie (Konkona Sen Sharma) is a prostitute soliciting at the signal. Dominic (Ranvir Shorey) is a drug addict who begs by playing a well-dressed software engineer who has just lost his wallet. Rani (Madhu Chandra) is a rustic girl who sells garments at the signal and romances with Silsila.

As with the other two films, there is an element of sleaze inserted into *Traffic Signal* on the pretext of showing how the poor are often made to live without dignity. Noorie is sometimes required to bestow sexual favours on a policeman free of charge; on the occasion shown to us, she tries to plead that she is menstruating but she is still forced to have sex. My observation here is that such a situation might even arise in an upper-class marriage but a film would hardly dwell on it unless it is dealing specifically with the plight of women. If it was dealing simply with the ways of the rich, it would hardly include such an event in a detailed manner. In another episode in *Traffic Signal*, a beggar woman breastfeeding her infant is ogled at by a respectable man in a car. One can imagine affluent women inadvertently exposing themselves at 'page 3' parties and being ogled at but dwelling on this would also be considered tasteless— it would take away the person's dignity without adding to our understanding. *Traffic Signal* is not voyeuristic but it views the poor in this way because it places itself outside their sphere. I propose that the film 'exoticizes' the poor because its gaze belongs to another class; the sense of responsibility for those it is depicting as in Nihalani's *Aakrosh* is absent.[13] To convey the essence of its attitude, if the film's gaze is a concerned one, it is not one of responsibility as much as of philanthropy.

By itself, the narrative around the traffic signal is too episodic to constitute a 'story'[14] and the director hits upon a way of narrativizing it. This strategy has to do with demands being made upon a builder by the underworld and the builder wanting a flyover to be constructed to bring up the value of his properties. The problem is that an honest official is standing in the way. The underworld therefore arranges for the honest official to be killed at the traffic signal—with Silsila and his friends innocently assisting. What they do not know is that, with the construction of the flyover, there will no traffic signal and they will be left with no livelihood.

A question which can be raised about the resolution in *Traffic Signal* is why the film-maker is unable to narrativize the lives of the poor and give them independent trajectories. If the lives of celebrities and corporate executives can be turned into stories, why cannot the lives of the poor also be treated thus? It can be argued that a story in a Hindi popular film is not autonomous but a thread in a grand narrative which relates to the progress/destiny of the Nation and this connection is explicitly made in most films. Munnabhai's moral trajectory in *Lage Raho Munnabhai*, for instance, points to the moral trajectory that the Nation itself will hopefully follow. Gurukanth Desai's rise in *Guru* is a strand in the story of the Nation's rise as an industrial power. This proposition can be viewed in another way: a story in a Hindi film is exemplary in some way because all stories, as Frederic Jameson would have it, are national allegories.[15] It can be argued that the hopelessness of the poor cannot be the viewpoint of a story in Hindi cinema because each film is necessarily about a Nation with hope. Still, the middle cinema of concern of the 1970s and 1980s resolved the difficulty by using a middle-class person's viewpoint. Regarded in this light, the stridently political middle cinema of the 1970s and 1980s was a warning against the apathetic road that the Nation might be taking. But if the focus in the films of this period is the liberal middle-class, the lives of the poor still have independent trajectories and develop on their own. *Ankur* may even be seen as a love story between the Dalit servant played by Shabana Azmi and her wayward deaf-mute husband who returns after a long absence and is overjoyed at finding his wife pregnant—although by the master. The narrativizing of the lives of the poor indicates a conviction that they need to be carried along by the Nation even if it needed help from the liberal middle-class.

A plausible conclusion to be derived from *Traffic Signal* is that since the destiny of the poor does not encroach upon the Nation they need not be carried along. The film beginning with a first-person voice-over from Silsila suggests that it will adopt the viewpoint of the marginalized but its inability to make a complete story of their lives—not endowing them with teleology—belies this. The director could, for instance, have turned it into a story of personal revenge—Silsila against the gangsters who involved him in the official's killing, and this would not have been implausible. But it would have been contrary to the grand narrative[16] implied by the film, which is the inexorable march of enterprise.

We have seen the increasing endorsement of crime as a legitimate extension of enterprise in Hindi cinema. Since the economic reforms are irreversible, enterprise will gain over indulgent state control and crime-driven enterprise will triumph over the weakening state. The film offers this scenario through the implication that the honest official is merely a temporary obstruction; it does not consider the possibility of his replacement by another honest official or the state pursuing his killers. It is presumed that once the impediment of an individual's personal honesty is removed, illegality will have its way—although this is duly wept over.

It is perhaps its ambivalent attitude towards enterprise that makes the film's philanthropy contradictory and empty. *Traffic Signal*, along with many others, is generally identified as a multiplex film.[17] This should give the reader a sense of the segment of the public it reflects the concerns of and, as I have argued earlier, its gaze belonged to a class above the one it was surveying. Since the sections that the film is addressing have been co-opted to the view that progress and development must necessarily proceed with the withdrawal of the state, no other path can be imagined for the march of enterprise except at the expense of state authority.

Fashion: Industry Exposé or 'Corporate Communication'?

One could say that with *Fashion*, Madhur Bhandarkar moves away from his earlier concerns inasmuch as he tries to look entirely at a single industry without aiming for the larger social picture. Considering that the film acknowledges the help of important fashion brands, one may also gather that it is not an exposé. The film is about an aspiring model, Meghna Mathur (Priyanka Chopra), from Chandigarh who goes to Mumbai against her family's wishes to seek a career. The film charts her trajectory in the fashion industry: her initial failures, her gradual rise, and her affair with Abhijit Sarin (Arbaaz Khan), the owner of a leading fashion brand named 'Panache'. The film plays up the glamour in the industry but also appears to look at its dark side, chiefly, top models being unable to handle public attention and becoming drug addicts (for example, the character of Shonali played by Kangna Ranaut). Meghna herself is unable to handle her success and, after an abortion, has a breakdown. The low point in her trajectory is portrayed dubiously: after a night of hectic partying, Meghna wakes up to find that she has had sex with a black man. The camera surveys the sleeping man's body from above and his colour is used to suggest the depths to which Meghna has sunk. Although this detail would hardly have escaped adverse reactions on international platforms, it has not attracted much attention in India.[18]

Having lost her self-confidence, Meghna now retreats to Chandigarh, broken and depressed. It is only after a year that she returns and tries to atone for her earlier displays of discourtesy. Shonali is an addict and an alcoholic and living on the streets in a disturbed condition and Meghna tries to help her rehabilitate. Meghna's initial attempts to return to the ramp are failures because of her low self-confidence but there are good people willing to give her a second chance and she gains poise. She modestly acknowledges that her return to the ramp is not due to her own efforts but due to Shonali who gave her the will to live and instilled a new self-confidence in her. At the moment of her dramatic return as 'show-stopper' for a top designer, she learns that Shonali is dead as a result of an overdose. Meghna is deeply distressed but she is still triumphant. The film ends with Meghna walking the ramp in Paris.

Fashion, as may be evident from the description, is entirely about personal aspiration. In fact, there is not even the customary romance coming to fruition which means that the closure is weak.[19] The director tries to deal with all those involved in the fashion industry: designers, editors of fashion magazines, and owners of brands, apart from fashion models. The industry has some of the makings of a 'community' because it deals with so many different categories: gay designers, struggling and successful models, photographers, philandering tycoons, and their families. At the same time, the fashion industry is not a 'community' in the sense I have defined it because it has no single purpose or destiny. Meghna Mathur climbs in her profession but her ascent has no bearing on the industry itself. Despite its promise to reveal the underbelly of the industry, the picture *Fashion* presents of it is so agreeable that it seems like an authorized biography approved by industry insiders. The absence of a romance and the film's conclusion with Meghna on the ramp in Paris has the appearance of a call for global competitiveness within the industry.

At the first glance, *Fashion* appears to be (except for the racist use of the black man's body) politically unrevealing but it is positioned as a politically conscious investigation of the industry. Madhur Bhandarkar had already made his reputation with various exposés and the audience, therefore, had expectations of the film along these lines. Secondly, he appears in the film as himself and a line of dialogue between two other people points him out with awe as a maker of 'realistic films'. Since he was a brand connoting 'social consciousness' when *Fashion* came out and this is consciously invoked, the audience are being invited to read the film 'politically'. In contrast to this claim of an exposé covertly made by *Fashion*, the film is even more benign towards the industry than Hollywood might have allowed. There is little of the exhibition of the jealousies, hatreds, cold rivalry, and ruthlessness that we find in Hollywood films, for example, *The Devil Wears Prada* (2006) which is about the fashion industry. Films about the workings of an industry cannot avoid being satirical at some point but *Fashion* studiously avoids such a possibility. A particular aspect of the film which deserves comment is the relationship between Meghna and Abhijit Sarin, the owner of Panache of which Meghna is the face. Abhijit Sarin is shown to be a powerful person in the fashion business and the issue being raised here is whether a young model entering into a sexual relationship with someone in his position has not been coerced into it. In *Page 3*, if the reader recollects, Gayatri yields to film-maker Charu Mohanty, not out of choice but because of coercion. The question is whether the same approach should not have been employed with regard to the fashion industry. Seen thus, rather than being the exposé that it claims to be, *Fashion* has the appearance of a public relations exercise for the fashion industry. Since so many industry players have been thanked by the film before the credits, there is reason to believe that this is exactly what it is. The fact that it is positioned as an exposé makes its methods insidious.

Another aspect of the film which merits scrutiny is the relationship between Meghna and Shonali. The two are rivals and Meghna replaces her as the top model and there is never any indication that the two are friends. Given this scenario, why does Meghna take it upon herself to rehabilitate Shonali? When Shonali is shown to be lying on a street in a drugged condition, a parallel is being drawn with Dominic in *Traffic Signal* but the two are hardly comparable. For one thing, Shonali is not in financial need while Dominic is a beggar living in a slum. It can be argued here that if the film had kept itself open to the larger world, it would have made the preoccupations of the fashion industry seem trivial. At the same time, without this exhibition of 'human concern', the industry might have appeared too uncaring. The film is perhaps trying to bring two incompatibles together—insularity and concern.

If there is a political lesson to be learned from *Fashion*, it is that Bollywood does not have Hollywood's independence and will be dictated to by sponsoring or financing interests in terms of the content of its films. This means that it may not be equipped to play a socially independent role but will acquiesce with business when required to do so. Film scholars have suggested that the nature of film production in the Hindi film industry has traditionally been different from Hollywood[20] and there are a very large number of small producers, some who produce only one film. This may have left Bollywood traditionally weak but corporate funding of cinema—funding of cinema by interests which are not in cinema—may further weaken it. The film was a significant success commercially but it has almost none of the characteristics of traditional Hindi cinema. Apart from the fact that it contains no heterosexual relationship taken to fruition, family relationships in it are of no consequence, it allows for no villains of any sort and deals almost entirely with one class, or presents all its characters as of one class with the same stake in the industry in which they are working. This last characteristic, it must be noted, is different from *Corporate* in which the central issue is that Nishi has a smaller stake in the Sehgal Group but is still more loyal to the company. Given that the conflicts it deals with are more in the nature of misunderstandings than a clash of interests, it is difficult to even read it as an allegory of the Nation. Considering these factors, *Fashion* can be compared to a house magazine pretending to be purveying general news to the public. This points to where a new danger to Hindi cinema could come from: instead of performing its traditional role of narrativizing the experience of the Nation (or a segment) and 'addressing a constituency', it could be assisting enterprise[21] as a service provider in 'corporate communication'.

This chapter has dealt with a film-maker who began by displaying social concern in the age of global enterprise but, as we follow his career trajectory, it begins to resemble a capitulation. As already brought out, the films feel none of the responsibility for society that middle cinema once felt. This is perhaps due to the general sense that the authority of the state has weakened as a result of losing power to the market and so no fruitful appeals for justice can be made to it. *Page 3* is not unproblematic because it exhibits concern while putting itself firmly in the camp of enterprise—which means that its concern is more a gesture of philanthropy than responsibility. Still, it admits to discomfort at enterprise gaining such dictatorial power that it subverts the authority of the state. *Corporate* is a strange exercise after *Page 3* because the corporate sector even replaces the Nation as an object of loyalty. It is not that human failings in the sector are not admitted but the abstraction of 'The Company'—justified by the shareholding public—reigns supreme. Dealing with the poor after two films about the more affluent classes, *Traffic Signal* has the appearance of a reversion to an earlier cinema of concern. But when examined more closely, it reveals contrary features. Firstly, it treats the poor, who are its subject, as outside the grand narrative of the Nation's progress, which is driven by enterprise—both legitimate and criminal. Enterprise is not a level playing field but favours the rich and powerful. Another aspect of the film is that it is not without faith in this 'progress' despite seeing the criminalization of enterprise and the weakening of the state as natural corollaries. *Page 3* and *Traffic Signal* are both pessimistic about the future of state authority—with the latter film being more extreme—but both films endorse the system (they regard as) subverting its design. The ostensible justification is that while enterprise may be responsible, it is also unstoppable. The consequence of endorsing the dominance of enterprise in the polity is to succumb to its power because this is Bhandarkar's undertaking in *Fashion* which emerges as a public relations exercise for the fashion industry.

If anything, the four films of Madhur Bhandarkar's discussed in this chapter provide evidence of the gaining power of enterprise. This might not have been alarming if 'enterprise' had been a level playing field but making this so are two features: the classes who are rich and powerful enjoy an unfair advantage and the meaning of the term 'enterprise' has been gradually extended to include crime. The strengthening of enterprise does not automatically imply the weakening of state authority but the endorsement of crime as an extension of enterprise certainly has this effect. Both *Page 3* and *Traffic Signal* received national awards[22] and this suggests that this message has the approval of the state, which may itself be a sign of its weakening authority.

Notes

1. M.K. Raghavendra, *Seduced by the Familiar: Narration and Meaning in Indian Popular Cinema* (New Delhi: Oxford University Press, 2008), pp. 183–7.
2. M. Madhava Prasad, *Ideology of the Hindi Film: A Historical Construction* (New Delhi: Oxford University Press, 1998), pp. 118–30.
3. Data obtained from IBOS Network (www.ibosnetwork.com) and Business of Cinema (www.businessofcinema.com). See http://ibos network.com/asp/filmbodetails.asp?id=Page+3; http://ibosnetwork.com/asp/filmbodetails.asp?id=Corporate; http://ibosnetwork.com/asp/filmbo details.asp?id=Traffic+Signal; and http://ibosnetwork.com/asp/filmbo details.asp?id=Fashion+%282008%29 (accessed on 17 July 2008).
4. None of the English language reviews of the film seem to find this problematic. This suggests that the film mirrors accepted attitudes among the Anglophone public.
5. Apart from a generous usage of spoken English in the film, *Page 3* was apparently a multiplex hit. See Namrata Joshi, in a review of Bhandarkar's next film *Corporate*, *Outlook*, 24 July 2006 available at http://m.outlookindia.com/story.aspx?sid=4&aid=231980 (accessed on 15 July 2012).
6. It has been noted that there is an institutional mechanism working in various spheres to separate the citizen-subject from his/her 'double' who is the subaltern. 'These exclusionary discourses of the secular 'citizen-subject' emerge from any different institutional locations (the police codes, the media, upper-caste/middle-class Hindu households, family planning agencies, etc.), in connection with a variety of subjects of 'public' interest (criminality, communalism, population, law and order, health, development, etc.).' See Vivek Dhareshwar and R. Srivatsan, '"Rowdy-Sheeters": An Essay on Subalternity and Politics', in Shahid Amin and Dipesh Charkrabarty (eds), *Subaltern Studies IX: Writings on South Asian History and Society* (New Delhi: Oxford University Press, 1996), p. 219.
7. The film bluntly shows us unclothed children sitting on the laps of near-naked men without making use of any of cinema's tricks of

illusion. One wonders if, instead of only being a sequence about child molestation, whether this would not itself constitute child molestation.

8. For a useful account of the political climate in which films like *Ankur* were made, see Aruna Vasudev, *The New Indian Cinema* (New Delhi: Macmillan, 1986), pp. 2–3.

9. Charu Mohanty is shown to be indifferent to Gayatri's initial refusal and simply shrugs it away. Evidently, he is not in want of women who are willing to submit to him.

10. In fact, one could say that Romesh Thapar subverts the state in the same way as the protagonist does in *Guru*, that is, through acquaintanceship with its functionaries.

11. Regardless of which political party is in power, there is a consensus that the economic reforms are irreversible. This has been widely acknowledged by scholars. For instance, see Rahul Mukherji, 'The Political Economy of India's Economic Reforms', *Asian Economic Policy Review*, vol. 3, no. 2, December 2008, pp. 315–31.

12. Business researchers start on the assumption that a negative portrayal of business conduct is the portrayal of an aberration. I am attempting to explain Nishi's ideal conduct as an aberration. See Tejas A. Desai, 'Contemporary Lessons in Economic Philosophy Drawn from Two Recent Indian Films', Working Paper Series, *Research and Publications*, Indian Institute of Management Ahmedabad, WP 2009-04-02, April 2009, pp. 4–5.

13. Govind Nihalani's subsequent film *Party* (1984) is actually about the responsibility of the partying classes. An activist is being brutally murdered in a tribal area even as the rich are preoccupied with their own petty problems.

14. Any telling or recounting of a string of events may be called narration. But not every narration yields a narrative, and not every narrative makes a story. By becoming a story, or pretending to be a story, a narration arrives at literariness of the fictive kind. A story is a narration that attains a certain degree of completeness, and even a fragment of a story or an unfinished story will imply that completeness as an aspect of its informing principle—the intentionality that governs its construction.

Robert Scholes, 'Narration and Narrativity in Film', in Gerald Mast and Marshall Cohen (eds), *Film Theory and Criticism: Introductory Readings*, 3rd edition (New York: Oxford University Press, 1985), pp. 392–3.

15. Frederic Jameson, 'World Literature in the Age of Multinational Capitalism', in Clayton Koelb and Virgil Lokke (eds), *The Current in Criticism* (West Lafayette, Ind.: Purdue University Press, 1987), pp. 65–88.

16. The causation in the film proceeds with the builder needing to pay off the underworld but not being able to because the value of his property needs to be pushed up—for which the flyover is essential. The impediment is the honest official. He, therefore, puts the ball back in the underworld's court and asks them to solve his problem. The underworld, therefore, 'removes the impediment' with Silsila to assist. The argument here is that this process represents the impersonal working of enterprise in the grand narrative of the Nation's progress and a story of personal revenge would have gone 'against the grain'.

17. Gita Viswanath, 'The Multiplex: Crowd, Audience and the Genre Film', *Economic and Political Weekly*, vol. 42, no. 32, 11 August 2007, pp. 3289–94. Also see, V. Vamshi Krishna Reddy, Ram Gopal Verma, 'Bombay and Globalization', *Asian Cinema*, vol. 22, no. 2, 2013, p. 162.

18. Some blogs have noticed this. For instance, Devdutt Pattanaik, 'Black Gods White Gods', *Verveonline*, vol. 17, no. 7, 2009, http://www.verveonline.com/75/morality/blackwhitegods.shtml (accessed on 22 July 2012).

19. For the role of romance in effecting the closure, see Raghavendra, *Seduced by the Familiar*, pp. 36–8.

20. Prasad, *Ideology of the Hindi Film*, pp. 48–9.

21. It is well known that financing in Bollywood comes partly from the underworld. But it can be argued that financing by the criminal underworld might leave the social content of Hindi cinema more secure than corporate sponsorship. For an enquiry into another aspect of Bollywood assisting the corporate sector—Bollywood's construction of international 'standards'—see Susan Runkle, 'Bollywood, Beauty and the Construction of "International Standards" in Post-liberalization Bombay', *Sagar: South Asia Research Journal*, vol. 11, 2004, pp. 37–57.

22. *Page 3* was awarded the 'Best Film' in 2004, while *Traffic Signal* received the Best Director Award in 2006.

9

Dystopia or Entrepreneurial Fantasy
Kaminey (2009)

Entrepreneurship and the Weakening State

Hindi cinema, as I have tried to demonstrate, takes up the motif of personal aspiration in real earnest in the new millennium and this shows itself gradually as a grand narrative, that of the Nation driven by enterprise. But making this motif unusual is the admission of illegality as a component of enterprise. *Lage Raho Munnabhai* (2006) which was widely regarded as a return to Gandhian values, dealt with an extortionist and a thug who remains an extortionist and a thug even after a 'soul altering experience' with Mahatma Gandhi's spectre—although he acknowledges small truths about himself. The film appeared to be blind to these implications but equally blind was its appreciative Indian public. As I argued, the film—and the wide-eyed responses to it—provided evidence that illegalities have been accepted as a fact of middle-class life in India. Other films like *Bunty Aur Babli* (2005) and *Guru* (2007) introduce the motif of the indulgent law: businessmen and even tricksters who owe their success to illegal practices do not face punishment but are acknowledged for their acumen and enlisted by the nation state. As elected governments go ahead with economic reform—and hasten the withdrawal of the state from areas in which it was once active— the inextricable association of illegality with entrepreneurship finds the state itself being progressively weakened, and the evidence is the helplessness of the law becoming a constantly repeated film motif. Apart from Madhur Bhandarkar's films which were dealt with in the last chapter, Om Shanti Om (2007) glosses over a fatal traffic accident in which the issue of culpability is not raised, apparently because of a private arrangement between the driver of the car and the dead person's family. These films constitute evidence of the weakening power of the state because 'lawlessness' is not their theme; they are set in milieus with other characteristics and yield this information despite themselves. A film actually showcasing a criminalized milieu—as the Batman films and Quentin Tarantino's Pulp Fiction (1994) do—is Vishal Bhardwaj's Kaminey (2009). As this means that Kaminey tries to turn the motif of lawlessness into a generic choice, it will be more difficult to argue that its vision of an urban dystopia constitutes social evidence. Yet that is the intention of this chapter.

Kaminey: The State, Politics, and Entrepreneurship

The story of Kaminey, despite its effort to appear elaborate and complicated, is simple enough. Charlie and Guddu Sharma (Shahid Kapoor) are identical but estranged twins with their family from Uttar Pradesh and while Charlie works with a gang that fixes horse races, Guddu works in a non-government agency. Guddu's girlfriend Sweety (Priyanka Chopra) is pregnant and the two get married but Sweety's brother Sunil Bhope, a hoodlum and a politician expounding Marathi language chauvinism, takes exception. That he has been agitating against north Indians in Mumbai and this will take away his electoral plank is the initial justification. But it later turns out that he has been offered five crore rupees by a builder for Sweety to marry his son and that is the real reason for his disapproval. Charlie, Guddu, Bhope, and Sweety are accidentally brought into contact with another gang run by a drug trafficker named Tashi, with whom the anti-narcotics squad is hand in glove. The object coveted by Tashi and his associates is a guitar case stuffed with cocaine and this falls accidentally into Charlie's lap. The film ends in a shootout over the cocaine and there is a bloodbath. The police who arrive to arrest the traffickers are tempted by the offer of a share in the drug money but even they cannot save the cocaine. Charlie, Guddu, and Sweety escape the carnage and live happily ever after: Charlie as a prosperous bookie with a glamorous girlfriend, and Guddu and Sweety as the parents of twins. There are also two Africans in the story who are negotiating with Tashi to exchange some blood diamonds for the cocaine and the two also perish in the shootout, leaving the diamonds to the protagonists. A motif omitted in this summary pertains to a flashback of the twins as children. Their father—generally an honest man—worked in the railways but was one day apprehended for stealing a wristwatch. The police demanded five thousand rupees to let him off but the twins could raise only three thousand. In any case, unable to bear the shame, their father killed himself and this was the moment when the twins drifted apart.

Kaminey is an unusual experience in Indian cinema—nearly as much a novelty as *HAHK* (1994). If that film was the first to evict the poor from the among the protagonists—providing spaces for them only as servants of the rich—*Kaminey* may be the first to do the same to law-abiding people who appear to exist only to be taken advantage of by the unscrupulous. Urban criminals, until the mid-1990s, were not glamorous figures in Hindi popular cinema and only people led astray (as in *Deewaar*, 1975) became criminals. As already mentioned in the Introduction, the film that changed this was Ram Gopal Varma's *Satya* (1999). *Satya* appeared 'realistic' but had a discourse interpretable in the context of the economic liberalization, initiated by P.V. Narasimha Rao and Manmohan Singh in 1991–2, which also marked the end of Nehruvian socialism. The police in *Satya* are given to illegality but they still act in defence of the law. In *Kaminey*, the police are acting only for themselves and with the motive of private gain. If

Lobo, the narcotics officer who gains custody of the guitar, is an agent of the drug mafia, the others who are not agents are also so tempted by the drugs that they participate in an open 'auction' on the street at the climax. Lobo is also shown as slovenly; he does not wear his uniform, which suggests that he is not acting on behalf of the state. In fact, it takes some time before he is revealed to be an anti-narcotics police officer because his conduct makes him seem a drug dealer. Drugs, it may be recollected, was treated as such dirty business in *Page 3*[1] that the extra-judicial killing of a drug dealer was treated as justifiable. Here it is represented as one more opportunity for enterprise.

Mumbai in *Kaminey* is designed as a dystopia resembling the Batman's Gotham City but the fact that it is an actual city, instead of an elaborate creation informed not only by an existing city but also various elements of design including German Expressionism and Art Deco,[2] gives it a different significance. There is also a view promoted by the media that Vishal Bhardwaj is the Indian Quentin Tarantino[3] because Tarantino is, likewise (*Pulp Fiction*; *Kill Bill: volume 1*, 2003; *Kill Bill: volume 2*, 2004), preoccupied with criminals, violence, drugs, and the underworld. But the difference between the two film-makers is important. Tarantino's world is a generic construct and he identifies no recognizable social groups in his stories. Elements like 'The Deadly Viper Assassination Squad' in *Kill Bill* and Mr Wolf in *Pulp Fiction* are essentially from other kinds of texts[4] and are, in a sense, placed within quotation marks. Tarantino also avoids subjects which might be taken to be socially pertinent (racism, for instance).[5] Bhardwaj, in contrast, is dealing directly with a recognizable city and recognizable socio-political issues. Guddu works in a non-government organization and the opening dance sequence involves an AIDS awareness campaign. He marries the sister of a politician/hoodlum standing on a 'Mumbai-for-Maharashtrians' plank. Bhardwaj's film is also steeped in grimy Mumbai—using actual locations saturated with social connotations—and it can hardly protest its innocence as Tarantino's films can. Where *Kill Bill* deliberately disengages with social issues, *Kaminey* treads a virtual minefield of them but uses them only to further a fantasy, one about advancement in a milieu in which enterprise is unregulated.

While being set in a real milieu and dealing with recognizable issues, *Kaminey* simplifies them considerable so that it fits its theme which is the pursuit of money by every section of society. To examine an issue about which the director apparently feels strongly, the story of the film includes a political party which has as its plank the idea of Mumbai for Maharashtrians. Sunil Bhope who heads the party takes exception to a north Indian marrying his sister because it is contrary to his own election rhetoric but quickly comes around to accepting the alliance when he is offered money. Sunil Bhope also asserts casually that he can abandon his political party and join another one if necessary. The observation here is that even corrupt politicians have compulsions which cannot be equated with money. Their power, for instance, depends on the constituencies they command and regardless of their real attachments they will find it hard to defy their constituencies at will. Seeing money and profit as the only motives is perhaps not the way of a politician but that of a businessman.

Celebrating 'Darkness'

A motif of importance in the film pertains to Charlie and Guddu's origins and their father. To those familiar with the past of Hindi cinema, the account of the film given earlier may make *Kaminey* look like an unusual cultural artefact but the film does not abandon Hindi film convention altogether and actually invokes Yash Chopra's *Deewaar* (1975). Charlie and Guddu are estranged, as the two brothers were in *Deewaar*. They are also from the working class and their father—a railway employee—took his own life when he was accused of being a thief. This motif carries forward the one in *Deewaar* in which the hero had the legend 'Mera baap chor hai' (My father is a thief) inscribed on his forearm and carried in his heart, thereafter, the hurt from the unjust accusation. But neither Charlie nor Guddu is a wounded soul (as *Deewaar's* protagonist was). Charlie is not living a life of illegality because of a deep sense of injustice but is cheerful about 'shortcuts' being necessary. Moreover, their dead father was not the exemplary figure that the father was in *Deewaar* and taught the twins that all people were *kaminey* (scoundrels). *Kaminey* has, by and large, been taken to be a 'dark' film and, while it is dimly lit, it is celebratory in its approach to corruption and social decay, which is heightened by the music. Huge sums of money are invoked casually and greed is portrayed as legitimate. For instance, Guddu is law-abiding but his disinclination to engage in criminal activity is not a moral quality but simply a quirk. In fact, Guddu needs Charlie to save him and the message is that social ethic is a hindrance. The vision promoted by the film may be roughly described as 'Social Darwinism', that society is a lawless jungle in which only the fittest survive. And one's 'fitness' is perhaps commensurable with one's willingness to shed moral scruples. The presence of the Africans means that the film's 'moral vision' is extended to include the global world in which criminality and thievery is the norm, a motif which echoes *Dhoom 2*.

The film cites 1984 as the year in which Guddu and Charlie's father came to Bombay for the first time and the flashback pertaining to their childhood is filmed in monochrome. The year has no particular significance in the film—although it was the year of Indira Gandhi's assassination — but has perhaps been hit upon to account for the age of the twins. There is no mention of their mother and an explanation for this can be that the mother might have needlessly brought in a moral angle[6] which *Kaminey* does well without. An important aspect is that their father being arrested for thievery is the first cause which has traditionally been crucial in the development of the story in Hindi cinema.[7] The 'first cause' is contained in the preamble (or flashback) and is the 'seed' from which the story emerges.[8] Examples range from Devdas' punishment by his authoritarian father in *Devdas* (1935), Raj's pregnant mother being cast out by his father on suspicion of her unborn child being someone else's in *Awaara* (1951), and Vijay's father being dubbed a thief in *Deewaar*. The first cause finds correspondence in the disturbance of the initial condition insisted upon by classical screenwriting from Hollywood.[9] But the first cause in the Hindi film is different from the 'disturbance' in that it does not create a condition that needs to be remedied. In *Guru* and *Bunty Aur Babli*, the first cause is a promise: the dissatisfaction of the protagonists with small-town dreams and their yearning to become entrepreneurs. If the first cause had a hurtful impact upon the protagonist, most films end badly for those concerned, such as in *Devdas*, *Deewaar*, and *Awaara*. This is because unlike the 'disturbance' in classical cinema which needs to be undone, the first cause is used to define an inviolable anxious condition, as in the case of the vengeful hero in Hindi cinema (*Agneepath*, 1990) who dies once vengeance has been obtained.[10] In *Kaminey*, the first cause does not lead to a condition of anxiety which makes one suspect that it has no negative connotations. It is, rather, only a pretense at justifying a dishonourable present.

Kaminey is curiously poised since the first cause—the father's suicide—is 'tragic' but the film itself is celebratory and this is an apparent contradiction that needs enquiring into. From the evidence of the dim lighting in *Kaminey*, we may presume that the film is intended to be 'dark' and the preamble ending with their father's suicide is probably devised to make it consistent with this dark vision. But the issue is this: if the fact of all people being scoundrels is cause for celebration—as the film suggests—how is the father's treatment at the hands of the crooked policemen appalling as that is the ethically valid conduct of all kaminey? If admirers of *Kaminey* deny that its vision of moral decay and corruption is celebratory, they will need to explain how Charlie can come out of the story phenomenally wealthy and also without undergoing a moral transformation.

Although dubbed as a 'semi-hit', *Kaminey* was lauded for its originality. But, in my reckoning, it only continues the celebration of enterprise in the films of the period in which no worthwhile distinction is made between legitimate business and illegality. I also propose that since the preamble deals with the mid-1980s in which Hindi cinema still subscribed to a completely different morality—that informed by Nehruvian socialism—it is even being untrue by portraying people in the light in which it shows them.[11] The explanation that suggests itself to me is that *Kaminey* tries to be 'dark'—as films about corruption on such a scale inevitably are—but is too taken up with contemporary attitudes to do this wholeheartedly. Emphasizing the triumph of traditional Hindi film values like honesty and loyalty might also have made it resemble the earlier cinema. A genre film—especially film noir—can be 'dark' only when it holds strongly to certain ethical values but finds them absent in society at large. Given the qualities exhibited increasingly by Hindi cinema in the new millennium the question to be asked is whether it has the propensity to be 'dark' at all since the new failings of society are only opportunities.

Kaminey's excellent box office showing in its first week was generally credited to big city multiplexes but its showing elsewhere and in single theatres apparently fell off subsequently. The film received much more unequivocal praise from the English language press than the Hindi one, in which the response was lukewarm. The English press was also clear that the film was intelligent entertainment, suggesting that it is the 'intelligentsia' it is meant for. If all this suggests that it was targeted at the aspiring urban classes, the discourse in the film tends to confirm it. For all the showcasing of the squalor and grime of the city—and its male protagonists being ostensibly from the working class—*Kaminey* does not indicate that making a living in the city is a difficult matter. The figures routinely invoked—crores or tens of lakhs of rupees—are not figures that one associates with working-class aspirations. This suggests that *Kaminey*'s vision is a low-life fantasy lived out by the aspiring, upwardly mobile classes who have a small idea of 'low life'. Why the aspiring, upwardly mobile urban classes need to live out a low-life fantasy is difficult to explain but it might be the best way to sustain their faith in 'Social Darwinism'. The films I mentioned at the beginning of this chapter implicitly treat illegality as a fact of everyday life but also concede that the chances of remaining unpunished are not evenly distributed across society. The casual killing of the drug dealer in *Page 3* while the rich businessman casually subverts the law provides evidence of this. I propose that the ascendant classes need a new mythology about a 'level playing field' within illegality and Social Darwinism is a self-justifying mythology enacted on behalf of those with advantages.

That India embraced the market wholeheartedly from 1991 onwards meant that there was a decrease in economic intervention by the state but Kaminey suggests that its meaning to those in the middle- to high-income brackets has also been a weakening of enforcement. To repeat my observations of the earlier chapters, the economic liberalization of 1991 was devised essentially to free the economy of the impediments of what was known as the 'control raj' but what is apparently not recognized is the miscalculation in this 'withdrawal'. While one must concede that freeing the economy from the shackles of control was necessary, it would have been appropriate at that point to strengthen enforcement in those areas where intervention was still necessary. 'Deregulation', it must be noted, cannot be equated with a failure to enforce. The strengthening of enforcement, unfortunately, did not happen and India became an enforcement nightmare.[12] But it is apparently a nightmare that allows the ascendant classes to dream.

Hindi popular cinema is now sufficiently differentiated to cater separately to various social segments but much of it still remains a fantasy or a 'collective daydream'[13] and speaks the language of myth. As per Roland Barthes,[14] myth is a kind of language, a set of conventions by which the exigencies of a historical moment are given eternal justification. The world of Kaminey is de-historicized because it treats its own vision of 'people as scoundrels' not as the creation of historical circumstances but as an eternally valid philosophy for 'pragmatists'. It is a depoliticized world in which even politics is only enterprise. Kaminey gives us an entrepreneurial fantasy disguised as a dystopia.

Notes

1. There is a view that drug dealing and sex are part of Hollywood's influence on Indian cinema. See Kuldip R. Rampal, 'Asia: The

Hollywood Factor', in Lee Artz and Yahya R. Kamalipour (eds), *The Media Globe: Trends in International Mass Media* (Lanham: Rowman and Littlefield, 2006), pp. 50–3. Seen thus, the difference between *Page 3* and *Kaminey* may correspond to the difference between *The Godfather* (1972) and *Pulp Fiction* (1994) in their attitudes towards hard drugs.

2. For an examination of the construction of Gotham City, see William Uricchio, 'The Batman's Gotham City™: Story, Ideology, Performance', in Jorn Ahrens and Arno Meteling (eds), *Comics and the City: Urban Space in Print, Picture and Sequence* (London: Continuum International Publishing, 2010), pp. 119–32. The Batman films, of course, need to be filmed in an actual city but it is still a city seen as an expressionist set.

3. Many of the best-known reviewers endorsed this view. Their comments are available on a blog called 'Bollymoviereviewz', http://bollymoviereviewz.blogspot.in/2009/08/kaminey-movie-review.html (accessed on 25 July 2012).

4. The epithet 'postmodern' used to describe Tarantino's films is largely because of his pastiche of other cinema, usually of the violent kind like kung fu action films and spaghetti westerns. Mr Wolf, I propose, could be taken from a manual on time management. For the significance of pastiche, see Frederic Jameson, 'Postmodernism and Consumer Society,' in E. Ann Kaplan (ed.), *Postmodernism and Its Discontents* (London: Verso, 1988), pp. 15–16. For a useful study of *Pulp Fiction*, a film from which *Kaminey* draws, see Eve Bertelsen, '"Serious Gourmet Shit": Quentin Tarantino's *Pulp Fiction*', *Journal of Literary Studies*, vol. 15, nos 1–2, 1999, pp. 8–32.

5. Marriages in *Pulp Fiction* are, for instance, deliberately indifferent to the issues of colour and race.

6. As film scholars have noted, the mother is traditionally the site of virtue in the Hindi film. Raj Kapoor's *Awaara* (1951) is the film usually cited although *Deewaar* would be an equally good example. See Ravi S. Vasudevan, 'Shifting Codes, Dissolving Identities: The Hindi Social Film of the 1950s as Popular Culture', in Ravi S. Vasudevan (ed.), *Making Meaning in Indian Cinema* (New Delhi: Oxford University Press, 2000), pp. 110–13.

7. See M.K. Raghavendra, *Seduced by the Familiar: Narration and Meaning in Indian Popular Cinema* (New Delhi: Oxford University Press, 2008), pp. 44–9.

8. Significantly, the plot material in classical Sanskrit plays is also seen to be present as a seed or a germ at the beginning and growing as the action develops. M. Christopher Byrski, 'Sanskrit Drama as an Aggregate of Model Situations', in Rachel Van M. Baumer and James R. Brandon (eds), *Sanskrit Drama in Performance* (New Delhi: Motilal Banarsidass, 1993), p. 144.

9. Hollywood screenwriting manuals have long insisted on a plot formula: an initial undisturbed condition, a disturbance, a struggle for elimination of the disturbance, and its actual elimination. See David Bordwell, *Narration in the Fiction Film* (London: Methuen), p. 157.

10. Raghavendra, *Seduced by the Familiar*, pp. 54–5.

11. In the Hindi films of the 1980s, policemen were not corrupt but weak and under threat from gangsters such as in films like *Tezaab* (1988), *Ankush* (1985), and *Pratighaat* (1987). See Raghavendra, *Seduced by the Familiar*, pp. 207–35.

12. A 2011 report indicated that India had dropped 11 places to be ranked 95th in the Transparency International Corruption Index. See *The Economic Times*, 2 December 2011, http://articles.economictimes. indiatimes.com/2011-12-02/news/30467987_1_corrupt-country-australia-shares-cases (accessed on 29 July 2012).

13. The first writer to use this phrase was Sudhir Kakar in *Intimate Relations: Exploring Indian Sexuality* (New Delhi: Penguin, 1989).

14. Roland Barthes, *Mythologies* (London: Paladin, 1973), p. 143.

10

The Exemplary Citizen

Education, *Taare Zameen Par* (2007), and *3 Idiots* (2009)

Kinds of Social Consciousness

Among the Hindi films dealt with hitherto in this book the ones which may be described as most 'socially conscious' were those of Madhur Bhandarkar's *Page 3* (2005), *Traffic Signal* (2007) and, to some extent, *Corporate* (2006). A more mainstream film-maker and actor who can also be described, thus, is Aamir Khan, who has also been rewarded by the state quite early in his career when he was accorded the Padma Bhushan in 2010. While this may convey some sense of how Aamir Khan differs from a film-maker like Madhur Bhandarkar, one could say that while the latter tries to address social issues by being 'critical' of the establishment and society, Aamir Khan is more 'constructive' in his approach. Aamir Khan made a film on primary education, *Taare Zameen Par*, and is also associated with one on higher education, Rajkumar Hirani's *3 Idiots*. Aamir Khan was so closely identified with 'education'[1] after the first film that the visiting United States (US) Secretary of State, Hillary Clinton, even shared a platform with him[2] on the subject in 2008 which could not have happened without consultation with the Indian state. Even if the Padma Bhushan was not awarded to Aamir Khan for his 'efforts in education' there is still the likelihood that they have contributed to his public image, which in turn has influenced the award.[3] 3 Idiots has been eulogized in the media as an 'assault on our apathetic education system'.[4] Rajkumar Hirani, who directed 3 Idiots also made Lage Raho Munna Bhai (2006), which has been discussed earlier. Both Hirani and Aamir Khan are, therefore, involved in entertainment considered 'meaningful' by their publics as well as the state. This chapter proceeds from the proposition that since the state has conspicuously approved of these 'messages' from Bollywood, the films and their viewpoints share an ideology with the Government of India in some way. If Taare Zameen Par tells us something about the meaning of primary education to Anglophone Indians, 3 Idiots, being a film on higher education, leads us to understand something about the state's attitude towards education and similar services, or at least provides us with a broad political perspective.

Taare Zameen Par: Dreaming and Competing

In Taare Zameen Par, Ishaan Nandkishore Awasthi (Darsheel Safary) is an eight-year-old boy, who dislikes school and fails every test or exam. He finds all subjects difficult and is belittled by his teachers and classmates. At home, his older brother, Yohaan, is both an athlete and a topper in most subjects and this makes Ishaan's position more difficult. Since he likes to wander around, he is caught bunking school one day and, since this is coupled with a poor report, his parents decide to send him to a boarding school, much against his protests. Ishaan's abject situation changes when a new art teacher, Ram Shankar Nikumbh (Aamir Khan), joins the school's faculty. Nikumbh's teaching style is markedly different from that of his strict predecessor, and he quickly observes that Ishaan is unhappy and contributes little to class activities although he has a friend in a physically challenged boy. Nikhumb reviews Ishaan's work and concludes that his academic shortcomings are indicative of dyslexia. On his day off, Nikumbh visits Ishaan's parents and asks if he can see more of their son's work. He is astonished by the sophistication of one of Ishaan's paintings, and tells his parents that Ishaan is an intelligent child who happens to process information differently. When Ishaan's surly father is sceptical, Nikumbh treats the man with mock severity demanding that he read some Japanese lettering on a video game and then admonishing him when he is unable to. He lets Ishaan's parents know of his suspicions that their son's difficulties are due to his being dyslexic. Back in school, he is able to win Ishaan's confidence and the boy, learning of the nature of dyslexia, gradually comes out of his isolation and his grades improve. At the climax of the film, Nikumbh organizes an art fair for teachers and students and Ishaan stands first. Ishaan's parents are overcome with joy at the change they see in the formerly intractable son.

It is evident that *Taare Zameen Par* is not simply about dyslexia but is coming out against the typecasting of children to perform roles determined by adults, their being made to compete at the school level and, most importantly, the way their imagination is killed even before it has had a chance to flower. But, almost perversely, it reveals what it understands of a child's imagination in the title sequence. Ishaan is an impulsive child happy doing whatever he wills and the film begins with the boy trying to catch fish in a drain. He catches two or three tiny fingerlings and places them in a glass bottle after which he is whisked away by an adult. The title sequence commences immediately after this and the film uses animation to show us what Ishaan is imagining. In the animated sequence representing the boy's imagination, the fingerlings are transformed into coloured tropical fish reminiscent of the aquatic creatures in *Finding Nemo* (2003). The sun also appears in this sequence in cartoon form as a circular yellow creature with a huge smile. This use of animation continues to denote the boy's dreams later in the film and the imagery representing Ishaan's imagination evidently owes to children's toys and animated films of the kind made popular by Walt Disney. The first question here is whether, in attacking the straightjacketing of the child's imagination, the film is not providing evidence of an imagination itself straightjacketed. It sets out to show that it is not only children of Ishaan's class but all children it is dealing with and the evidence is a sequence in which Nikumbh comforts a boy worker in a roadside restaurant with biscuits and tea as well as a song which also reinforces the sense of universality. Still, regardless of the film's claim of universality for its concerns,[5] the animation imagery commented upon earlier clearly bears the stamp of an affluent Anglophone class. The child of a farmer in a hot dry district, for instance, is unlikely to imagine the sun as a smiling yellow orb.

While the film appears to be decrying 'competition' by showing us Ishaan's father's attitude, the issue of 'success' is nonetheless brought in by the back door. It is only when Ishaan wins a prize that he is integrated into the community within the school and accepted by his own family. Ishaan's only friend, Rajan Damodaran, who is physically challenged, is also a top student in his class. There is a sense here that it would only be right for talented people[6] and 'toppers' to be associated and a hierarchy reigns. This means that the film—regardless of its protests to the contrary—is actually about individual aspiration rather than about the freedom to imagine and dream. A protagonist topping the class is hardly a new occurrence in Hindi cinema since every possible virtue was traditionally attached to the protagonist—especially the male one—but the notion of ascent within a classroom hierarchy is a new motif and is in evidence only now. This motif takes on new significance in 3 Idiots, one of the biggest successes of Indian cinema in the last decade.

3 Idiots: Oneself as the Other

3 Idiots begins with two former classmates, Raju Rastogi (Sharman Joshi) and Farhan Qureshi (R. Madhavan,) going in search of Rancho (Aamir Khan) whom they lost touch with after graduating as engineers from the 'Imperial College of Engineering'. The college is an elite institution which admits only the brightest students. Although its ownership is not specified, Raju comes from a poor

family and is also not doing well enough for a scholarship and this suggests a government-run institution, perhaps modeled on the Indian Institute of Technology (IIT).[7] This, however, is disingenuous because Raju's poor family circumstances are used for humour. One joke which is repeated, for instance, is that his home is filmed in black and white when everything else is in colour and Raju is not seriously offended at their frequent quips about his family's station and the humble food he eats at home. The argument here is that even the mélange of classes in a government-run institution like the IIT is absent in the 'Imperial College of Engineering' suggesting that (as in *Taare Zameen Par*) the film is presenting the affluent class experience as universal. This might not be exceptionable in a light comedy but *3 Idiots* is positioning itself as a vehicle for concern.

The film alternates between the present and the past. Rancho comes from a wealthy business family in Shimla and was the non-conformist, while the other two were inspired by him. Another classmate was Chatur Ramalingam—less inventive but openly ambitious—and the three friends often clashed with him. With the conclusion of their course, the latter were openly challenged by Chatur on the success of their future careers. When Farhan and Raju return to their alma mater after ten years, Chatur joins them, fresh from the US and full of his achievements and possessions. He is now concluding a business arrangement with a fabulous inventor named Phunsukh Wangdu, which will make him successful beyond their wildest dreams. It is Chatur who now reminds the two of his challenge ten years back.

Many of the flashbacks in the film deal with the figure of authority in the Imperial College, Professor Viru Sahastrabuddhe (Boman Irani), whom the boys have nicknamed ViruS. The Professor was a hard taskmaster who believed in competition and success at any cost. ViruS had been so unsparing that his implacability led to a boy's suicide. ViruS, nonetheless, remained unmoved and cited his continued application to work after his own son's death. Particularly galling to ViruS was the fact that while Rancho was always playful it was still he who stood first and Chatur came only second. Because of Rancho's influence, Farhan eventually abandoned engineering as a career and became an international wildlife photographer, while Raju, despite his poor showing in the final examination, impressed potential employers with his confidence and found employment.

Raju, Farhan, and Chatur now set off for Shimla to meet Rancho. Rancho's name is actually Ranchoddas Shamaldas Chanchad and they find the enormous Chanchad mansion without much difficulty. When they find Ranchoddas, however, they discover that he is not their Rancho but someone else. Their graduation photograph hangs on the wall with this man's face on it instead of Rancho's. Who was Rancho really, they wonder, and it comes out that 'Rancho' was a gardener's child in the Chanchad household who showed an aptitude for learning. Since the boy wanted 'learning' and the actual Ranchoddas only a degree, the boy was admitted to the Imperial College as 'Rancho'. When they finally locate 'Rancho' he is teaching local children in Ladakh's wilderness, bringing creativity to his 'model school'. The crowning bit of information is that 'Rancho' is actually Phunsukh Wangdu—with hundreds of patents in the US—and Chatur is thus humbled.

The fact that 3 Idiots has a large number of comic moments does not detract from its being a film with a serious message on education. The message pertains to higher learning in India being rendered painful because of the emphasis placed on competition and the rat race. Creativity is the casualty, the film says, because of people having to submit to a straightjacketed notion of education. This is the apparent message but 3 Idiots, nevertheless, relies on Rancho coming first to fully convince us of his abilities. His doing so effortlessly has a parallel in the dyslexic boy in Taare Zameen Par suddenly demonstrating his prowess. 'Dog eat dog' and 'rat race' are disparaging terms for market-induced competitiveness but the films show little faith in the possibility of being indifferent to competition. For all his affinity to the poor children of Ladakh, the former gardener's boy, Phunsukh Wangdu, can only be judged on the basis of his American patents.

Films like 3 Idiots are strangely positioned inasmuch as while they endeavour to deal with the 'real issues' of today, they still depend on the elements of the Bollywood fantasy. Since they conveniently shift from one mode to the other, it is difficult to say what aspects should be taken seriously. For instance, Rancho/Wangdu has established a school in Ladakh. Anyone who has seen the terrain in Ladakh understands the difficulty that finding drinking water—let alone establishing a 'model school'—represents. The film shows the protagonists driving from Manali to Leh (known to be the second highest motorable road in the world) as easily as one might between two suburbs in Mumbai, perhaps taking its notion of the Manali–Leh highway from an automobile advertisement. If *3 Idiots* is a film with social concern, it can be criticized for not being adequately concerned with the actual conditions in the world it is depicting. If it is a 'fantasy', it shows itself incapable of imagining existence in a far-flung corner—except as extensions of middle-class city life.

It is perhaps in its failure to imagine that *3 Idiots* reveals its hidden self, eventually. Most of the protagonists in the film are given families and pasts that help us to understand and locate them. Farhan is a middle-class boy and Raju Rastogi's pensioner father is paralysed and his complaining mother is trying to put her son through college. Even Pia, as the daughter of a professor in an elite institution, is a credible figure. But there is an evident 'absence' in the way Phunsukh Wangdu/ Rancho is imagined because the film does not give him any kind of recognizable past. He is simply a 'gardener's child' and we get to see nothing of his background or his family. If mainstream Hindi cinema never gave us accurate pictures of working-class life, it was nonetheless able to imagine the working class plausibly, but this appears no longer so. Even when Phunsukh Wangdu (as 'Rancho') arrives in an elite college he has a confidence far beyond that of someone accustomed to the life of a servant's child. He grimaces at the abject conditions in Raju Rastogi's home and, moreover, the film betrays its lack of faith in his credibility by associating him with a name that would sound outlandish to city audiences. Also, Phunsukh Wangdu has 'hundreds of patents' to his credit but there is not even a hint about how he acquired them. Bollywood abounds in fantasy but in this inability to imagine Wangdu lies an uncomfortable truth: that such a person is unimaginable. It is unimaginable that a servant's child in India will become a celebrated inventor. Elite educational institutions are not for his kind even when the institutions have been established by the state.

3 Idiots proposes that 'servants' and their children can become inventors without being able to imagine their journey from their origins. It supposes higher education without considering the level of primary education made available to their kind. Still, the film does not stand alone and is from a milieu in which 'education' is synonymous with elite education. The 'rat race' in education is the preoccupation of only a small segment but it gets disproportionate attention from the state. If one is unconvinced, one needs only to look at the reported statements of the Ministry of Human Resource Development (HRD) at around the time of release of *3 Idiots*. In June 2009, the HRD minister Kapil Sibal suggested foreign direct investment in education to make it easier for those intending to go to Harvard or Yale to avoid visa problems: 'India has the potential to be a global provider of quality graduates,' he reportedly added.[8] In August 2009, his proposed plan to introduce grades instead of marks at the 10th board exam level in Central Board of Secondary Education (CBSE) schools caused consternation and some wondered what would happen if 90 per cent and 99 per cent were bunched together. How would the schools differentiate merit[9] because higher education depended on it, was the major anxiety. In February 2010, Kapil Sibal discussed a plan for an Education Finance Corporation which would extend loans for higher education.[10] By the minister's own admission, only around 2.5 per cent of school children pursue higher education in India[11] but the HRD ministry appeared to be giving a substantially larger proportion of its attention to it. Primary education also seems to be attended to as a report says that with the passage of the Right to Education Act, the expenditure on primary education is estimated at Rs 70,000 crore per year.[12] The dissimilarity in the attitude towards higher and primary education is significant. While minute attention is given to *issues* in higher education, primary education is regarded generally in terms of outlay.

If the recipients of the concern in 3 Idiots are mainly those who have scraped together enough finance for their children to get into higher education, many of the HRD minister's statements address the same issue. One of them was the decision to put IIT fees on hold until the government put in a mechanism that would provide students with access to funds.[13] Considering that Kapil Sibal has also been appealing to parents to stop pressurizing children,[14] it would appear that the Government of India and Bollywood have the same concerns. A minister's reported observations may not be conclusive evidence of where the government's attentions are directed but there is still a sense to be gained that the Government of India's HRD ministry is principally addressing the same public as 3 Idiots. It has been necessary to dwell at such length on state interventions in education here only because of the evidence that among Bollywood personalities, Aamir Khan's concerns have earned him a privileged position in the corridors of the government, implying that there is some reflection of the concerns of the Government of India in 3 Idiots.

An aspect without which any examination of 3 Idiots would be incomplete is the persona that Aamir Khan has constructed for himself. I have already indicated the star's ascendancy with the Congress government and this may have been assisted by the hostility he encountered in Gujarat with BJP strongman Narendra Modi.[15] It is perhaps his secular credentials together with his social concern that makes him politically favoured. Aamir Khan, it would seem, is tending to represent for the elected Congress government after 2004 what Raj Kapoor meant to Nehru's Congress. Although Raj Kapoor's films were critical of society and the establishment, he had a privileged position in the film industry by the early 1960s because of his closeness to power.[16] There were other film-makers in the same period—like Bimal Roy (Do Bigha Zamin, 1953) and Ritwik Ghatak—who had exhibited similar concern but were not favoured. The question is if social concern, per se, is not adequately appealing, how did Raj Kapoor earn his privileges. Raj Kapoor's political importance, it can be argued, owed to his star persona more than his directorial importance and his positing the 'exemplary citizen' as other actors did not when the Nation was being constructed in the 1950s.[17] For one thing, apart from the social criticism they engage in, his two most important films of the 1940s and 1950s, *Barsaat* (1949) and *Awaara* (1951) are about reconciliations: the ethnic minorities with urban India in *Barsaat* and state authority with its dispossessed children in *Awaara*.[18] *Awaara* adopts the viewpoint of someone born privileged but thrown out on to the street and whose 'experience on the footpath provides the moral justification for the action';[19] there is an effort to make the privileged live the life of the 'other'. The social discourse in *Shri 420* (1955) can also be associated with an actual political process underway: Jawaharlal Nehru's reformist efforts against feudal power entrenched in the state. Nehru's efforts to usher in modernity conflicted with Sardar Patel's traditionalist views and were resisted within the Congress even after Vallabhbhai Patel's death[20] by the entrenched middle-level leadership. Raj Kapoor takes sides with 'reformism' because *Awaara* shows a judge (an emblem of state authority) as living lavishly and being unmindful of those dependent on him. *Shri 420* is, equally, a diatribe against the wealthy and decadent opponents of Nehruvian modernity. At one point, Raju in *Shri 420* calls upon a million people to protest against hoarders and while this is much stronger than a comparable exhortation in *Mother India* (1957) which was censored, it was allowed.[21] Hindi cinema had other stars after Raj Kapoor who personified the exemplary citizen: Manoj Kumar, who embodied the Indian of the Green Revolution in *Upkar* (1967), is perhaps the most identifiable one.[22] To use the terms earlier employed, Raj Kapoor was being 'constructive', while film-makers like Bimal Roy and Ritwik Ghatak were merely 'critical'.

The 'exemplary' quality of a hero perhaps only arises when his position finds correspondence in an actual political conflict. As indicated in *Shri 420*, the conflict is between entrenched money/feudal power and Nehru's reformist/modernizing vision[23] because there is such a discourse in Raju being a graduate and his sweetheart

(Nargis), a teacher. The farmer hero of the Green Revolution, similarly, comes into conflict with those in trade—who wielded great financial power before India attained self-sufficiency in food grains due to state action and the larger farmers suddenly gained economic power. *Upkar*, in fact, makes the conflict between the farmer and the hoarder/trader the central one. Both these 'exemplary citizens', it must be noted, are aligned with the social action of the state and they are exemplary because they justify its agenda. This is not true of, say, the 'Angry Young Man' played by Amitabh Bachchan or Rajesh Khanna's romantic heroes. The question now is whether Aamir Khan of *3 Idiots* can be explained in such terms.

Aamir Khan is a more versatile actor than Raj Kapoor and has played a variety of roles such as in *Fanaa* (2006) and the action film *Ghajini* (2008). But the roles in *Rang De Basanti*, *Taare Zameen Par*, and *3 Idiots* may be taken to represent a stable screen persona since they are also closest to his talk-show self in *Satyamev Jayate*. The Aamir Khan of the films is Anglophone, irreverent but also earnest, the last attribute gaining after *Rang De Basanti*. The association of irreverence with the exemplary is unusual but that is the connection he makes especially in the last two roles. If one were to ask what Ram Shankar Nikumbh in *Taare Zameen Par* and Rancho in *3 Idiots* are irreverent about, the immediate answer is traditional education with its emphasis on 'cramming'. As already indicated, competition is not decried in the two films but a different path in which it is not 'mindless' is advocated.

A refrain in recent years is the notion of 'global standards' needing to be attained in various fields and this is associated with moves to usher in international players into India: in insurance, journalism, education, and retail trade to name only a few and most of these have been resisted. In the field of education, Indian education has been constantly compared unfavourably to education in the US[24] and Rancho's eventual achievement, the one that helps him vanquish his rival, Chatur, who 'crams', is his registering patents in America. This, it can be argued, finds correspondence in the conflict between those who seek to invite foreign universities into

India and those who oppose it. Less than a year after the release of *3 Idiots* the cabinet approved a bill to allow the entry of foreign universities into India—The Foreign Educational Institutions (Regulation of Entry and Operations) Bill, 2010[25]—but this was opposed by both the Left and the BJP on grounds that a 'level playing field' is necessary to protect Indian institutions. There is, hence, an actual conflict in which Aamir Khan as the exemplary citizen is taking sides.

India is spending 3 per cent of its gross domestic product (GDP) on education, which compares with that of Thailand, Indonesia, and Korea. But when it comes to primary education, India's expenditure is half of these countries and, in this connection, it has been noted that systems with excessive bias towards higher education are less equitable.[26] As an explanation, the dominant factor for governmental decisions has gradually become 'viability' after 1991 and since higher education serves those with more wherewithal it is more viable than primary education. The issue is whether this emphasis on viability does not imply that the government is equating the public to a clientele. This does not mean that there is actually effective state intervention in higher education because, increasingly, due to the breakdown of the state system, higher education (like primary education) has been passing into private hands,[27] but the class pursuing higher education—that with the greatest economic power—apparently merits the most attention from the elected government. Regarded in this light, the gardener's boy Phunsukh Wangdu is, at the very least, exemplary for moving into this privileged class with little assistance from the state. Since the state has been 'withdrawing' since 1991–2, such personal initiative is apparently welcome.

Notes

1. In 2012, he made news with the television talk show *Satyamev Jayate*, running into its second season in 2014, in which he takes up a different social issue each week—alcoholism, caste and untouchablity, malpractice in the medical profession, domestic violence, and so on.

2. See 'Aamir Khan to Share Dais with Hilary Clinton', *The Indian Express*, Mumbai, Friday 17 July 2009, http://www.indianexpress.com/news/aamir-khan-to-share-dias-with-hillary-clinton/490646/ (accessed on 10 August 2012).

3. Aamir Khan's efforts have been endorsed by psychiatrists as well. For instance, see T.S. Sathyanarayana Rao and V.S.T. Krishna, 'Wake Up Call from "Stars on the Ground"', *Indian Journal of Psychiatry*, vol. 50, no. 1, January–March 2008, pp. 2–4.

4. Baradwaj Rangan, '3 *Idiots*', *The New Indian Express*, 27 December 2009. The review can be found on the following blog: http://baradwajrangan.wordpress.com/2009/12/26/review-3-idiots/ (accessed on 8 August 2012).

5. The tagline for the film, 'Every child is special', also bears this out.

6. There is a hypothesis that creative ability and language disability often occur together and the film has been commended for this reason. See Ambar Chakravarty, '*Taare Zameen Par* and Dyslexic Savants', *Annals of Indian Academy of Neurology*, vol. 12, no. 2, April–June 2009, pp. 99–103.

7. The film was shot at the Indian Institute of Management Bangalore, which is as glamorous as any government-run educational institution.

8. Chetan Chauhan and Ruchi Haleja, 'FDI in Education Soon: Kapil Sibal', *Hindustan Times*, 26 June 2009, http://www.hindustantimes.com/india-news/newdelhi/fdi-in-education-soon-kapil-sibal/article1-425416.aspx (accessed on 29 March 2014); and 'FDI in Education Top Priority: Kapil Sibal', *Thaiindian News*, 25 June 2009, http://www.thaindian.com/newsportal/uncategorized/fdi-in-education-top-priority-kapil-sibal-interview_100209235.html (accessed on 29 March 2014).

9. Mansi Sharma, 'Schools, Students Wary of Educational Reforms', IBN Live India, 31 August 2009, http://ibnlive.in.com/news/schools-students-wary-of-govts-education-reforms/100305-3.html (accessed on 10 August 2012).

10. See 'Centre Mulling over Education Finance Corporation: Sibal', *DNA*, 1 February 2010, http://www.dnaindia.com/india/report_centre-mulling-over-education-finance-corporation-sibal_1342120-all (accessed on 10 August 2012).

11. Ibid.

12. 'UPA Government: Report to the People 2009–2010', Ministry of Information and Broadcasting, Government of India, Sabira Chaudhuri,

'Primary Education Central to Upcoming Budget', *Mint*, 18 February 2010, http://www.livemint.com/Politics/QrXCBjlbVqYY4rhOS71B3O/Primary-education-central-to-upcoming-Budget.html (accessed 29 March 2014).

13. See 'IIT Fee Hike Put on Hold: Sibal', *The Hindu*, 5 February 2010, http://www.thehindu.com/news/national/article100973.ece (accessed on 10 August 2012).

14. See Arun Prabhudesai, 'Woohoo..Another Salvo from Mr Kapil Sibal—Suggests No Preschool before Age of 4', *Trak-In*, 16 February 2010, http://trak.in/tags/business/2010/02/16/no-pre-schooling-before-age-4-kapil-sibal/ (accessed on 30 March 2014)

15. After 2002, that is, after the infamous riots apparently instigated with the connivance of the state government, Aamir Khan has repeatedly taken on the Gujarat government on various issues including the Narmada dam issue and this has seen his films—*Fanaa* (2006) and even *Taare Zameen Par* being banned in Gujarat. Although it raises some pertinent questions about Muslims and Indian nationalism, *Fanaa* is an innocuous film about terrorism in Kashmir but its banning in Gujarat apparently helped its collections elsewhere. See Shahnaz Khan, 'Nationalism and Hindi Cinema: Narrative Strategies in *Fanaa*', *Studies in South Asian Film and Media*, Vol. 1, No. 1, 1 May 2009, pp. 85–99.

16. *Sangam* (1964) was filmed partly in Europe and Raj Kapoor was the first Hindi film-maker to get permission to film abroad. See M. Madhava Prasad, *Ideology of the Hindi Film: A Historical Construction* (New Delhi: Oxford University Press, 1998), p. 86. Also see Ritu Nanda, *Raj Kapoor Speaks* (New Delhi: Viking, 2002), p. 107.

Once after Jawaharlal Nehru returned from the Soviet Union which included a meeting with Stalin, he happened to bump into Papa ji. Nehruji did not watch many movies but knew my father well. He took my father aside and said, 'What is this film *Vagabond* (*Awara*) that your son has made? Stalin was talking about it all the time.'

Stalin died in 1953, a year and a half after *Awaara*'s release. Also, according to reliable sources, Stalin never met Nehru personally, not even the Indian Ambassador, Vijayalakshmi Pandit who was Nehru's sister. Amit Gupta, *Global Security Watch–India* (Santa Barbara: Praeger, 2012), p. 2.

17. Dilip Kumar has also been described as 'Nehru's hero' in Lord Meghnad Desai, *Nehru's Hero: Dilip Kumar in the Life of India* (Delhi: Roli, 2004). Desai's view that he represented the quintessential romantic hero for people born in the mid-to-late 1920s is certainly true. As argued elsewhere, Dilip Kumar's naturalistic performances in the period endows his characters with an unusual freedom of choice—in a cinema in which fates are determined—which allegorizes 'independence' in the years following 1947 and the films are remarkably open-ended. See M.K. Raghavendra, *Seduced by the Familiar: Narration and Meaning in Indian Popular Cinema* (New Delhi: Oxford University Press, 2008), pp. 105–8. Also see Sumita S. Chakravarty, *National Identity in Indian Popular Cinema, 1947–1987* (New Delhi: Oxford University Press, 1998), p. 99. Raj Kapoor's films may not embody the experience of independence as much as they become ideological tools for the construction of an inclusive national identity. If Dilip Kumar's heroes were those with whom the audience of the period could identify, Raj Kapoor's heroes perhaps represented the exemplary Indian. The famous song 'Mera joota hai Japani' in *Shri 420* provides some evidence here.

18. For analyses of *Barsaat* and *Awaara*, see Raghavendra, *Seduced by the Familiar*, pp. 112–14, 117–24.

19. Ranjani Mazumdar, *Bombay Cinema: An Archive of the City* (Ranikhet: Permanent Black, 2007), p. 3.

20. See Sunil Khilnani, *The Idea of India* (New Delhi: Penguin 1998), pp. 33–4, 37–8, 78–9.

21. Patrick Colm Hogan, *Understanding Indian Movies: Culture, Cognition and Cinematic Imagination* (Austin: University of Texas Press, 2008), p. 158.

22. Raghavendra, *Seduced by the Familiar*, p. 171.

23. Sunil Khilnani, *The Idea of India*, pp. 75–80.

24. Here are two reports in the media which make the comparison: Geeta Anand, 'India Graduates Millions but Few Are Fit to Hire', *Wall Street Journal*, India News, 5 April 2011, http://online.wsj.com/article/SB100014 24052748703515504576142092863219826.html (accessed on 13 August 2012); and Praveen Iyer, 'A World of Difference', *The Hindu*, 14 March 2012, http://www.thehindu.com/life-and-style/nxg/article2994398.ece (accessed on 13 August 2012).

25. For the progression of events that led to this, see Livemint.com, 'Timeline: Foreign Education Institution Bill', 15 March 2010, http://

www.livemint.com/2010/03/15162548/Timeline-Foreign-Educational.
html (accessed on 14 August 2012).

26. Jee-Peng Tan and Alain Mingat, *Education in Asia: A Comparative Study
of Cost and Financing* (Washington, DC: World Bank Publications,
1992), pp. xiv, 145. Also see, Jayati Ghosh, 'Public Spending on
Education in India', MR Zine, *Monthly Review*, 29 June 2011, http://
mrzine.monthlyreview.org/2011/ghosh290611.html (accessed on 15
August 2012).

27. Devesh Kapur and Pratap Bhanu Mehta, 'Indian Higher Education
Reform: From Half-Baked Socialism to Half-Baked Capitalism', Center
for International Development at Harvard University, Working Paper
No. 108, September 2004. As this paper brings out, middle-class Indians
are willing to pay handsomely for higher education. This has gradually
seen private institutions thriving without enough state supervision or
control. A major portion of this private education is, therefore, of low
quality. 'The Imperial College of Education' is, simply, what higher
education pretends to be.

11

Politics and Enterprise
Raajneeti (2010)

The Politician in Hindi Cinema

The professional politician has been a relatively recent entrant into Hindi film stories. The earliest representation of the politician that one recalls is Radha's younger son dressed in white khadi in the framing sequence of Mehboob Khan's *Mother India* (1956) and inaugurating a new irrigation channel. Politicians in that period were still denoted as 'statesmen', as generally people from the freedom struggle who had entered public life. Although gangsters had taken to politics by the 1980s in *Pratighaat* (1987), the criminalized politician may have officially entered Hindi cinema only in the late 1990s with films like *Satya* (1999) and *Shool* (2000), in which they derive their power from being in politics. As indicated earlier, the forces of law enforcement behave as private agencies around this time because of the perceived withdrawal of the state from the public space after 1991–2. Politics, like crime, becomes an extension of enterprise in the new millennium.

The appearance of the corrupt politician in the late 1990s was a novelty although middle cinema, films such as *Ardh Satya* (1983) and *New Delhi Times* (1986), had already dealt with his kind. The difference between 'middle films' like Govind Nihalani's *Ardh Satya* and mainstream films like Ramgopal Verma's *Satya*, both of which invoke criminality in politics, is that while the former are basically aligned against a real state of affairs,[1] mainstream films create a mythology around the politician by seeing him/her as an archetype. This distinction may become clearer if it is further added that the protagonist of Nihalani's *Ardh Satya* is not heroic but an individual with weaknesses, while the one in *Satya*, even when inhabiting a world made to seem physically 'real', is exemplary in some way. Prakash Jha's *Raajneeti*, the largest 'political' offering from Bollywood in the past few years, admits the larger-than-life characteristics of popular film characters when it adapts the Mahabharata to tell a story of intrigue within a political family. It is significant that the politician is no longer simply an obstacle as in the other films but someone central and with gravity like Arjuna or Karna of the *Mahabharata*, or Michael Corleone from *The Godfather* (1972), the texts from which *Raajneeti* draws to portray a powerful family.

Raajneeti

In *Raajneeti*, Bhanupratap Singh and his younger brother Chandraprakash Singh head the Rashtravadi Party which has been out of power but is now supporting the government. Elections are due shortly but at this point Bhanupratap Singh has a paralytic stroke and the party needs a leader. Instead of nominating his own son Veerendra Pratap (Manoj Bajpai) as the leader, Bhanupratap names his brother Chandraprakash, thus incensing Veerendra Pratap. Chandraprakash has two sons: Prithviraj Pratap (Arjun Rampal), who is a politician and Samar Pratap (Ranbir Kapoor), who is working on his PhD on 'Victorian poetry' in the US. Brij Gopal (Nana Patekar), who is also Chandraprakash's brother-in-law, is a senior functionary and strategic advisor in the party. The conflict between the two branches of the family surfaces when a candidate is needed for a Dalit-dominated constituency. The cocky, Sooraj Kumar (Ajay Devgn), is the son of the family chauffeur but is locally popular because of his prowess at the game of kabaddi. When he stakes a claim for candidature here, the aggrieved Veerendra Pratap supports him against the party's official candidate. This catapults Sooraj to the top rung of the party and he becomes Veerendra Pratap's trusted lieutenant. Unknown to everyone, Sooraj is actually the stepbrother of Prithviraj Pratap and Samar Pratap, the result of their mother's secret liaison with a radical of the 1970s (Naseeruddin Shah). In the early part of the film Samar Pratap returns home from the US for a visit but is soon embroiled in the fratricidal war that engulfs the family.

The bloodshed in *Raajneeti* begins on the evening when Samar Pratap is due to return to the US. His father, Chandraprakash, drops him off at the airport but is liquidated the same evening on Veerendra Pratap's orders because of the latter's fear of being politically sidelined. Samar Pratap therefore cancels his return and remains behind with his family. Another development in the narrative includes the trumped up rape charges against Prithviraj Pratap which forces a split in the party, with the Prithviraj faction forming the Janashakti Party. Indu (Katrina Kaif) is the daughter of a tycoon and she loves Samar, although he does not reciprocate her feelings because he has an American girlfriend named Sarah. In order to raise funds the family contracts Prithviraj Pratap's marriage with Indu—her father would like her to be the wife of the future chief minister. Once again blood is shed, limits are abandoned, and Samar Pratap shows his hand as a strategist in the mould of Michael Corleone. Prithviraj Pratap kills the police officer enlisted by the opposite side and also some others but he and Sarah are also killed by a car bomb. As the climax, Samar and Brij Gopal organize an ambush and both Veerendra Pratap and Sooraj Kumar are killed. The film concludes with the Janashakti Party sweeping the polls and Indu being installed as chief minister. Samar does not stay on in politics but returns to the US to pursue his true vocation.

Politics as Soap Opera

Raajneeti is unusual among the films dealt with in this book as it has the feel of soap opera although this may be because of the fact that it draws from an epic. To cite a few of these characteristics which distinguish it from other Hindi films, although Samar and his brother are victors, there is little that makes them the 'good guys'. In the Mahabharata, the Pandavas are wronged but Samar and Prithviraj Pratap cannot make such a claim. In *The Godfather* as well, it must be recollected, Vito Corleone's refusal to get into the drug business marks him out morally from the other gangland chiefs. Soaps cannot empathize too much and too exclusively with one or a group of characters because they are aired as serials in which sympathies should shift. This fact forces them to make the audience intimate with several characters equally[2] but *Raajneeti* is meant to be shown in one screening and there is no reason for it to be morally even-handed. Given its neutrality, the apparent moral justification for Samar and Prithvi being given a larger share of empathy—rather than Veerendra Pratap and Sooraj Kumar—is that the bloodshed commences with their father's assassination, but Prithviraj Pratap has already played dirty when that happens. But there is, possibly, another covert reason for why Samar and Prithvi are made the protagonists and this will be taken up later.

The consequence of the film not taking sides adequately by naming one group as 'good' makes it seem that politics itself is a contaminated space and this is reinforced by the idealistic radical, Bhaskar Sanyal, played by Naseeruddin Shah not getting enough importance. Sanyal could have provided a moral fulcrum to the film but he does not. His rhetoric may mark him out as a 'radical' but we are unsure of what he represents and why he is idealistic. The ease with which he abandons politics because of a stray sexual liaison also has us wondering. His former paramour—Samar and Prithviraj's mother—also shows no memory of either him or his 'ideals'. The film, it must be concluded, refuses to be nostalgic about a past 'good' period in political life although electoral politics is categorically bad in the present. But, strangely enough, the film shows no distaste for the 'political life' because it plays up the glamour—upscale cars, palatial houses, immaculate clothes, and servile associates. More than all this, it celebrates strategy although 'strategy' is only geared towards self-advancement.

There are two successful strategists in the film and while Brij Gopal is placed in the advisory position of Sri Krishna in the *Mahabharata*, Samar Pratap goes through the same transformation as Michael Corleone in *The Godfather* and loses his (foreign) wife/ partner similarly. Brij Gopal is a problematic creation because while Sri Krishna's 'wisdom' (some might call it ruthlessness) comes from his confidence that he is on the side of dharma, Brij Gopal can have no such confidence and is simply on Samar and Prithviraj's side because he is their mother's brother. It is significant that just as Sri Krishna—being god-incarnate—is not made a deliberate target by the enemies of the Pandavas, neither is Brij Gopal identified as such by Veerendra Pratap and Sooraj Kumar, although it is on Brij Gopal's advice that Samar Pratap later kills the unarmed Sooraj Kumar. The attributes of 'neutrality' and 'wisdom' with which Brij Gopal is endowed are, therefore, false but the film appears to believe in them because their falsity is not problematized.

An even more problematic aspect of the film is Samar Pratap's moral tainting,[3] which is designed to mirror Michael Corleone's in *The Godfather*. As Michael was in that film, Samar is drawn more and more into killing. One, therefore, needs to explain why *Raajneeti* should conclude, after the killings are over, with Samar Pratap returning to the US to complete his work on Victorian poetry. Samar Pratap, after personally killing the unarmed Sooraj Kumar, in effect returns to 'innocence'. To make the scenario even stranger, he returns to look after his dead partner Sarah's mother. The information that Sarah was pregnant when she died does not change the unexpected nature of the act. It is well known to the Indian audience that there are places in the US where the aged are looked after but the director is making a deliberate point of Samar's regained innocence by having him undertake this responsibility. It should be noted here that in the

Mahabharata, Arjuna also kills the unarmed Karna at Sri Krishna's behest but the latter is a god, which absolves Arjuna of guilt. With Brij Gopal not being a 'god', the issue is whether Samar Pratap can similarly get absolution. Since such a release cannot be claimed by Samar, a key question is how his culpability for killing Sooraj Kumar (who is his stepbrother) can be put aside so casually. Michael Corleone, it must be recollected from *The Godfather*, Part III (1990), was haunted by his killing of Fredo. If Samar has to bear this guilt and/or face retribution, how can he return to the US, an innocent man, that is, go back to Victorian poetry and tend to Sarah's mother? This is problematic but, as Vijay Mishra points out, the absence of a fully articulated (and personally accountable) tragic sense in Indian literature and film is not unusual[4] and that is what Samar Pratap is riding on.

Politics as an Exclusive Domain

Samar's regained innocence also owes to the spaces in India and the US having different moral connotations and the US actually 'imparting innocence' to its citizens. As already argued while dealing with *Kaminey*, big crime with which one can get away has gradually come to be regarded as morally defensible within India but this approval is only locally valid and without universal implications. America's moral difference is supported by Sarah's appalled responses to the abduction she witnesses and the announcement of the death of someone in a car bomb—someone she saw in Samar's company the previous day. Even though Sarah is not at the moral centre of the film, she is the only one with a strong enough moral sense to be shocked by the happenings around her. Sarah's presence actually makes us see that Samar Pratap, in fact, is two people—the ruthless killer that politics makes of him in India and the blameless student of poetry that he is in the US. Although there is also some uncertainty here because murderers have rarely got away in Hindi cinema in this fashion, moral transformation of the kind posited in *The Godfather* is actually disallowed in Hindi cinema in which people are 'in essence' not transformable.[5] One could therefore propose that Samar Pratap—despite the political killings—has no moral connotations in himself but is simply the product of circumstances—the 'Social Darwinism' promoted in the milieu. If a parallel is to be drawn from Hindi cinema, he is not very different from the poor man rendered arrogant by sudden wealth (as in *Maine Pyar Kiya*, 1989) who regains his humility eventually.

The sense of political life in India not merely as corrupted but its corruption as without a remedy is a difficult one to explain. Even *Rang De Basanti* portrayed its heroic protagonists as having ideals in politics. Lakshman Pandey (Atul Kulkarni), it must be recollected, was an idealistic worker in a political party. But this sense of irremediability can perhaps be understood through the choice of texts that the film brings together—the *Mahabharata* and *The Godfather*. While *Raajneeti*'s 'Godfather side' makes politics appear like enterprise on the edge of illegality, its 'Mahabharata side' gives it the sense that its first families are entitled to their power, influence, and wealth as a royal family might be. Although the film is nominally about democratic politics, it conveys the sense that the political space is off limits for the classes not actually born into it. The evidence is that while both Sooraj Kumar and his adoptive father are inducted into political life, only the 'well-born' son gets a stable foothold. Sooraj is drawn as a parallel to Karna in the *Mahabharata* but other evidence can be found in the woman—Prithviraj Pratap's mistress—who attempts to obtain a party ticket to contest an election but is shooed off derisively. She is also disposed of casually later on as though to illustrate the fate befalling upstarts who cannot estimate how far their labours will fetch them. If political life is earmarked as an exclusive territory it is perhaps disingenuous to call it 'irremediable', but 'corrupted' would still imply the possibility of entering and cleansing it. Political corruption, it would seem, cannot be eradicated because politics is the exclusive territory of a political class.

The sense that political positions are inherited is not true of India, where only a few families like the Nehru family have been able to ensure dynastic succession over generations. Businessmen, film stars, and criminals alike are frequently seen entering electoral politics and embarking on successful careers without a history of politics in their families. This being the case, the question is why *Raajneeti* portrays electoral politics in this 'feudal' way—inherited positions and loyalties, and outsiders being kept strictly out. According to industry accounts, *Raajneeti* had a predominantly multiplex viewership although it also did very well with audiences in the diaspora.[6] Also, the fact of the titles appearing only in English needs to be taken note of. These aspects suggest that the classes addressed by the film are largely from metropolitan/urban areas and, predominantly, Anglophone and the supposition finds support in Samar Pratap 'regaining his innocence' in academic life in the US—because higher education in the US is central to Anglophone aspiration in India.[7] This attitude towards politics is different from the one in *Rang De Basanti* (2006) which, while addressing the same class, showed more faith in the democratic basis of electoral politics. This suggests that between 2006 and 2010, electoral politics—which once permitted 'amateurs' admittance—is seen to have become the exclusive domain of professional politicians.

At this point, I should revert to something only hinted at earlier—that there is another reason for why Prithviraj and Samar are chosen as the protagonists of *Raajneeti*. The two are set apart from Veerendra Pratap and Sooraj Kumar by their Anglophone associations. Apart from Sooraj Kumar being a Hindi-speaking Dalit and the adopted son of a car driver, while Samar is a literary scholar in the US with an American girlfriend, Arjun Rampal who plays Prithviraj is a former fashion model associated with several up-market brands and is partly Dutch. Katrina Kaif who plays Indu is half British and was brought up by her English mother. Manoj Bajpai, who plays Veerendra Pratap, is an actor who was born in a small village in Bihar. Although it is difficult to see more than an implication here, my contention is that the backgrounds of the actors influence their gestural vocabulary and make us read the associations of the characters they play. The henchmen associated with Veerendra Pratap—S.P.

Sharma, Babulal, and Prithviraj Pratap's party worker mistress who joins the enemy—who are killed or punished brutally also have no Anglophone associations. The argument being offered here is that it is not their moral qualities as much as their class associations which make Samar and Prithviraj the protagonists of *Raajneeti*. If *Raajneeti*, in addressing the upwardly mobile Anglophone class gives voice to its political attitudes, it follows that the viewpoint of electoral politics being closed off to them belongs to these classes, which are vocal in their regret of politics being entirely directed towards the unlettered 'other'.[8] It is this class which favours the 'market' as the determining factor in economic decisions because market-dictated decisions—as opposed to populism which is targeted entirely at the 'other'—are economically sounder. From another perspective, this proposition echoes Partha Chatterjee who argues that large sections of the population in most democracies exist in 'political society' in which the 'extra-legal' is a way of negotiating livelihoods. If the market-favouring public represents 'civil society' which likes to see itself as rule-bound, its other is represented by the cheering groups of people in *Raajneeti*, a token representation of what 'political society' may be.[9]

Raajneeti is set in the world of politics but there is no sign of an electorate, except the cheering crowds, which make demands. It is significant here that the election meetings and the mobilizing of votes appear always to be in open areas away from the metropolises or urban slums, *as if the electorate does not include the well-to-do and educated from the cities.* The rival parties have no ideology, no strategy against their rivals, and their energies are all directed within, as if the electorate did not have to be wooed with a programme. When the election takes place it is as though the contest was a family affair even though the ruling party led by a political veteran named Ramnath Rai is not implicated in the family's doings. Samar Pratap is a 'political strategist' but his energies are directed against his cousins rather than towards the polity. In fact, the rivalry between the two parties is like a competition between business houses. The film, in fact, bears comparison with Shyam Benegal's *Kalyug* (1981)[10] although the action in it takes place at a heroic level unlike Benegal's film which strives for realism.

Politics is competitive but the question is whether the difference between the workings of even an opportunistic political party and a business enterprise does not lie in politics having to contend with an electorate. The 'electorate' may appear to have correspondence with the 'market' but there are still distinctions to be made. A key difference is that the 'electorate' is not flexible but fixed while the 'market' is variable and can even be created. A product can find a completely new market but there can be no 'new electorate' although the constitution of an existing electorate changes over time. This not only means that a political party cannot be as adventurous as an enterprise but also that, in the long term, the strategies of a political party should be stable and backed by an outlook. The national electorate in India may be dominated by unlettered people but it imposes terms upon political parties, which cannot be run like businesses only through entrepreneurial skills. Also, while the electorate may be susceptible to manipulation, its choices are so unfathomable that not only psephologists but even exit polls have rarely been entirely correct.

Having taken stock of the various aspects of *Raajneeti*, we come up with a strange mix of discourses: (a) politics is the exclusive criminal domain of a wealthy/powerful political class, (b) politics is big business but it is not a business opportunity available to the public at large, (c) the electorate (which does not include the Anglophone Indian) has no will and can be manipulated just as the consumer can be persuaded by business, (d) the real challenge before politicians is not to win over an electorate but to get the better of their rivals, and (e) Indian politics has come to mean crime and that invoking moral issues in politics is naïve.

Considering the audience that *Raajneeti* is addressing, it would appear that the Anglophone classes from the metropolitan cities have been alienated from politics and the political life. Their understanding is that it is an enterprise involving violence and crime. But since they have already conceded that crime is a legitimate extension of enterprise, they cannot take moral exception to it. As already noted, since the cheering crowds in *Raajneeti* exclude their kind, these classes do not see themselves as being part of the electorate. Although politics is understood to be of one hue—opportunistic and entrepreneurial—the Anglophone urban classes exhibit some empathy towards the Anglophone politician—'their own kind'— even though the spoils of politics accruing to these politicians does not trickle down to them. But if 'their own kind' is defined not only as English-speaking politicians but also as politicians uncommitted to the electorate and without a constituency, there are other issues involved and indirect advantages to be had. This is where the arrival of 'CEOs' in politics become relevant, those who have gradually distinguished themselves from 'mere politicians'.

The Politician and the CEO

After the economic liberalization of 1991–2 the economic options confronting a political party are largely illusory and, regardless of its professed ideology, each political party carries forward the agenda of economic reform, that is, move away from state intervention. If there is some respite now and then, this is either because of worldwide recession weakening 'market forces' or the arrival of elections when political parties move towards populism. Since the long-term agenda is generally held to be non-negotiable, political parties have a need for 'managers' or 'administrators' who are distant from electoral politics but are still nominally 'politicians'. The economic options available to political parties are few but, while there is only a token difference between the economic agendas of the 'left' and the 'right', there is still a demarcation between the 'CEO' and the 'politician' in the political class. The clandestine fight in the political arena is perhaps the one between the two categories. In contrast to the politician who is interested in building and nurturing a constituency, the CEO favours 'governance'. The emphasis on governance may appear apolitical but it implies the fixed long-term political agenda just described. It is evidently the CEO who is favoured by funding institutions like the World Bank and the International Monetary Fund (and the global financial system), chiefly, because a well-managed economy is of primary importance to a lender.[11] The Rajya Sabha route into government favours the CEO but the two types denote mindsets that the players carry into politics and the point of entry may not distinguish between them. It would seem that the CEO in politics, increasingly, has private business interests.[12] The corporate/business sector, it must be noted here, is among the most powerful votaries of continued economic reform in India. Anglophone Indians are among those most involved in the doings of private businesses, as employees, vendors, and investors, and the relationship between the two is evidently a strong one.

Raajneeti is about electoral politics at the state level and does not, therefore, invoke the CEOs in politics who have made their mark largely at the centre. It is also about political parties not yet in power and who have not commenced to govern. But we must recollect that after the politicians from both sides have killed each other in the film, the person who inherits the leadership is Indu, the daughter of a powerful business family. This is a 'happy' ending because Indu has not been 'political' as the others were. There is an implication here that after politics has exhausted itself the state can finally get down to governance by an apolitical leader.

While *Raajneeti* focuses on the violence and crime associated with electoral politics, it would not be correct to describe it as being 'disenchanted' with politics. It portrays the political class as glamorous and it does this by making comparisons with two epics dealing with different kinds of empires which have both excited the Indian imagination. *Raajneeti* treats the most brutal kind of opportunism in politics as understandable if not legitimate, although it also, nominally, has a moral resolution in which the politicians eventually destroy each other.

More importantly, however, the film appears to echo the attitudes of an urban Anglophone class which has found itself alienated from electoral politics. The media pitches the elections to this class as if it was a spectator sport[13] and the attitude of the class to the electoral process is that of consumer rather than participant. This may explain why the politicians in *Raajneeti* conduct themselves like gladiators rather than people nurturing constituencies. The fact that the Anglophone class is a class of consumers makes it more important to the market and, therefore, to the CEOs in politics as well as the global financial system. The film shows electoral politics essentially as an unproductive distraction in which political programs are short-term rhetoric. But if only a market-dictated long-term economic plan is legitimate, an issue to be resolved is the position occupied by a hopelessly disadvantaged electorate in the long-term economic programme—since India is a democracy.

Notes

1. This is perhaps why some critics have been confused by *Ardh Satya* not having a 'message' or a moral discourse unlike popular cinema. See Kishore Valicha, *The Moving Image: A Study of Indian Cinema* (Hyderabad: Orient Longman, 1988), p. 107.

2. Noël Carroll suggests that soap operas encourage speculation on whether characters should do this or that and provide objects for gossip, like real people do. This is very different from the Manichaean moral polarization of the Hindi melodrama. Noël Carroll, 'As the Dial Turns: Notes on Soap Operas', in *Theorizing the Moving Image* (New York: Cambridge University Press, 1996), pp. 122–4.

3. The film is aware of the moral implications of Samar's actions because he declares that politics brings out the devil in oneself.

4. Vijay Mishra, *Bollywood Cinema: Temples of Desire* (London: Routledge, 2002), p. 42.

5. See M.K. Raghavendra, *Seduced by the Familiar: Narration and Meaning in Indian Popular Cinema* (New Delhi: Oxford University Press, 2008), p. 49.

6. This is suggested by its overseas performance. See Ray Subers, 'Arthouse Audit: Raajneeti Coninues Bollywood Blitz', Box Office Mojo, 7 June 2010, http://boxofficemojo.com/news/?id=2810&p=s.htm (accessed on 29 March 2014).

7. For instance, see Andrew White, 'Indian Students Flock to the US', *Forbes*, 13 August 2007, http://www.forbes.com/2007/08/05/india-america-students-oped-cz_aaw_0813students.html (accessed on 26 September 2012).

8. There have also been scholarly treatises on the relationship between education and the conduct of politicians. For instance, see Timothy J. Besley, Rohini Pandey, and Vijayendra Rao, 'Political Selection and the Quality of Government: Evidence from South India', Centre for Economic Policy Research Discussion Paper No. 5201, Social Science Research Network, August 2005.

9. Partha Chatterjee, *The Politics of the Governed: Reflections on Popular Politics in Most of the World* (New York: Columbia University Press, 2004), pp. 40–1.

10. Shyam Benegal's *Kalyug* (1981) tried to look at a contemporary business rivalry through the Kurukshetra war in the Mahabharata. Madhur Bhandarkar's *Corporate* (2006) also resembled *Kalyug* although it did not invoke the Mahabharata. The Mahabharata has been used by modern Indian writers and film-makers to illuminate the present. See Pamel Lothspeich, 'The Mahabharata's Imprint on Contemporary Literature and Film', in K. Moti Gokulsing and Wimal Dissanayake (eds), *Popular Culture in a Globalised India* (London: Routledge, 2009), pp. 82–94. But these 'modernist' works (which include *Kalyug*) play down the heroic aspects of the Mahabharata suggesting that the 'dharmic morality of the epic seemingly does not hold sway in contemporary globalizd India'.

11. In the Congress party, the prime minister and the former home minister P. Chidambaram appear to be CEOs, while those like Pranab Mukherjee—until he was elected president—and Digvijay Singh are politicians. For instance, Digvijay Singh's remarks against the former home minister's handling of the Naxalite problem points to the difference in approaches between the politician and the CEO. See 'Rethink Counter-Maoist Strategy: Digvijay Singh to P. Chidambaram', *Economic Times*, Politics/Nation, 14 April 2010, http://articles.economictimes.indiatimes.com/2010-04-14/news/27579710_1_maoists-dantewada-naxalites (accessed on 21 September 2012).

12. Chandrababu Naidu, former chief minister of Andhra Pradesh, who was perhaps the first chief minister to describe himself as a 'CEO', is an

entrepreneur. P. Chidambaram hails from a well-known business family and Sharad Pawar was chief of the Board of Control for Cricket in India (BCCI), one of the biggest money-spinning organizations.

13. A study of the way television channels reported the 2009 elections suggests this. See Romit Raj, 'How Indian TV Channels Pitched the 2009 Elections to Their Audiences', *Phalanx: A Quarterly Review for Continuing Debate*, October 2009, http://www.phalanx.in/pages/open_page_current.html (accessed on 25 September 2012).

12

The Anthropological Gaze

Agrarian Issues and *Peepli (Live)* (2010)

Agrarian Issues in Hindi Cinema

The economic condition of farmers is not a subject that Hindi cinema has concerned itself with in the recent past. Agrarian issues, to the best of one's knowledge, were last dealt with as long ago as the late 1960s although the dacoit (*daku*) genre still thrived in the 1980s. Where earlier agrarian films like *Mother India* (1957) and *Ganga Jumna* (1961) dealt with rural poverty and the exploitative zamindar/moneylender, *Upkar* (1967) explored the manipulation of the peasant by the trader. The daku film—essentially, the Indian 'Curry Western'—does not take up agrarian issues (at least after *Ganga Jumna*) but relies on themes like personal vendetta, as films like *Mera Gaon Mera Desh* (1971) and *Sholay* (1975) testify. The daku film has been attributed by film historians to the perceived nexus between the landed class and the police which saw dacoits as being heroic,[1] but after *Ganga Jumna*, the dacoit is increasingly a villain rather than someone who has been wronged.[2]

Why agrarian issues disappeared from Hindi cinema is difficult to explain but India had been plagued by agrarian unrest/militancy in the 1950s and measures were initiated to effect structural changes in the property order. Both *Mother India* and *Ganga Jumna* draw upon this factor and try to be sympathetic to the rebel—who is nonetheless punished.[3] Perennial food shortages were also the order of the day until the Green Revolution of the 1960s finally made India self-sufficient in food grains. In areas like Punjab where the state had invested heavily in irrigation, this led to the farming community gaining in strength—especially the middle category farmers.[4] *Upkar*, which is basically about a strong middle farmer no longer in debt to the moneylender but drawn into another conflict with the middle-man trader, is a phenomenon which reflects this development. From the late 1960s onwards, no nationally significant developments within the farming community were in evidence although there were movements restricted to certain regions.[5] Since Hindi mainstream cinema is a national cinema, we may surmise that these local agrarian issues were no longer considered significant enough to be narrativized by Hindi cinema.

Another factor to be considered is that in the 1990s, the most important national development impacting on various aspects of Hindi cinema, which was economic liberalization, did not have a significant impact on agrarian issues. Since agriculture has not assumed more importance in the global age, the first question which needs to be asked is why Aamir Khan–produced *Peepli (Live)* should bring up agrarian issues, and whether they are really at the centre of the film. While the three films dealing with agrarian issues cited earlier are 'political' in the sense that they are driven by the conflicts informing agrarian life in India, *Peepli (Live)* is a different kind of film which exhibits humanist concern without being 'political' in a comparable way. Where each of the earlier films is high melodrama and uses stars conspicuously in the role of the rural working class, *Peepli (Live)* (2010) is different.

For a mainstream film, *Peepli (Live)* gives us a view of rural India that is without precedent in its authenticity. At the same time, it is addressing a more segmented audience than Hindi cinema traditionally did. Where the titles of most mainstream films, by and large, appear only in English today, *Peepli (Live)*—apart from having its titles only in English—also has a concluding English legend (about the migration of farmers to the cities). Since this legend is important to the thrust of the film, it can be argued that the film is addressing only those who can read English. In effect, therefore, *Peepli (Live)*'s authentic vision of agrarian life is consumed by another class than the one the film is about.

Many of the rustic protagonists of *Peepli (Live)* could well have been played by actual rustics and this is very different from films like *Mother India* and *Upkar* in which the village folk played by Nargis and Manoj Kumar looked city bred. Even the rural exuberance of Dilip Kumar in *Ganga Jumna* is feigned when compared to Natha and Budhia in *Peepli (Live)*. At the same time, the authenticity of the rustic protagonists of *Peepli (Live)* is limited to their speech and gestures. The film declines to construct fiction around them relating to the intimate circumstances of their lives. Where Radha's family life was central to *Mother India*, for instance, we know little about Natha and Budhia's families, or their antecedents. Where we were made to identify with Radha in *Mother India* and almost thought her thoughts, *Peepli (Live)*—while exhibiting concern—also prevents empathy. We are not allowed to get into the minds of the protagonists or empathize as *Mother India* allowed us to. *Peepli (Live)* is clear that its rural protagonists and its audience belong to completely different worlds and there is little reason to confuse the two.

Peepli (Live)

Peepli (Live) is set in a small village named Peepli in central India and the film begins with two poor farmers Natha (Omkar Das) and his brother Budhia (Raghubir Yadav) in danger of losing their land because of unpaid loans. The two are desperate but a local politician mentions casually that the government has announced compensation of one lakh rupees for every indebted farmer who kills himself. This has the brothers thinking and it is finally agreed that Natha will sacrifice himself. The film successfully turns the choice of

Natha as an unwilling 'martyr' into black comedy of a kind not often seen in Hindi cinema. As chance will have it, however, Natha voices his decision to kill himself in a public space and this is overheard by a media person. Peepli is located at a political fulcrum because it is the constituency of the chief minister of this state of 'Mukhya Pradesh' and local elections are imminent. Also, the central government is trying to manipulate political forces to ensure his defeat. The political conflict around Peepli means that Natha's proposed suicide is especially newsworthy. Hordes of television personnel therefore descend upon Peepli to catch his demise on camera. Natha is the first 'live suicide' they have known because every other farmer's suicide came to be known only after the person's death.

Peepli (Live) is rich in satirical detail. Apart from the television crews preoccupied with 'eyeballs' and ratings, there are the local Thakurs who insist that Natha should kill himself when he begins to have second thoughts. The off-camera bonhomie between the minister for agriculture, Saleem Kidwai (Naseeruddin Shah), and the television show hosts is caught well as is the glibness of the minister who casually devises new yojnas (plans) which cannot be implemented. The secretary for agriculture is a different kind of person who would prefer to wait until the High Court has taken a view on Natha's declared intent. Also caught intelligently are the rumblings in Natha and Budhia's family—especially the shrewish, screaming women. Rather touching is the impoverished farmer digging for mud to sell and dying from exhaustion, quite unnoticed. Perhaps the episode in which Natha needs to relieve himself but cannot escape the cameras and the television crews, who scrutinize even the excrement he has left behind a rock while sheltering from the camera and speculate about it, is excessive. In any case, Natha cannot take any more of all this but by some quirk of fate, his death is announced when someone else (a newsperson named Rakesh) is killed in an accidental fire. The chief minister had announced an inducement of one lakh rupees to prevent Natha from killing himself but his death by accident means that his family will get no relief. Natha, however, is now actually away, working on a construction site in the city and the film ends with an announcement of the millions of Indian farmers who have thus migrated in the past decade.

The striking aspect of Peepli (Live) is the complete absence of drama in it. There are two categories of people in the film: those belonging to the media, the bureaucracy, and the political class who are all fundamentally disconnected from the local people, who constitute the second category. Each of them is constructed as a separate community and the way the members relate to each other is the evidence. In the privileged group, for instance, the media personnel are shown to be on partying terms with the minister for agriculture at the centre who is called up by the chief minister (from another political party) during the parleys underway when they are awaiting Natha's suicide. In the same way, the 'local' people include farmers, their families and local politicians/strong men. The term 'community' just used for the two groups does not mean that they bear comparison with the 'community-as-nation' with common loyalties; they are simply people who are socially connected to each other. The film does not identify with the privileged group but neither does it do so with the local villagers. Lack of empathy with any person or group is broadly characteristic of a certain kind of satire but this does not explain the absence of drama. Peepli (Live) neither convinces us that anything matters deeply to anyone nor that the course of events can be altered. The rivalry between the political parties does not force either side to take measures affecting the outcome of events and Natha's impending death does not lead his family to see its future as likely to be different. The intended suicide is an accidental development but his family does not respond to it or its own approaching penury as a woeful or horrific development. Natha also abandons his family as though he could easily live without it. Having a house, he has not represented the poorest of the poor in the village but he is virtually destitute on the construction site in the city. Still, he embraces this fate as if only out of irritation at those plaguing him. The plot of Peepli (Live) is overwhelmed by a strange listlessness but a pertinent observation is that this is not simply an aesthetic failure on its part; it is even a natural consequence of the kind of social concern exhibited by it.

The Concerns

Peepli (Live) is directed by Anusha Rizvi and Mahmood Farooqui but it bears the hallmark of the 'cinema of concern' heralded by Aamir Khan (who produced the film) within mainstream Bollywood which includes Taare Zameen Par (2007). My earlier remark that the film was 'humanist' rather than 'political' can be elaborated upon now as meaning that it does not identify the issues to be confronted. The film is about rural indebtedness and there are a number of paths it might have taken and questions it might have raised. Normally, it is not fair for a critic to comment about what a film *might have been* but Peepli (Live), I propose, makes itself 'humanist' as a deliberate ploy by which to evade economic and political issues. In examining the predicament in which Natha and Budhia have been placed, the film looks upon indebtedness as a 'human' concern rather than an economic one and this causes its listlessness. We do not know under what circumstances the two fell into debt although 'alcohol' is offered half-heartedly as a cause. If the film had identified a clear economic reason[6] for the misery of the protagonists, a clear villain would also have emerged as would the essential teleology.

The other major concern of the film revolves around the methods of the media, for example, television channels, and it may be useful to compare its approach with that of Madhur Bhandarkar's Page 3 (2005) which was discussed in an earlier chapter although that film was about the print media. An important aspect of Page 3 is the power associated with the media, largely its capacity to do good by investigating social/political evils. The film argues that the primary role of the media should be a moral/social one. Another film dealt with in this book, Rang De Basanti (2006), also portrays television as a moral agent.

In Peepli (Live), the television channel is neither in possession of any power nor is it an agent of social morality; it is a business enterprise. Even if this is legitimate, the film is being inauthentic when the people of Peepli are portrayed as indifferent to the arrival of the television crews, television presence being only an intrusion and not an opportunity. One of the key deficiencies faced by agrarian India is media attention and I propose that it is far from likely that when the crews do arrive, their presence will not be taken advantage of. The mere presence of media journalists is, in a sense, adequate to render them 'moral agents' in a democracy since those accountable are their natural quarry.[7] This being the case, the question is why the film portrays Peepli's response to television as cool. The television crews, correspondingly, focus on inane matters—like Natha relieving himself—when they might have used the occasion to pursue the more interesting/revealing stories, of which there could not have been paucity. Exaggerations of this sort may be permissible in satire but this also conveys the sense that those in Peepli are in the position of the 'other', as a tribe outside civilization might be to an ethnographic documentary, in the making of which the tribe wields little influence. If those in Peepli had 'transacted' freely with the television crews — that is, tried to find advantage in their presence—this sense would perhaps have been dispelled and Peepli might have 'integrated'.[8]

Peepli (Live) may be well meaning and humanistic but its humanism is not inclusive, that is, not accompanied by an admission that those to whom one should extend sympathy are essentially as one is. This, in a way, carries forward some tendencies noticed in Madhur Bhandarkar's Traffic Signal (2007) examined in an earlier chapter. The lives of the urban poor not being narrativized in that film suggested that they were perceived as outside the pale of the Nation. Peepli (Live), in addressing a public increasingly confident that it is the Nation, demarcates the space of the agrarian poor as belonging to the 'outside'. When we reflect upon the relationships, we find that those working in the television crew have commitments of some sort: Rakesh (who is killed later) and the presenter Nandita even debate the ethics of what they are doing. Natha and Budhia, on the other hand, are less sincere in their deliberations over their course of action; each of them insists on killing himself but is covertly manipulating the other to take the step. This ploy may succeed as black comedy but it also makes it seem that there is more cohesion within the television crew than there is in Peepli village. Business ethics are more binding than loyalty to one's 'community'—which is how the village was once represented in Hindi cinema.

When Hindi cinema dealt with the agrarian poor in the era in which Nehruvian socialism was the accepted political creed, it had stars playing the poor. Since film stars are naturally people in whom the public projects itself, one can say that the public at large identified with the poor. It must also be observed that when film stars portrayed the working class, they were shown working with their hands. Radha (Nargis) in *Mother India* wields a plow, while Vijay (Amitabh Bachchan) carries crates as a dockyard labourer in *Deewaar* (1975). Neither *Mother India* nor *Deewaar* could be described as 'humanist' because audiences were made to follow the drama in the stories rather than simply feel for the central characters.

Humanism—if it implies the absence of drama and only a desire to make the audience feel or empathize—was never a genre in mainstream cinema until the new millennium. Why the genre arose in the global age needs explaining and a hypothesis is that drama came from the film taking sides politically as in *Mother India* and *Upkar*. The ascendancy of economic reform to the status of sole political agenda assisted in the process of de-politicization because every other political issue which informed Hindi cinema earlier was rendered irrelevant.[9] The waning of the political and its compensation by 'feeling' may have engendered the apolitical 'humanist' category in mainstream cinema where a disadvantaged person is the focus. Illustrations are *Taare Zameen Par* in which the focus was a dyslexic boy and Sanjay Leela Bhansali's *Black* (2005), about a deaf-mute and blind girl. These are humanist in a different way from *Peepli (Live)* because the object of sympathy belongs to the same social segment as the middle-class audience and they deal with a kind of disadvantage which cannot be as 'political'. Still, *Peepli (Live)* is comparable because it deliberately overlooks the possibility of political causes, like microfinance, which are the actual causes of suicides in agrarian India.

In conclusion, it will be helpful to speculate briefly about why, despite its concern, *Peepli (Live)* is more timid in its social criticism than films like *Mother India*, *Ganga Jumna*, and *Upkar*. The reason, I propose, is that the corporatization of the economy has lent versatility to capital that it did not possess in the 1950s and 1960s. To elaborate, it might have been possible for film production to be more independent earlier because it was not reliant on other sections of the economy, for instance, moneylenders, landowners, and traders, who are attacked in the these three films. Now, on the other hand, corporate entities and groups have a wide range of economic interests and most of them are also increasingly involved in the media. Even more importantly, the Anglophone public is implicated in the doings of enterprise as vendors, employees, and/or shareholders, and seeing causes (and villains) in microfinance or retail chains is extremely inconvenient; the new 'humanism' is perhaps an escape from responsibility. This implies that capital and the Anglophone classes present a united front against social and economic criticism, as it were. If this is granted, there is apparently a greater degree of censorship today—at the level of ideation—although the censoring authority is perhaps not the state but the economy.

Notes

1. Fareed Kazmi, *The Politics of India's Conventional Cinema: Imaging a Universe and Subverting a Multiverse* (New Delhi: Sage, 1999), p. 100.

2. In later dacoit (*daku*) films like *Batwara* (1988) and *Ghulami* (1985), the narration is once again sympathetic to the criminal but the reasons for his turning a criminal are personal and can be traced to caste antagonism. The plot of social injustice forcing an innocent farmer into crime is included in films like *Ganga Jumna* (1961) as well as *Paan Singh Tomar* (2012), which will be examined in a later chapter.

3. See M.K. Raghavendra, *Seduced by the Familiar: Narration and Meaning in Indian Popular Cinema* (New Delhi: Oxford University Press, 2008), p. 144.

4. Sunil Khilnani, *The Idea of India* (New Delhi: Penguin, 1998), p. 31.

5. A movement of some importance in the Hindi-speaking belt was the one led in western Uttar Pradesh by M.S. Tikait in the 1990s. For a useful political study, see K. Lerche, 'Agricultural Labourers, the State and Agrarian Transition in Uttar Pradesh', *Economic and Political Weekly*, vol. 33, no. 13, 26 March 1998, pp. A29–35.

6. As two possible causes, there are agencies persuading farmers to alter their cropping plans with the lure of windfall profits, and some are enterprises in the retail trade. A film about the unfulfilled promises of a big retailer leading to indebtedness would have been more forceful. It is now coming to light that microfinance is usury of a severe kind and this could also have been cited as the source of Budhia and Natha's misery. See David Bornstein, 'Profiting from the Poor: The Ethics of Microfinance', *Dowser*, 14 April 2010, http://dowser.org/profiting-from-the-poor-the-ethics-of-microfinance/ (accessed on 15 October 2012).

7. For instance, see Shakuntala Rao, 'Accountability, Democracy, and Globalization: A Study of Broadcast Journalism in India', *Asian Journal of Communication*, vol. 18, no. 3, August 2008, pp. 193–206.

8. As commentators on television have pointed out, the proliferation of private television channels and the creation of a television public had significant implications for democracy in India where the state-run Doordarshan had largely been an 'insipid propaganda machine'. See Nalin Mehta, 'Breaking News, Indian Style: Politics, Democracy and Indian News Television', in K. Moti Gokulsing and Wimal Dissanayake (eds), *Popular Culture in a Globalised India* (London: Routlege, 2009), p. 31.

9. Here are a few broad political issues which informed Hindi cinema in the earlier decades: Nehruvian modernity in the 1950s, admitting the marginalized into the mainstream in the 1970s, and caste identity in the 1980s. Secularism is also an issue which has lurked in virtually every Hindi film from 1940s onwards but even this has now become a non-issue in Hindi cinema today with religious affinities not being problematized in films like *3 Idiots* but treated as an 'irrational prejudice'. In actual political life, however, religious identity is more important than ever.

13

Resisting the Anglophone Nation

Rab Ne Bana Di Jodi (2008) and *Dabangg* (2010)

The Other Hindi Cinema

In the previous chapters, we have analysed the Hindi cinema which addresses Anglophone Indians but there exist Indians who are not Anglophone and who need another kind of cinema which attends to their concerns. The question arises, therefore, whether there is a cinema received in smaller towns like Jhansi and Moradabad but not especially favoured in the city multiplexes. Part of the difficulty here is that while there is such a cinema, it is mostly small budget cinema and is too local to be nationally significant.[1] During a trip to rural Rajasthan a few years ago, it became apparent to me that actors popular in the 1980s like Sunny Deol feature in many of these films (for example, *Veerta*, 1993; *Khuda Kasam*, 2010) but the International Movie Data Base does not acknowledge these films and information about them is also hard to come by. The actors themselves seem reticent to acknowledge these films despite their success locally, perhaps, because their production values will not do them credit. As an instance of a bigger film, one listed as an 'all-time blockbuster' in Rajasthan and Bihar is Sooraj Barjatya's *Vivah* (2006)[2] which is virtually unknown in the cities. Since my concern is primarily with the Nation and its constitution today, I will here confine myself to examining films popular across India but with no perceivable Anglophone bias. A film which answers to the description is Aditya Chopra's *Rab Ne Bana Di Jodi*. Before going on to examine this film, however, it may be useful to identify the signs by which one may conclude whether a film addresses an Anglophone public or otherwise. Since much of this has already been dealt with, this is in the nature of a summary coming at the appropriate moment.

As already explained, since all films are in the Hindi language, the fact of a film's 'Anglophone' inclination is conjecture based on our understanding of city audiences in the new millennium. An observed characteristic of Anglophone Hindi cinema is the notion of 'aspiration' which implies a certain slant in the vocations chosen for the male protagonists. In *3 Idiots* (2009), for instance, Rancho is associated with engineering patents registered abroad, while his friend is an international photographer. In *Raajneeti*, Samar Pratap is working for his PhD in the US. There is thus a sense that global associations are preferred and this is true even when the films deal with crime as in *Bunty Aur Babli* (2005), *Dhoom 2* (2006), or *Kaminey* (2009). Indians travelling abroad as tourists in the earlier cinema, of course, were a different category as were non-residents. The protagonists of *DDLJ* (1995) are not 'global Indians' although they live and work in London, while Rancho in *3 Idiots* is, although he works in the remotest of India. Being 'global' is therefore less a matter of where a person is stationed than how he/she is connected to the rest of the world. NRIs may live abroad but they are not globally mobile and do not 'aspire' although they are usually wealthy. Seen thus, the protagonists of *KANK* (2006) are not 'global'.

A corollary to being Anglophone implying 'aspiration' is the accompanying absence of the 'community'. As already elaborated, the 'community' implies allegorizing the Nation as a microcosm and the global mobility of aspiring Anglophone Indians effectively prevents them from being a community; in *KANK*, the characters, live in New York and are a part of community, while there is no corresponding student community around Rancho in *3 Idiots*. The distinction here, however, is not as clear as one would like because there is a community of youth in *Rang De Basanti* (2006) and the group is Anglophone without the accompanying provision of their 'aspiring' in any way, if aspiration is associated with personal advancement. A plausible explanation is that the individual notions of the 'global', the 'Anglophone Indian', and 'aspiration' emerged separately—perhaps through the same socio-political stimuli—but came together in later cinema.

Although the Anglophone category may not regard itself as a 'community' in itself, it sees its own trajectory as signifying the trajectory of the Nation. As already argued in the book, individual lives have no particular meaning in Hindi cinema, they gain significance only in relation to the grand narrative of the Nation. There is also no non-Anglophone category recognized in Anglophone cinema and the 'others' are only the poor. Since the fate of the poor is not seen to impinge upon the narrative of the Nation after 1991–2, the films find no teleology in their lives. The poor, when they appear in Anglophone cinema, have lives which are not narrativized. Evidence of this was found in films like *Traffic Signal* (2007) and *Peepli (Live)* (2010).

Another aspect of Anglophone Hindi cinema, perhaps, seen first in *Rang De Basanti*, is its tendency to become 'political' —by expressing its abhorrence of electoral politics and the political life. Since this goes hand in hand with a eulogy of 'enterprise' one could understand the Anglophone class as being frustrated by electoral power being wielded by the 'uneducated', usually portrayed as susceptible to political manipulation as in *Raajneeti* (2010). There is an inconsistency here because while illegality is seen as a legitimate component of enterprise, it is frowned upon in electoral politics. Side by side, the state is also regarded as an obstacle to aspiration, and evidence can be found in films like *Bunty Aur Babli* in which employment in the railways is brushed aside as a demeaning possibility. How or why this came about can only be speculated upon but it is a characteristic that distinguishes the Anglophone from the non-Anglophone, to whom the 'community' and the state still have value. I shall try to demonstrate this. Before continuing, however, it must be clarified that there is no evidence of any hostility between the Anglophone and the non-Anglophone classes in cinema. There is, for instance, no lampooning of Anglophone ways as there is of modernity in Guru Dutt's *Kaagaz Ke Phool* (1959) in the character played by Johnny Walker. The same producers are frequently responsible for both kinds of films although the two categories address different (though overlapping) audiences and publics.

Rab Ne Bana Di Jodi

The film (directed by Aditya Chopra) begins with Surinder 'Suri' Sahni (Shahrukh Khan) taking home his bride, Taani Gupta. She is the daughter of his former professor and he married her entirely by accident. It happened when he went to attend her wedding and was introduced to her. So spirited was Taani that he immediately fell in love with her. Taani's father had always held the introverted Surinder to be the ideal young man for Taani and had made this known to his daughter, who nonetheless chose to marry someone else for love. When a tragedy strikes and Taani's fiancé and his family are killed in a road accident while on their way to the wedding, the mortally stricken Professor Gupta extracts a promise from Surinder that he will marry Taani. After the professor's death, therefore, he marries her in an impromptu wedding and they return to Amritsar, where he works in a state undertaking named Punjab Power. Taani has not married Surinder against her will but there is still an emotional gap between them that Surinder is unable to bridge. Surinder's best friend is Balwinder 'Bobby' Khosla (Vinay Pathak), a hairdresser, who offers him counsel now.

Taani is an ideal wife except that she lets him know that she does not love him. She is also not the bubbly girl Surinder fell in love with and is much graver in her demeanour. For his part, Surinder is considerate and tries his best—given his diffidence—to make her happy. The turning point in their relationship comes when dance instructors from Mumbai set up an establishment in Amritsar and Taani asks Surinder to allow her to take dancing lessons. Surinder consults Bobby on the matter and, after some thinking, realizes that this presents him with an opportunity as well. With help from Bobby, therefore, he takes off his moustache, abandons his glasses, alters his hairstyle, and enrolls in the same dance class as 'Raj Kapoor'. In *Om Shanti Om*, as well, the surname 'Kapoor' was synonymous with sophistication.

The reader may recognize a few other features in common between *Rab Ne Bana Di Jodi* and *Om Shanti Om* (2007). The first similarity is the motif of a man assuming a more glamorous persona to win a woman and this involves role playing. Secondly, both Om Makhija in *Om Shanti Om* and Surinder live unexciting lives, although *Rab Ne Bana Di Jodi* does not convey the impression that Surinder is 'ordinary' as Om Makhija is made out to be. But the differences between the two films are more pertinent from my perspective. A key difference is that Om 'aspired'—he tried to advance his career—while Surinder, modestly, wants only to win his own wife's heart. There is also a greater feeling of community here than in *Om Shanti Om*, which also had a group of friends/colleagues around the protagonist. This sense of community in *Rab Ne Bana Di Jodi* may not be evident at first glance because a community is usually given a common purpose. But so many people from Amritsar—shown as a bustling and prosperous city—taking dancing lessons from Mumbai can be understood as an entire city seeking sophistication. There is, consequently, a feeling that the city itself is a thriving community[3] and this gets emphasis with the privileging of the Golden Temple as a place for congregation. Further, Surinder is not at the centre of the group as Om is placed in *Om Shanti Om* and the lack of a sense of vicarious participation in their leader's efforts seen in that film is absent here.[4]

In the dance class, each student is paired off with someone and, as luck will have it, Taani and Surinder become partners. 'Raj' is closer to Shahrukh Khan's screen persona than Surinder—where the star is required to 'act'—and Raj's flirtatious conduct has Taani gradually transforming, although she does not fail to chide him when his flirtation becomes excessive. The two are just friends until Raj expresses his love to Taani and suggests that they elope, if she does not love her husband. Her response is uncertain and 'Raj' recognizes the impending catastrophe in her reciprocating his love. At the last moment—the minutes before the final dance competition— Taani realizes that Surinder 'held her hand when she was alone' and tells 'Raj' that she cannot go with him. She is certain that, after this revelation, Raj will fail to turn up. Raj, however, appears at the last moment, but as Surinder, and reveals the deception he has been practising. 'Mr and Mrs Surinder Sahni' duly win the dance competition.

To revert to my comparison of the film with Om Shanti Om, Shahrukh Khan effectively plays two roles here, as in that film. If at first glance it appears that, as Raj, he is projecting his favoured screen persona—corresponding to Om Kapoor in the earlier film—it nonetheless becomes apparent that 'Raj' is more of a caricature. We are also prepared for parody in the role by Bobby Khosla's comic flamboyance. Overall, 'Raj' is deliberately pitched so that Taani will understand Surinder's constancy and reliability and Raj's persona is unstable although it is not the instability of Buddy Love from The Nutty Professor (1963).[5] This sense of Raj's instability is confirmed when Taani chooses Surinder over him. In Om Shanti Om, it is Om Kapoor rather than Om Makhija who is the more stable.

The motif of the woman confronted by two avatars of the same man and choosing the less flamboyant one is a familiar one. In the Hindi film Ponga Pandit (1975), the wife rejects the man she is married to, who belongs to the priestly caste in Varanasi, because she is 'modern'. The husband appears in the shape of a Bombay pop singer to win back her heart, only to subsequently teach her a lesson and get her to take her place as a traditional wife. This film was made when, under the influence of Indira Gandhi's ideological rhetoric, Hindi cinema had embraced anti-Western nationalism with a vengeance.[6] The metropolis as a symbol of the Western–modern is also present in *Rab Ne Bana Di Jodi*. The Western–modern may have no evident negative connotations here as in *Ponga Pandit* but there is still an ambivalence in the portrayal of Bollywood dancing as an emblem of sophistication. Surinder's mentor in 'glamour' being a hairdresser rather than, say, a fashion designer (as in Madhur Bhandarkar's *Fashion*, 2008) is also significant because, in India's persisting caste hierarchy, barbers are lowly placed.[7] Although the film's discourse may be too gentle to be a satire, we still detect a sense of Anglophone culture being kept at a distance in *Rab Ne Bana Di Jodi*. The film may, therefore, be seen as an affirmation of traditional 'non-Anglophone' values although a stronger statement perhaps comes from *Dabangg*. Before going on to examine *Dabangg*, however, it is necessary to examine another aspect of *Rab Ne Bana Di Jodi* which sets it apart from most of the other films dealt with hitherto: the reappearance of the parent as an emblem of moral authority.

Reaffirming the Moral Authority of the Parent

Hindi cinema, for much of its history, used the parental presence—especially the mother—as the conduit through which ethical values enter the narrative[8] though filial loyalty or *dosti* could also serve as a substitute. A key factor here is that the moral significance of parental presence is made evident in a 'first cause' which sets causality in motion.[9] Even in the new millennium, the mother's presence and her invoking of his spirited father in *Lagaan* (2001) provided the hero with the moral impetus to resist the British in cricket.[10] Contrarily though, in most of the films dealt with in this book, when the parental presence is not insignificant or weak, it represents a standpoint (ethical or otherwise) that the protagonists reject. In *Gadar: Ek Prem Katha* (2001) and *Veer-Zaara* (2004), the strong parent is from the Pakistani side and the protagonists (who reject Pakistan) break away from them. In *Rang De Basanti*, the parent with the strongest presence is a corrupt arms dealer and he is assassinated by his patriotic son. In *Bunty Aur Babli*, the protagonists are ambitious and do not concur with their parents' plans for their futures and this motif finds a place in *Guru* (2007) and *Fashion* as well. Even in *3 Idiots*, Rancho's principal adversary is the heroine's father. The parent, in an overwhelming majority of these examples, is primarily an obstruction to aspiration.

As argued elsewhere,[11] the parent has represented tradition and, in the light of this factor, one could say that Anglophone cinema represents a self-conscious break with tradition and the past.[12] This decisive break did not come about with the end of Nehruvian socialism (that is, the economic liberalization of 1991–2) and many films of the 1990s (*HAHK, DDLJ*) still respect parental authority deeply. An explanation for the subsequent shift is that while occupations were traditionally passed on from father to son and one's birth dictated what kind of vocation one followed, the rise of the new economy signals the moment when this was broken. Young people—regardless of their caste or birth or the traditional occupations of their family—began to find occupations in cities which were new, having to make themselves Anglophone to do this.[13] *Rab De Bana Di Jodi* reverts to the older cinema since its moral thrust revolves around a dying man's plea to his former student not to abandon his only daughter but to make her his wife. This is the key moral issue in the film because it becomes the reason for the wife remaining loyal to her husband.[14] This concept of loyalty in the film will become pertinent again later but for now it is enough to say that Abhinav Kashyap's *Dabangg* introduces some of these issues.

Dabangg

One of the most durable narrative devices in Hindi cinema before 1991–2 was the preamble which contained the first cause: a childhood sequence in which characters or relationships are defined forever. For instance, the sacred dosti between Sundar and Gopal in Raj Kapoor's *Sangam* (1964) is defined in an opening segment set in their childhood. In *Deewaar* (1975), Vijay's anger at social injustice is caused by his being shamed by workers who believe that his father has betrayed them. In nearly every version of *Devdas*, it is located in the boy Devdas' punishment at the hands of his authoritarian father. The preamble is crucial in each film because a key event in it determines the eventual development of the story. Gopal is committed to Sundar's happiness in *Sangam* because of this first event, Vijay remains 'angry' through the length of *Deewaar*, and Devdas remains weak until his death from excessive drinking of alcohol. *Dabangg* continues the same tradition.

Dabangg begins in the childhood of Chulbul Pandey (Salman Khan) and Makhanchand Pandey aka Makhi (Arbaaz Khan). Chulbul's mother (Dimple Khanna) married Prajapati Pandey (Vinod Khanna) when her first husband died and Makkhi is her son from this marriage. The preamble defines the characters of Chulbul and Makkhi as fearless and weak, respectively, as well as, Chulbul's love for his mother who understands their qualities. Also brought into focus is Chulbul's resentment towards his stepfather although Prajapati Pandey 'gives him his own name' and tries to treat him as his son.

In the next segment, Chulbul and Makkhi are grown up, with Chulbul being a police inspector. Newspaper reviews describe Chulbul as 'corrupt' but he sees himself as a Robin Hood. To help the audience understand the character of Chulbul, '21 years' after the preamble, Chulbul apprehends a gang of bank robbers but allows them to get away after he appropriates the stolen money. When a constable is disappointed at missing a promotion because of such benevolence, Chulbul shoots him in the shoulder and compensates him with a lakh of rupees; the injury, thus, becomes evidence of 'valour' and justifies the constable's promotion. In this way, Chulbul gets money to spend usefully as well as the devotion of his subordinates.

But if Chulbul takes dirty money and uses it, it is because he has a 'constituency' to nurture rather than to spend on himself. He is dressed impeccably and is very different from police inspectors in films like *Kaminey* who look sloppy as they bring disgrace to their uniform. To show that there are also other kinds of policemen, there is a corrupt one named Kasturilal Vishkarma (Om Puri) who is associated with the villain. While Chulbul Pandey is adored by his subordinates for his numerous endearing qualities, Kasturilal operates alone. Other motifs in the film include a senior politician named Dayal Babu (Anupam Kher) and his villainous youth-wing associate Chedi Singh (Sonu Sood), who tricks Makkhi into assassinating Dayal Babu. Also in the film is a drunkard named Haria whose daughter, Rajo (Sonakshi Sinha), Chulbul wants to marry. Makkhi romances with Nirmala whose father, Masterji, resists the alliance but later consents. The film is far from impeccably plotted and relating the numerous sub-plots in it would make it seem neater and much more cogent than it actually is. Moreover, many of the motifs appear to have no purpose at all and appear even capricious.[15]

But after all these excesses in the narrative have been put aside as difficult to interpret event-wise, what remains is still considerable. In the first place, while Chulbul is a fearless police officer, it is difficult to see him as an emblem of the state in the abstract as policemen once were in the Hindi cinema because he is given too many personal eccentricities. Moreover, if his fearlessness represents the strength of the state, an unanswered question will be what does Kasturilal Vishkarma represent—as he is shown as servile before political power and also in uniform?

The preamble houses the 'message' relayed by any film and, when legality and state authority are part of the message as in *Zanjeer* (1973), the notions are introduced in it.[16] The preamble in *Dabangg* is only about Chulbul, his personal qualities, and his family circumstances, and the issue of legality and the state are not brought into it in any way. This being the case, it can be argued that Chulbul being a fearless policeman in *Dabangg* does not imply that state authority is itself strong. I propose that the message relayed by the film is quite the opposite, that with the state having so little authority on its own, the personal qualities of its functionaries play a large part in identifying illegalities and in upholding the law. Apart from this leading to different kinds of conduct from Chulbul and Kasturilal, Chulbul himself is not finicky about separating the personal from the official in his dealings. If Chulbul wears his police uniform with genuine pride, he also uses the power imparted by it to assist him in his personal dealings. For instance, he woos Rajo when he is in uniform and conveys the sense that she cannot refuse his—because of his authority.

Another aspect of the film that needs to be taken note of is that whatever crisis Chulbul faces and overcomes is within his family although many of them should justly have had public connotations. The most important one is Makkhi's unwitting hand in Dayal Babu's assassination—at the behest of Chedi Singh—being an extension of the conflict between Chulbul and Makkhi. At the highpoint of Chulbul and Makkhi's enmity for each other, Chulbul publicly thrashes Makkhi for ill-treating a worker in his father's factory. A high-ranking police official makes Chulbul tender an apology to Makkhi and the matter is resolved. The observation here is that the affairs of the Pandey family are treated as public events in the town. One actually gets the sense that the life of the town revolves around the Pandey family and resolving family disputes would set the town right. After Chulbul is finally victorious against the villain, Chedi Singh, and celebrates this by presiding over Makkhi's wedding to Nirmala, Prajapati Pandey addresses him as 'Pandeyji'—virtually acknowledging that Chulbul is the master of the Pandey household.[17] A public servant's success culminating in the conquest of his own family is evidently a singular occurrence. To phrase it differently, in the rural family dramas of the past (for example, Mother India, 1957), family issues were brought out into the open because public life was what was ultimately at risk. Radha kills her son in Mother India because he goes against the laws of the village. If Radha's act against her son has public purpose, Chulbul's public acts seem intended to assist in winning him his position in his family. One wonders if this does not point to a deep erosion of the sense of public life and if this is not due to the systematic obliteration of the dividing line between private and public ends.

A factor that cannot be lost sight of while dealing with Dabangg is the role of the mother. The mother is traditionally the site of virtue in Hindi film narrative[18] but unlike the strong mothers in the earlier films who had to conduct themselves to deserve the reverence with which they were regarded,[19] Chulbul's mother appears to do little to deserve her sacred position in the narrative. Since the sacred mother who made sacrifices on behalf of her children allegorized the Nation, the reverence towards her was understandable. Moral transgression by the protagonist was also judged most strongly when the mother disapproved and this is not only true of *Mother India* and *Deewaar*, but also of *KANK* in which the mother remains with her divorced daughter-in-law when her son has engaged in adultery. My proposition here is that the weakness of the mother in *Dabangg* should be read in conjunction with the discourse pertaining to the weakness of state authority—since the state assists in the imagining of the Nation-as-Community. With the weakening of the state, the question is whether the Nation itself does not weaken as a community in the imagination of its constituents[20]—and whether the weak mother in *Dabangg* does not point to it.

Another observation about *Dabangg* can be made when Chulbul announces the fact of his being of the Brahmin caste. 'Pandey' is a Brahmin name but Hindi cinema traditionally used caste names without attaching much significance to them, except for a period in the 1980s.[21] Even then, caste was simply a fact, sometimes for the purpose of banding together and not necessarily a matter for pride. In *Dabangg*, not only is Chulbul proud of his Brahmin caste status but his stepfather and his family appear to enjoy social status in the town because of their caste. It is significant that none of the others have discernible caste surnames except the crooked policeman Kasturilal Vishkarma, who has a surname also with caste associations—that of the artisan caste which includes blacksmiths, goldsmiths, and carpenters. In effect therefore, Chulbul's people are the only denoted Brahmins[22] in the town and their centrality in the town affairs may owe to this. When we regard the two policemen in relation to each other, we are also made to take note of their respective positions in caste hierarchy. To show how this is a regression for Hindi cinema, in an earlier film from the 1980s, J.P. Dutta's *Batwara* (1988), in which a policeman asserts his caste identity as a Thakur (or Kshatriya), the man is the villain who tries to bring about enmity between two friends from different castes—a Thakur and a Jat. At the conclusion, a suitable end is arranged for the villain—the friends 'skewer him like a pig'.[23]

Chulbul's 'Brahmin-ness' does not relate to his attributes but to his blood and this is where the film differs from some regional films—usually south Indian—in which 'Brahminhood' is associated with certain innate qualities. The south Indian regional cinemas—chiefly Tamil and Kannada—have been more preoccupied with caste than Hindi cinema in which caste names have been affixed casually without much significance. In Tamil films, the Brahmin–non-Brahmin divide has also repeatedly shown up, indicating that cinema is often a caste battleground. For instance, the Tamil film *Anniyan* (2005), it has been convincingly demonstrated,[24] constructs the ideal citizen as a Brahmin, rather than as a deracinated individual. *Dabangg* is different from *Anniyan* inasmuch as Chulbul is not an exemplar of citizenhood. While the protagonist of *Anniyan* represents a social ideal, Chulbul, although heroic, is not a vehicle for polemic. His caste-ness is more in line with jati than varna—emphasizing birth rather than social function—and this finds confirmation in the local flavour of the film, that is, in its depiction of rural India.[25]

Part of the complications in *Dabangg* owe to the number of characters in it whose relationships with each other are difficult to chart. But overall, one's sense of it is that the society it depicts is hierarchically structured although this is implicit rather than explicit. The leading players in this milieu are mainly Chulbul's kin, existing and prospective. There are others, such as workers, police constables, and so on, who represent the minions and whose hierarchical positions appear to be a given. Chedi Singh has no position in this hierarchy and may be understood as a rogue element who has forced his way into it. The highest-ranking person in the narrative is Dayal Babu, a senior politician from outside the milieu and, if anything, Dayal Babu recognizes that the local structures cannot be tampered with except at one's own peril. He sees Chedi Singh as a dangerous nuisance which needs to be checked although very carefully. Correspondingly, the higher-ranking police officials above Chulbul appear to regard him as the 'local state' rather than their subordinate, the only explanation accounting for the free hand he is given is maintaining local law and order although he is unorthodox. If one were to compare *Dabangg* to many 'Anglophone' Hindi films (like *Kaminey*, which also has a large number of characters and a confusing plot), one could say that in contrast to them, it represents the triumph of local insularity where Anglophone cinema tries to be global. As if to confirm this, where most recent films identify with people who are comfortable with the English language—also as betokened by film titles like *3 Idiots*, *Wake Up Sid*, *Peepli (Live)*, and *No Problem*—Chulbul is not Anglophone and pronounces even English words proudly in local ways (for example, 'confuse' as 'confuj').

Coming to the portrayal of politics in the film, it may be taken to represent the opposite of what it does in *Raajneeti*. Dayal Babu represents the class that *Raajneeti* is about but in contrast to that film, the local politician-goons in *Dabangg*, far from being subservient and manageable, have entered into illicit/criminal local arrangements which the senior leaders have no control over.

Lastly, if Chulbul emerges, from the description of *Dabangg* just provided, as a morally flawed individual, this is hardly the sense conveyed by the film. In the terms of the imagery employed he is even exemplary. I propose at this point that there is nothing in his conduct to suggest that he is deviating from the code of dharma.[26] He is not greedy and lives in the ramshackle family house. If he uses stolen money for his own ends rather than returning it to the authorities, it simply means that he is not bound strictly by legality, and there is no reason to believe that the dharmic codes are synonymous with legality.[27] While the reader may be sceptical about the notion of a policeman keeping a stash of stolen money to be used for 'good purposes', it becomes credible when we compare Chulbul to Chedi Singh, who uses stolen money to build his own business enterprise, a brewery. It must be noted that the milieu is responsible for many of the illegalities, which also appear to get social approval. Dayal Babu is an honourable politician but he admits that he needs Chedi Singh and the criminals under him. The bank robbers thrashed by Chulbul in the first sequence described earlier are designated 'party workers' by Chedi Singh when he makes a claim upon the stolen money for the 'party'. Thus, the film is dealing with a milieu in which one uses whatever strengths one possesses (for example, caste, official position, political connections, and marital ties) to one's advantage and 'illegality' is a fact of everyday life. If a policeman using his position to his own ('good') ends would have been frowned upon in early Hindi cinema, it is not incompatible with dharma in *Dabangg*.

The two films dealt with in this chapter, *Rab Ne Bana Di Jodi* and *Dabangg*, appear dissimilar. Yet, they have two important aspects in common. The first is that both of them deal with local milieus in which there is either faint evidence of the global ('Mumbai' dancing in *Rab Ne Bana Di Jodi*) or none at all, as in *Dabangg*, in which the local rules itself, however imperfectly. In contrast to the village in Hindi cinema—as in the oft-cited *Mother India*—which represented the Nation-as-Community, the small town in *Dabangg* is within a larger Nation (signified by politicians like Dayal Babu and the senior police officials) to which it is increasingly impervious.[28] This suggests the erecting of a wall against the national as well—and not only against the global—a barrier of which there was little evidence in the earlier cinema, which embraced the Nation more wholeheartedly. The second aspect common to both films is their foregrounding of the notion of loyalty since the first causes in both films invoke it. As already indicated, the first cause in *Rab Ne Bana Di Jodi* is the dying teacher requesting his student to marry his daughter and the daughter's steadfast loyalty to her husband is due to his having acceded to this dying plea. The preamble of *Dabangg*, in which the first cause resides, invokes the notion of loyalty but in a more convoluted way. The film begins with the mother portrayed as an object of love and loyalty to the boy, Chulbul, and the stepfather being resisted. The stepfather is not blamed but neither is he made an object of sympathy. While the mother may not allegorize the Nation as in films in which she is portrayed as sacred, I propose that we are still induced to read her presence in the context of past representations—as an embodiment of tradition if not the Nation. Chulbul refuses her demand that he show deep respect for his stepfather but, immediately afterwards, the adult Chulbul is seen in uniform. A connection may, therefore, be surmised between Chulbul not acknowledging his stepfather as parental authority and his wearing his uniform proudly, and so, state authority is perhaps placed in the position of surrogate father. When the stepfather addresses Chulbul as 'Pandeyji' at the conclusion, he is perhaps acknowledging its acceptability. It should be noted here that there are precedents for the allegorizing of mother and father as Nation and state, respectively, in Hindi cinema and the film is only following the footsteps of films like Awaara.[29] It can also be argued that since Chulbul's biological father is neither named nor his caste status hinted at, his mother's remarriage—unusual in itself—is only a ruse to provide Chulbul with a Brahmin stepfather.

Since the uniform is deemed worthy of respect, a question that may engage the reader is how an 'exemplary' policeman in a Hindi film may be shown to stash away illicit money obtained from a robbery for appropriate private use, to use the power given to him by his position to personal ends but still transmit the message to the audience that state authority is to be respected. To understand this, we must begin by recognizing that the action in popular cinema takes place in an exalted, heroic plane like that in the epics, which have been described by Vijay Mishra as precursor texts, the founders of Indian discursivity and the minimal starting point for a systematic analysis of Indian cinema.[30] In Dabangg, apart from the action sequences, there are a number of elements which can be described as 'heroic' and an instance is Rajo's drunkard father killing himself because his daughter will not marry as long as he lives as he has to be cared for. Indian popular cinema is not mimetic but is part of a tradition of performance, literature, and art in which the artefact is not subordinate to external reality but truer and greater.[31] Phrased differently, popular cinema has not attempted to show the milieu as it is but, rather, as it 'should be'. This being the case, the question is how the imperfect milieu as portrayed in *Dabangg* can be accounted for, and it may be useful here to compare the film to *Kaminey*, which also portrays an 'imperfect milieu'. The difference is that while the 'imperfections' in *Dabangg* are accepted as the conditions under which dharma should still be fulfilled, those in *Kaminey* are celebrated as conducive to the pursuit of *artha*. This suggests that neither film envisages that the milieu might be reformed—or even as in need of reformation.[32] The morally impeccable protagonist of the earlier Hindi cinema and the 'corrupt' Chulbul Pandey are perhaps both fulfilling their respective dharmas equally, but with the latter conducting himself only as would befit an upright person the kind of milieu he inhabits. Both *Kaminey* and *Dabangg*, in portratying their milieus, are not being 'mimetic' because that has not been the way of Hindi cinema. They, rather, install their seemingly imperfect milieus as ideals—not social ideals but 'ideal' conditions for the pursuit of dharma or artha.

Rab Ne Bana Di Jodi and *Dabangg* have been described as 'resisting the Anglophone Nation' in the title of this chapter and this 'resistance' is offered by them partly through envisaging the 'local' as independent and partly by eschewing aspiration—which is synonymous with artha—and upholding traditional dharma. Both these films also introduce 'loyalty' as a key notion as most of the other films in this book do not. In *Raajneeti*, in which loyalty is a virtue, it is exhibited by Sooraj (Ajay Devgn) towards Veerendra Pratap (Manoj Bajpai), neither of whom the film is in sympathy with. An association is now being made here between loyalty and dharma and since loyalty has already been associated with the imagined Nation, one might conclude that the invoking of dharma—even when it is not named as such—in Hindi cinema can be related to the Nation, if there was not another possibility.

The strengthening of the local in *Dabangg* is a development without precedent in mainstream Hindi cinema especially because we have understood Hindi cinema as a national cinema. This book is dedicated to a new development after 2000 which is the arrival of the Anglophone Indian nation—with global associations—but it is inevitable that this will be resisted, and *Dabangg* points in that direction. If, at first glance, Chulbul Pandey in *Dabangg* seems a return to old values in Hindi cinema in which the state was deeply respected, a closer scrutiny has revealed that Chulbul Pandey, although in uniform, gets his authority from local traditional structures and administers according to hierarchical imperatives which are older than the independent Indian nation state. Anglophone cinema, in films from *Lage Raho Munna Bhai* to *Kaminey*, pointed to a weakening of the state and taking advantage of this for personal advancement is even lauded in *Guru*. In films like *Dabangg*, we see the flip side of this development, which is, the strengthening of local authority to a position of dominance. When dharma reappears as a value in Hindi cinema, it is perhaps only a response to the privileging of 'aspiration' in Anglophone India. While 'enterprise' is the mantra of the ascendant urban classes, it is simplistic to assert that all will be swept away before it because 'traditional India' with its hierarchies and caste affiliations is still very much alive, if *Dabangg* is any indication. But the attendant fact is that the dharmic codes as publicly perceived— since they have little bearing on legality—may not be as progressive as one would like. The proposition here is that dominant local authority in the villages and small towns also take advantage of the weakening state as urban Indians involved in enterprise might but in a different way. If illegality has become part of 'enterprise' to the Anglophone Indian, caste dharma and hierarchical imperatives may have become part of 'justice' in rural and semi-urban India.[33] The uniform Chulbul Pandey wears was taken to represent state authority but it has become more identifiable with the authority unwittingly ceded by the weak state to local structures of traditional power.

It must be noted here that when India is compared to other societies of the south, the most striking thing often observed is the depth that the modern idea of the state and its institutional practices have gained in the political imagination of ordinary Indian people.[34] The gaining of authority by local structures of power indicated by *Dabangg* must therefore be regarded in this light.

Notes

1. Although India makes the largest number of films, records are hardly available for most films. Unlike Hollywood, Bombay's film industry was not dominated by a handful of autocratic moguls. The Film Inquiry Commission Report of 1951 noted that unlike the concentration of production in the hands of a few concerns in Hollywood, Indian cinema was distinguished by a plethora of producers, averaging one to two films per producer. See M. Madhava Prasad, *Ideology of the Hindi Film: A Historical Construction* (New Delhi: Oxford University Press, 1999), p. 34.

2. *Vivah* had a higher adjusted gross than films which are much better known, like *Munnabhai MBBS* (2003), *Dhoom* (2004), and an adjusted gross comparable to *KANK* (2006) and *Guru* (2007). See Box Office Results, 'Top Grosses by Decades and Years—2000s', http://ibosnetwork.com/asp/topgrossersbyyear.asp?year=200 (accessed on 30 March 2014).

3. It did seem in the Hindi cinema of the 1950s—especially those of Guru Dutt like *Aar Paar* (1954)—that Bombay was a happy community in some sense. Ravi S. Vasudevan gives us an account of the street scene in the films of the 1950s which suggests this. See Ravi S. Vasudevan, 'Shifting Codes, Dissolving Identities: The Hindi Social Film of the 1950s as Popular Culture', in Ravi S. Vasudevan (ed.), *Making Meaning in Indian Cinema* (New Delhi: Oxford University Press, 2000), p. 115. It is now impossible to imagine any of the metropolises as a 'community' in the same sense.

4. The term 'leader' is actually not appropriate for Om Makhija in *Om Shanti Om* because a leader aims at a common purpose while Om Makhija seeks only to advance himself. Pappu Master (Shreyas Talpade) plays second fiddle to the protagonist—as the vidhushaka does in traditional theatre—but without a comic side, which is also provided by Om (Shahrukh Khan). Pappu Master seems only to participate vicariously in Om's efforts and successes, perhaps, to universalize the notion of aspiration. In *Rab Ne Bana Di Jodi*, Bobby Khosla hardly 'looks up' to Surinder.

5. *Rab Ne Bana Di Jodi* also bears comparison with Jerry Lewis' *The Nutty Professor*, which is also about a diffident man (a chemistry professor) who becomes the smooth, handsome skirt-chaser Buddy Love after consuming a potion. In that film, the two personae are placed in

opposition to each other. At the climax, the instability of Buddy Love is made publicly evident—his persona breaks down when he is onstage. In *Rab Ne Bana Di Jodi* the two personae reinforce each other and Taani chooses a 'hybrid' bearing Surinder's name.

6. The most famous nationalist film of the 'anti-Western' era was Manoj Kumar's *Purab Aur Paschim* (1970). Indian cinema moved considerably from this anti-Western position to a eulogy of NRIs after the economic liberalization of 1991–2 which continued into the new millennium. For an examination of the shift, see P. Mankekar, 'Brides Who Travel: Gender, Transnationalism and Nationalism in Hindi Film', *Positions: Asia Critique*, vol. 7, no. 3, Winter 1999, pp. 731–62.

7. For instance, see McKim Marriott, 'Caste Ranking and Food Transactions: A Matrix Analysis', in Milton B. Singer and Bernard S. Cohn (eds), *Structure and Change in Indian Society* (New Jersey: Transaction Publishers, 1968), p. 134.

8. See M.K. Raghavendra, *Seduced by the Familiar: Narration and Meaning in Indian Popular Cinema* (New Delhi: Oxford University Press, 2008), pp. 37, 61.

9. Ibid., pp. 44, 48.

10. This takes the form of a fleeting flashback before the hero scores the winning runs off the last ball. The implication is that victory owes to inspiration taken from a parent.

11. Raghavendra *Seduced by the Familiar*, pp. 33–8.

12. In the older cinema, the parent or friend who is not exemplary is the one who has abandoned tradition. Wealth, at least before 1991–2, often proves a moral obstacle. For instance, the male protagonist's rich parents in Raj Kapoor's *Bobby* (1973) not performing their duties as parents conscientiously. In *Maine Pyar Kiya* (1989), the friend who grows rich (the male protagonist's father) similarly moves away from loyalty to his poorer friend (the heroine's father) who helped him when he was in need. An explanation for this discourse in the older cinema is that wealth is seen to distract a person from her/his dharma. Tradition dictates that artha be subordinated to dharma, that is, one must not allow material desires to overpower one's commitment to social obligations. See Louis Dumont, *Homo Hierarchicus: The Caste System and Its Implications* (New Delhi: Oxford University Press, 1998), p. 196.

13. A study of the occupation of woman characters in Tamil language cinema in the new millennium suggests this because the same arguments would apply to Hindi cinema. See Joyojeet Pal, 'Between Goddesses, Vamps and Software Engineers: Women and Jobs in Tamil Cinema in an Era of Economic Liberalization', *Phalanx: A Quarterly Review for Continuing Debate*, July 2011, http://www.phalanx.in/pages/article_i006_Between_Goddesses_Vamps_Software_Engineers.html (accessed on 14 November 2012).

14. It may also be fruitful to compare this respectful attitude towards a teacher with the irreverence of Rancho's towards ViruS in *3 Idiots*.

15. A turn in the narrative occurs with Chulbul, being the older brother, wanting to marry before Makkhi does. He is due to marry Rajo while Makkhi is to marry Nirmala. Since Chulbul's money has been appropriated by Makkhi, he proceeds to the latter's wedding ceremony and asks his prospective father-in-law to attend to his marriage first. Since there is no elder relative to bless Chulbul, he places his own palm over his head and blesses himself. This enrages the old man and Makkhi's wedding is stopped after Chulbul's is over. This capriciousness could also be Chulbul's rather than that of the story and may be demonstrating (with approval) the capriciousness of someone who wields power and authority.

16. Raghavendra, *Seduced by the Familiar*, p. 182. The proposition of the meaning being 'relayed' in Hindi cinema is M. Madhava Prasad's. See Prasad, *Ideology of the Hindi Film*, pp. 50–1.

17. Makkhi's culpability in the assassination of the honourable Dayal Babu is not examined and it is as though this was a matter for the brothers to resolve among themselves.

18. For instance, see Vasudevan, 'Shifting Codes, Dissolving Identities', p. 110.

19. Three mothers most often cited by theorists are those from *Awaara* (1951), *Mother India* (1957), and *Deewaar* (1975). All of the three mothers suffer great hardship in order to bring up their children.

20. Partha Chatterjee acknowledges a theoretical problem in the nation as an imagined community: 'If the nation is an imagined community and if nations must also take the form of states, then our theoretical language must allow us to talk of community and state at the same time. I do not think our present theoretical language allows us to do

this today.' Partha Chatterjee, *The Nation and Its Fragments: Colonial and Post-colonial Histories* (New Delhi: Oxford University Press, 1997), p. 11. My own enquiry is not as concerned with the Nation being an imagined community or not as much as with Hindi cinema having represented it as such.

21. For example, films such as *Qayamat Se Qayamat Tak* (1988) and *Batwara* (1988) deal with the Kshatriya caste. For its significance, see Raghavendra, *Seduced by the Familiar*, pp. 224–7.

22. Both Chulbul and Makkhi contract marriages with women whose caste backgrounds are not specified although Rajo could belong to the potter caste. But Nirmala's father is called 'Masterji' implying a teacher. Rajo's father is a drunkard but he wears spectacles hinting at education. Her brother is also well-educated. One can sense an implication that the women are also from Brahmin families since being educated or/and being teachers is traditionally associated with the priestly caste.

23. *Batwara* and another film by J.P. Dutta *Ghulami* (1985) were read as anti-Thakur although Dutta himself, apparently, belongs to the same caste. *Ghulami* created a furore in Rajasthan where it was set. See Lalitha Gopalan, *Cinema of Interruptions: Action Genres in Contemporary Indian Cinema* (New Delhi: Oxford University Press, 2002), pp. 75, 82.

24. Rajan Krishnan and M.S.S. Pandiyan, 'The Brahmin and the Citizen: Shankar's *Anniyan*', *Economic and Political Weekly*, vol. 41, nos 27–8, 8–15 July 2006, pp. 3055–60.

25. In dealing with caste, jati can be described as a local level representative of the *varna* model. Since there is a proliferation of local jatis and some confusion over which jati represents what varna (that is, whether Brahmin, Kshatriya, Vaishya, or Shudra), one could also say that the jati is the local approximation of a universal 'ideal' which is the varna. Jati is determined by birth, while varna pertains to an abstract system specifying function. See Dumont, *Homo Hierarchicus*, pp. 72–4.

26. Dharma is perhaps a more durable notion in Hindi cinema than morality and ethics because it deals with one's conduct in traditional relationships. Dharma is defined as action conforming to the universal order and artha as action conforming to selfish interest. 'Universal order' involves hierarchy and, if anything, the relationships in *Dabangg* involve hierarchy through various institutions, official or unofficial, such as caste, the machinery of the state and official hierarchy, marriage networks, and

so on. See Dumont, *Homo Hierarchicus*, p. 259. Chulbul honours these relationships and, to all appearances, does not act selfishly.

27. Dharma has, in fact, more to do with the notion of genealogical purity than ethics as we understand them. See Vijay Mishra, *Bollywood Cinema: Temples of Desire* (London: Routledge, 2002), pp. 5–6.

28. Most of *Rab Ne Bana Di Jodi* is set in Amritsar but Taani comes from another town which is not named. Since she is alienated from that town after her father's death there is a deliberate move to make Amritsar an independent town with its own mores.

29. See Raghavendra, *Seduced by the Familiar*, pp. 120–2. In *Awaara*, the mother is less the Nation than 'Land as the Bread-provider' (an affiliate of the Nation like 'tradition' and the 'community'), while the father is portrayed as a judge, a standard way of allegorizing the state in the 1950s. A noted film theorist describes virtue and respectability as the mother's and father's domains, respectively. See Vasudevan, 'Shifting Codes, Dissolving Identities', p. 110.

30. Vijay Mishra, 'Towards a Theoretical Critique of Bombay Cinema', *Screen*, vol. 26, nos 3–4, 1985, pp. 133–46.

31. Raghavendra, *Seduced by the Familiar*, pp. 52–3.

32. *Rang De Basanti* was perhaps the first mainstream Hindi film to propose reforming the milieu. In the cinema termed 'reformist'—that of the 1930s and 1940s—the 'reform' that one witnesses are only changes of the heart. It is difficult even to recall a Hindi film from the earlier cinema in which someone cleanses the social milieu of criminals, as in vigilante or lawman films from the West. This may owe to dharma being a personal ethic with little bearing on public morality. For a broad enquiry into this last aspect, see Richard Lannoy, *The Speaking Tree: A Study of Indian Culture and Society* (London: Oxford University Press, 1971), pp. 295–340.

33. The rise of honour killings on the directives of *khap panchayats* in Haryana points to the increasing power of local authority. See 'Honour Killings Persist because Police and State Agencies Fail to Take Them Seriously', *The Times of India*, 28 November 2012, http://m.timesofindia. com/home/opinion/edit-page/Honour-killings-persist-because-police-and-state-agencies-fail-to-take-them-seriously/articleshow/17391934. cms (accessed on 7 December 2012).

34. Sudipta Kaviraj, *The Trajectories of the Indian State: Politics and Ideas* (Ranikhet: Permanent Black, 2010), p. 68.

14

Transactions

Friendships in *Dil Chahta Hai* (2001) and *Zindagi Na Milegi Dobara* (2011)

Interpreting Love and Friendship

Farhan Akhtar's *Dil Chahta Hai* is perhaps too early a film to represent the Anglophone cinema this book is about, but it prefigures it in an essential way. Moreover, comparing it to a later film from the same stable—produced by Farhan Akhtar and directed by Zoya Akhtar—which owes its motifs to *Dil Chahta Hai* could help us understand a basic transformation of Hindi cinema in the first decade of the new millennium. Both *Dil Chahta Hai* and *Zindagi Na Milegi Dobara* are about male bonding and belong to the same category as *Rang De Basanti* although without the political objectives of that film. Male friendships traditionally went under the term 'dosti', a sacred relationship[1] which can perhaps be described as 'surrogate brotherhood' and replaced the filial one as a basis of deep loyalty. For instance, *HAHK* (1994) is about marriage ties between two families necessitated by dosti.[2] This observation about dosti may be regarded alongside the interpretation given to 'loyalty' in the Introduction and will become pertinent in this chapter.

HAHK is also important in another way. The film came after the economic liberalization of 1991–2, that is, after the state decided to abandon its interventionist policies and, as already indicated, in the 'Introduction', this made Hindi cinema much simpler. The stories in the earlier Hindi cinema had been marked by profligacy, largely, because of the signifiers in the narrative corresponding to the state and deriving from various kinds of state action. One has only to imagine Raj Kapoor's *Awaara* (1951) with the protagonist's father *not being a judge* to understand how diminished the story would become without the state as a participant. With the withdrawal of the state from the public space, the signs representing it (chiefly the police and the legal system) also vacated film stories. The narrative profligacy of *Dabangg* in relation to *Rab Ne Bana Di Jodi* (films dealt with in Chapter 13) is evidence of the presence of the state—as a signified entity—making the former film hermeneutically richer. *HAHK* was perhaps a film that actually brought simplicity into Hindi cinema in the 1990s.[3] It allegorizes the Nation as a happy family gathering—with due representation given to the minorities and the marginalized classes—but the state is conspicuous by its absence in the narrative. This continues in Hindi cinema after 2000 and both films examined in this chapter have very little 'plot' to fall back on, being largely about friends 'having fun'.

Before going on to examine *Dil Chahta Hai*, a few observations should also be made about interpreting relationships in the Hindi film. It should be reiterated that a large number of Hindi films are labelled 'love stories' but love is not the subject matter; it is simply a closure strategy, when reciprocated and taken to fruition.[4] For 'love' to be interpretable, it should occur in conjunction with other factors, for instance, between people of different classes or religions, as in *Bobby* (1973) and *Bombay* (1995), respectively. While dealing with *Rab Ne Bana Di Jodi*, the modern wife regarding her loving husband as too dull, and striving for Mumbai-style sophistication, was interpreted by considering it along with the husband's employment in a government-run power company.

The second aspect about love is that it gains significance when the issue of loyalty is associated with it because, as observed in the Introduction, loyalty is towards a sacred relationship—that love itself is not regarded as being.[5] In *Rab Ne Bana Di Jodi*, loyalty is introduced through the male protagonist's professor who requests him to marry his daughter. Any relationship demanding loyalty implicates the Nation overtly or covertly, at least through affiliated notions like the community, the state, and tradition. In the film, *Race* (2008), for instance, two brothers attempt to kill each other and this is made possible by the story being set outside India, that is, in a space that tradition and the Nation have vacated. Male friendship, like heterosexual love, also gains significance only when loyalty is associated with it, and it develops to become dosti. This is a crucial factor to be considered while analysing the issue of male friendships in two films from the new millennium, *Dil Chahta Hai* and *Zindagi Na Milegi Dobara*.

Dil Chahta Hai

Farhan Akhtar's *Dil Chahta Hai* is focused on three friends—who were together in college—displaying different attitudes towards love. Akash (Aamir Khan) is flippant about romantic attachments and does not keep girlfriends for over two weeks. Sameer (Saif Ali Khan) is genial, well-meaning, and romantic but keeps falling in love much too readily. Siddharth (Akshaye Khanna) is a talented artist who develops a deep attachment for Tara (Dimple Kapadia) who is fifteen years older than himself, a divorced single woman, and also an alcoholic. *Dil Chahta Hai* begins with Siddharth rushing to hospital because Tara is dying of cirrhosis, and Sameer visiting him later. Akash does not come because of some acrimony in their past which they have not yet overcome. The story of their past relationship is then related in flashback.

Much of *Dil Chahta Hai* is given to the pranks played by Akash chiefly on his friends but also on other people. The most important prank is his conduct towards Shalini (Preity Zinta), whom he sees in a restaurant and pretends to 'woo'. Shalini's fiancé, Rohit, happens to be around and gives Akash a black eye. Another event is Akash engineering a break-up between Sameer and his overbearing girlfriend. Akash and Siddharth fall out when Akash makes slighting comments about Siddharth's relationship with Tara. Almost half of *Dil Chahta Hai* goes by in this way with Siddharth and Sameer's romantic attachments leading to no significant development and the film waiting for Akash's love story to get it moving. The friends spend their time with one another but their involvement remains inconsequential until 'loyalty' is made an issue. This appears to happen in two ways, although one of them eventually proves to be a false lead.

Firstly, Siddharth's commitment to Tara turns the film in a direction that Hindi cinema rarely takes—the motif of the 'adult' relationship. The relationship between the two is defined by the film as 'adult' since Siddharth, being an artist, paints Tara in the nude. Siddharth's mother and Akash do not understand this relationship which is founded on 'art appreciation' and Akash's response is to cast aspersions on its 'purity'. The film attempts to demarcate itself from mainstream films through this relationship and announces its difference but, by the end, this adds up to nothing. *Dil Chahta Hai* makes it appear that the relationship between Siddharth and Tara is crucial (by commencing with it) but, in actual effect, the motif has little impact upon the plot. Tara is disposed of and despite his 'maturity' Siddharth arrives at the same emotional intersection as the others—as a single man ripe for a conventional romance. But the question of why the film seeks to demarcate itself from the rest of Hindi cinema remains. The answer is perhaps that it had sighted a new audience—the Anglophone one—which had not yet become a determining factor in the success of Hindi films.

The notion of loyalty does not emerge successfully through Siddharth and Tara but more conventionally in the story of Akash and Shalini. Akash is packed off to Australia by his parents to manage the family business and he encounters Shalini once again on the aircraft. In Australia, the two meet again and Akash's emotions turn into love although he does not admit it even to himself. Shalini also falls in love but cannot marry him and this is when loyalty becomes the issue. Shalini's parents, it turns out, were killed in an accident and his father's partner brought her up like his own daughter. This partner's son is Rohit and Shalini must marry the possessive Rohit out of gratitude for what she has received from his parents.

Dil Chahta Hai, at this point, resorts to the same strategy as *HAHK* to resolve the crisis. In the latter film, the heroine is due to marry the elder brother of the man she loves because that is the family's decision. But the family has decided on this because it mistakenly believes that the girl would not object to marriage with the older brother—who would help take care of the baby—and reverses its decision when it realizes that her heart lies elsewhere: that is, she would object if she was given the chance. In *Dil Chahta Hai* too, Rohit's parents want Shalini to marry Rohit because they believe that is what she wants. When Shalini reveals that she loves Akash and not Rohit, they direct her to marry Akash.

The three protagonists from *Dil Chata Hai* prefigure those from the Anglophone Hindi film but there is nonetheless a key aspect that tethers them to the cinema of the 1990s—particularly *Diwale Dulhania Le Jayange* (1996)—and this is their ultimate respect for parental authority. Since there are no issues the film raises which are not associated with 'love', it is in love that obedience shows itself. Akash is from a wealthy business family and does not resist his father's instruction that he should manage the family business in Australia. His marital plans with Shalini have her adoptive parents' blessings and, since they belong to Akash's class, his own parents' consent may be presumed. As for the others, Siddharth has formed another attachment likely to get everyone's approval and Sameer has 'fallen in love' with the very girl whom his parents wanted him to marry. If this return to obedience places the film with the older Hindi cinema, a motif which is new in *Dil Chahta Hai* is the three-way friendship (rather than the two-way dosti). Since films like *3 Idiots*, *Zindagi Na Milegi Dobara*, and *Delhi Belly* (2011) exhibit it later we need to scrutinize it more closely.

The Three-way Friendship and the 'Transaction'

Dosti, as reiterated, is a relationship which sometimes replaces the filial one in Hindi film narrative. Dosti and parenthood, in the earlier Hindi cinema, represent the attachments of the past and tradition and also serve the same purpose that historical context serves in films from Hollywood[6] because they stretch back in time to before the commencement of the story. Since parenthood and dosti are the contextual foundations on which the story is laid, they help to secure the story[7] formally but also ethically, since right conduct is prescribed by tradition. But unlike dosti, the three-way friendship has no moral basis and it is often (as in 3 Idiots) contracted within the duration of the story. My own hypothesis is that 'three' is a structural ruse to give the central relationships a degree of stability, as the story cannot rely on genealogy and tradition for support. In all the films involving the three-way friendship—and Rang De Basanti, which uses its four-way counterpart—there is a loosening of the parental hold upon the story because of the weakening of tradition and genealogy and the ruse is necessitated. As already indicated, the weakening of tradition finds correspondence in Anglophone Indians breaking with the occupations handed down by their families—from the last years of the 1990s onwards—to take up employment in new economy businesses.

The difficulty with the strategy of the three-way friendship in Dil Chahta Hai is that while it may be useful as a structural device, it is not effective at the moral level and this is because the three friends do not 'transact' among themselves. The issue of 'loyalty' has been discussed but even when loyalty is not demanded by an entity (a person, a community, or an institution) from another, people need to 'transact' with each other in productive relationships. They may not yet constitute a community or exhibit loyalty but they must still 'transact'. The three friends in 3 Idiots, for instance, transact with each other when they imbibe education from ViruS and jointly prove him wrong. A 'transaction' is identifiable through the effort that a person makes towards another in a relationship, creates a debt to be repaid in some way; even antagonisms and love need to become 'transactions'. Revenge, for instance, is transactional. In *HAHK*, it is only through the incident in the engagement party— when the man saves the woman from embarrassment by letting her have the ceremonial shoe which both of them have been trying to capture—that love develops. 'Loyalty' is perhaps like a debt which can never be repaid because it is embedded in the essence of specific relationships. In *Dil Chahta Hai*, loyalty is expected to be exhibited by Shalini towards her adoptive parents until they exercise their authority in Akash's favour. Akash and Shalini also transact with each other (Akash helps her overcome her obligations) but the three-way friendship involves no 'transaction' since none of the friends owe to one another.

It would appear that Hindi cinema has been aware of the need for transactions and important relationships have proceeded only through them.[8] The significant aspect here is not the significance of the 'transaction' as such but the absence of the transactional in the male friendships in *Dil Chahta Hai*—and this is exceptional. The film was a flop everywhere except in Bombay[9] where it apparently made up. It connected exceptionally well with urban youth and diasporic audiences[10] who were more in tune with the changes wrought by globalization upon Indian society. The film is now widely regarded as a cult classic and *Zindagi Na Milegi Dobara* which derives directly from it also became a colossal success.[11] This suggests that the absence of the transactional in male friendships —although it violates traditional story construction—has been accepted by audiences because it finds correspondence in the social experience of the Anglophone class.

Zindagi Na Milegi Dobara

Zoya Akhtar's *Zindagi Na Milegi Dobara* commences with Kabir (Abhay Deol) proposing to Natasha (Kalki Koechlin). At their engagement party, Natasha learns that Kabir is planning a three-week bachelor road trip to Spain with his school friends, Imraan (Farhan Akhtar) and Arjun (Hrithik Roshan). Kabir explains that the three have a long-standing pact, and that during the road trip, each of them will have to pick an adventure sport, which all three will try together. Initially, Arjun is reluctant to take part in the trip due to his excessive attachment to his profession as a financial broker in London. It is later revealed that Arjun's ex-girlfriend left him for this reason. Imraan has an additional personal agenda on the trip, that is, to find his biological father Salman Habib (Naseeruddin Shah), an artist in Spain. The rest of the film is about the friends' adventures in Spain—their meeting with Laila (Katrina Kaif), their diving instructress who takes them deep-sea diving, the La Tomatina festival in Buñol, and skydiving near Seville. The three are also pranksters and this leads them to a night in jail until they are bailed out by Imraan's father. Imraan bonds briefly with his father who regrets abandoning him but nonetheless asserts that he was (and is) not prepared for a son. The film ends with the friends participating in the bull-run in Pamplona. Arjun and Laila have fallen in love and Arjun has decided to give up financial broking. Imraan, who is a copywriter, has decided to publish his poetry, while Kabir has decided not to marry the possessive Natasha, since his engagement was caused by a misunderstanding.

Zindagi Na Milegi Dobara is constructed as a road movie and is episodic but one is hard-pressed to discover much 'development' in the unfolding events. Yet, it is not as though the film does not try to introduce conflict in some ways. The earliest is the suggestion that Imraan once had an affair with Arjun's ex-girlfriend and this is brought up after an event that should have been momentous, but is not. Arjun has been attending to clients on his mobile phone and at one moment, quite casually, the irritated Imraan flings it out of the car. The way this is eventually sorted out is that Imraan buys Arjun a cheap mobile phone a little later to compensate. The observation here is that common experience tells us that a phone is crucial today, and more so, to a financial broker. What the information stored on a mobile phone can represent to a professional does not engage the film at all and the two men remain friends. In a milieu as fiercely competitive as today's such an act might destroy a career and generate fierce hatred but *Zindagi Na Milegi Dobara* sees 'lifestyle' as a strong enough binding element. The absence of the transactional is true of the other relationships as well: Arjun and Laila 'fall in love' as easily as Kabir dumps Natasha. Kabir and Natasha remain 'friends' without the terms of their 'friendship' being renegotiated through an appropriate transaction. This last observation is not a demand for 'realism' but simply a reminder of the conventions of the earlier cinema in which a tentative attachment is abandoned only when a new, 'truer' one is found because the story must be brought to full closure.[12]

Zindagi Na Milegi Dobara was made a decade after *Dil Chahta Hai* and many things have evidently changed for the Anglophone Indian. Where, in the earlier film, parental authority—although weak—is still to be respected, the protagonists of *Zindagi Na Milegi Dobara* are all self-made with parents hardly in sight. They are well employed enough to holiday in Europe with cost not being an issue.[13] If the film is among the very first in Hindi cinema to propose an equal friendship between adult professionals, like *Dil Chahta Hai* it proposes 'lifestyle' alone as the basis of stable homosocial attachments. Even if *Zindagi Na Milegi Dobara* is targeted at urban youth with heavy consumption-based lifestyles, this does not account for its avoidance of the issues of work and livelihood. When Hollywood films play up affluent lifestyles, like *The Firm* (1993), they also glamorize the kind of work which makes such lifestyles possible. But to appreciate where *Zindagi Na Milegi Dobara* stands we need to look at Hindi cinema's past and its treatment of work-related camaraderie.

While examining Hindi film convention closely, we find that even when it has dealt with the working class as in the 1970s or with farmers earlier, there has never been a sense of people brought together by work. Relationships revolve almost entirely around families and familial associations. The exceptions are few and fleeting and one can cite the students in *3 Idiots* and the brief relationship in *Deewaar* (1975) between Vijay and the Muslim dockyard coolie with the armband bearing number '786'. In *Mother India*, Radha and her children do not enter into relationships with the other farmers and neither does Bharat in *Upkar* (1967). Those brought together by work are either soldiers (as in *Border*, 1998) or policemen and in both cases the Nation or state brings them together and not work. In romances involving people in specific professions as in *Upkar* (between doctor and farmer) the discourse is that love of the Nation brings them together. Thus, regardless of the economic changes underway in the milieu, genealogy is the only reliable cementing force in Hindi film relationships. When the family weakens in the new millennium, as would appear from Anglophone cinema, work does not substitute it as a cementing factor in stable relationships, and the absence of 'transactions' within interpersonal dealings can perhaps be attributed to this factor.

Between *Dil Chahta Hai* and *Zindagi Na Milegi Dobara*, we see genealogy weakening in relationships—and 'lifestyle' bringing people together physically but not binding them. This is not only true of *Zindagi Na Milegi Dobara* but also of *Delhi Belly* (2011), which appeared at around the same time. As in *Zindagi Na Milegi Dobara* the protagonists of *Delhi Belly*, conceived as an irreverent comedy, are also ostensibly employed. Tashi (Imran Khan) is a news reporter, Nitin Beri (Kunal Roy Kapur) is a photographer, and Arup (Vir Das) is into advertising and the three share quarters in a ramshackle apartment. Their employment is, however, only intended as background information because the nature of their work plays no part in the drama which involves diamond smuggling. *Delhi Belly* does not play up the glamour as *Zindagi Na Milegi Dobara* does and the characters live squalid lives but their relationships have still more to do with how they live rather than what they do—lifestyle rather than livelihood.

Zindagi Na Milegi Dobara and *Delhi Belly* may belong to a consumerist society but so do the films from Hollywood and this is apparently not an adequate explanation for the trend they represent. A reason could be that the Indian films are targeted at a class of young people and students who have not yet begun to earn their livelihood and are not familiar with the issue of work. Since the prospect of work has not engaged them, they have not considered the basis of their relationships. Another reason could be that new economy businesses are increasingly given to eliminating the human interface, bypassing interpersonal 'transactions' at the everyday level. But whatever the reasons underlying the phenomenon, it points to the ephemeral nature of interpersonal relationships even within the same class and reflects upon the growing instability of a social order—although one cannot be certain.

There is another key difference between *Dil Chahta Hai* and *Zindagi Na Milegi Dobara*, which has not been discussed so far and this has to do with the spending power exhibited by the protagonists of the latter film in Spain and the touch of pride on the film's part in Indians being able to spend, even more than Europeans. Indians have been shown travelling abroad in the earlier cinema but rarely did one get a sense of the dealings involved. In the films of the 1990s, such as *Hero No. 1* (1997) and *DDLJ* (1995), and even *Dil Chahta Hai*, the protagonists are shown to be rich enough to travel abroad but in *Zindagi Na Milegi Dobara*, the protagonists are shown as entering classy hotels and surveying the rooms with the air of clients. In one town, the protagonists stay in a fully furnished villa—so large that it is almost a castle—equipped with a swimming pool and extensive grounds, overlooking the countryside. To drive home the point that cost is not a consideration, the friends bicker more than once on the car they should hire, the implication each time being that 'having fun' is the only consideration. The friends are also shown acquiring diving equipment and transacting with a pilot to go skydiving. At the same time, the film gives no indication that its protagonists are especially wealthy, unlike the one in *Hero No. 1* who was described as a millionaire. Kabir is from a builder's family and Arjun is a financial broker in London who may be expected to be well off but Imraan is a junior copywriter whose salary can only be modest. Still, it is Imraan who insists on hiring an antique car which is 'more fun'. After spending apparently huge amounts on their trip, two of the friends— Arjun and Imraan—abandon even the professions they have been pursuing as too demeaning, to 'follow the wishes of their heart'. The observation here is that the film not only shows ordinary Indians as having enormous spending power but also takes considerable pride in this. An explanation for this emphasis on Indian spending power is that by around 2005–6, Indian businessmen had started acquiring assets abroad in a big way and spending lavishly enough to get global attention, and this was duly celebrated by the English language press in India.[14]

Most Anglophone Indians are, of course, hardly as routinely wealthy as the film makes it appear and even the more affluent may have to be content with modest exhibitions of carefree living like the La Tomatina festival visited briefly by the film.[15] If this celebration of the spending power of the Anglophone Indian is motivated by the success of Indian enterprise, *Delhi Belly* goes a step further when it gloats over the ruthlessness of the Indian criminal in an elaborate ('comic') sequence in which the smuggler Somayajulu (Vijay Raaz) tortures a Russian gangster. This may be attributed to crime being admitted as a legitimate component of enterprise in the new millennium—evidenced in films like *Dhoom 2*—and the torture sequence is perhaps only an extension of Indian enterprise being celebrated by Anglophone cinema. 'Not only can we outspend Europeans in Europe but we can also out-brutalize the Russian mafia', is the apparent refrain of the two films together.

Unwelcome although this assertion may be, it will be difficult to deny that the cited aspects of *Zindagi Na Milegi Dobara* and the torture sequence in *Delhi Belly* are celebrations of nationhood, although the Nation celebrated is a far less inclusive one than that celebrated by *Mother India* and *Upkar*. At the same time, the weakening of the transactional in mainstream Hindi cinema suggests that the imagined Nation itself is weakening in the consciousness of the Anglophone Indian. Instead of the ethic of capitalism gradually replacing 'tradition'—that is, people being brought together by work rather than genealogy in film stories—we find interpersonal relationships becoming lost in consumerist fantasies.

But the important question here is whether a stable social order can be taken for granted when the generation addressed by the films comes into its own and rules India. Whatever the outcome, Hindi cinema appears to have a parallel in contemporary Nigerian popular cinema (Nollywood) in which one rarely gets the sense of a stable community or serious work ethic. Characters in contemporary Nigerian films seem not to belong to communities, they do not transact with each other—like those in *Zindagi Na Milegi Dobara* and *Delhi Belly*—and even personal loyalties appear non-existent.[16] Indian cinema was hugely popular in countries like Nigeria and Senegal because it was perceived to be 'non-Western' and upheld the same virtues important in African society, for example, the subordination of the individual to the welfare of the community, respect for elders, and so on,[17] but with Indian cinema itself being transformed, this could be changing.[18] The sense of nationhood is generally not to be found in African popular cinema[19] because creating a country does not ensure a Nation, which has to be imagined together by a sizable public—which will be assisted in the process if the state delivers the Nation to it through various services. Not surprisingly, most of the failed states of the world are in Africa. The contention here is that nearly 70 years after Independence, Indians cannot take their Nation as a given because, judging from *Delhi Belly* and *Zindagi Na Milegi Dobara*, the Anglophone public—which includes the segment wielding the greatest political power—is losing the capacity to imagine an inclusive one.[20] The reader should be reminded that this is only over two decades after the Indian state commenced on its path of 'withdrawal'.

Notes

1. See M. Madhava Prasad, *Ideology of the Hindi Film: A Historical Construction* (New Delhi: Oxford University Press, 1999), pp. 83–6.
2. The pertinent point is two friends once loved the same woman who, eventually, married one of them. Since the other man stepped aside for his friend's sake, their relationship is founded on loyalty to one another, which is why their families must be together through thick and thin and brought together once again through marriage. See M.K. Raghavendra,

Seduced by the Familiar: Narration and Meaning in Indian Popular Cinema (New Delhi: Oxford University Press, 2008), pp. 247–8.

3. Although widely welcomed, this new simplicity was also denounced at the time as a 'claustrophobic denial of narrative possibilities'. See Rustom Bharucha, 'Utopia in Bollywood: *Hum Aapke Hain Koun..!' Economic and Political Weekly*, vol. 30, no. 15, 15 April 1995, pp. 801.

4. Raghavendra, *Seduced by the Familiar*, pp. 36–9.

5. This is a difference between Bollywood and Hollywood: the nuclear family is sacred in Hollywood films where the staunchest kind of loyalty is demanded in marriages even when they are not stable. See Heather Gilmour, 'Different, Except in a Different Way: Marriage, Divorce and Gender in the Hollywood Comedy of Remarriage', *Journal of Film and Video*, vol. 50, no. 2, Summer 1998, pp. 26–39. In contrast, Bollywood traditionally demanded it for one's parents and for the joint family, or for the all-male 'dosti' which is best seen as surrogate brotherhood. A similarly binding relationship between women or sisters is not possible because when sisters marry, they are seen as belonging to different families.

6. For how time and history feature in Hindi cinema, see Raghavendra, *Seduced by the Familiar*, pp. 31–40.

7. Even in fantasy films like *The Lord of the Rings* trilogy (2001–3) where there is no historical context, there is a need to erect a whole fictional context in the form of the history of Middle Earth. Hindi films, in contrast, consistently used genealogy as the context in the earlier periods.

8. An exception may be another associated notion—'station'—in which two individuals are placed in a relationship in which one owes to the other. An illustration would be the obedience of a junior officer in the military to a senior one, as in *Haqeeqat* (1964). A relationship dictated by 'station' is different from one dictated by *dharmic* codes—which is also hierarchical—in that it is not as sacred. The issue of 'loyalty' is also not invoked with regard to relationships based on station since it is not a component of 'tradition'.

9. Derek Bose, *Brand Bollywood: A New Global Entertainment Order* (New Delhi: Sage, 2006), p. 26.

10. See Anne Tereska Cieko, 'Introduction', in Anne Tereska Cieko (ed.), *Contemporary Asian Cinema: Popular Culture in a Global Frame* (New York: Berg, 2006), pp. 2–3.

11. The film is listed as eighth among the top 20 net grossers of all time. The film had an adjusted gross of nearly Rs 90 crore which makes it as much of a hit as *Bunty Aur Babli* and nearly as big as *Rang De Basanti*. See http://ibosnetwork.com/asp/filmbodetails.asp?id=Zindagi+Na+Milegi+ Dobara and http://ibosnetwork.com/asp/topgrossersbyyear.asp?year=200 (accessed on 20 December 2012).

12. There is never any doubt in the character's mind with regard to which love is true (*Andaz*, 1949). The solution found in most 'dumpings' is either for the other woman to turn out evil or a seductress (*Imtihan*, 1974), or have her meet a tragic end (*Baazi*, 1951). In *Devdas* (1935), Chandramukhi loves Devdas but he loves only Parvati, and it is Devdas who dies. Another option is for the other woman to find the true love of her life in another person, although this course is rare.

13. To fully grasp this, one needs to compare the film to *Ek Tha Tiger* (2012) in which the state-employed protagonist's expense account is so limited that he uses only public transport when in Britain/Ireland. See M.K. Raghavendra, 'The Resurgence of Salman Khan', *Talk*, 3 October 2012, http://www.talkmag.in/cms/culture/movies/item/229-the-resurgence (accessed on 23 December 2012).

14. For instance, see Sucheta Dalal, 'Mittal versus Arcelor: The Hypocrisy Within', *The Indian Express*, 6 March 2006, http://expressindia. indianexpress.com/news/columnists/full_column.php?content_ id=89048 (accessed on 24 December 2012).

15. In this festival people fling ripe tomatoes at each other. After *Zindagi Na Milegi Dobara* appeared, there was a move to hold a similar festival in Bangalore, perhaps the most Anglophone of Indian cities, but it was promptly banned after several protests. See 'Karnataka Government Bans La Tomatina Festival', Zeenews: Showbiz, 16 September 2011, http://zeenews.india.com/entertainment/and-more/karnataka-govt-bans-la-tomatina-festival_96482.htm (accessed on 25 December 2012).

16. Evidence can be found in a typical Nollywood comedy, *Early Marriage* (2012), directed by Chika Onu, also found on YouTube. This film exhibits many of the characteristics of the films dealt with in this chapter. Relationships are conducted entirely through casual conversations about marriage and love; romances are perfunctorily terminated and formed without the new relationships being negotiated.

Portrayal of affluence is favoured and denoted through emblems—like the Mercedes—without attention to how such affluence was acquired. The film is set both in a village and in Lagos, and communities are noticeably absent in both places. See http://www.youtube.com/watch?v=qTumKX1OLw8 (accessed on 26 December 2012).

17. Gwenda Vander Steene, 'Bollywood Films and African Audiences', in Anjali Gera Roy and Chua Beng Huat (eds), *Travels of Bollywood Cinema: From Bombay to LA* (New Delhi: Oxford University Press, 2012), pp. 303–6.

18. It is being suggested that love for Bollywood in Africa is declining because Indian directors are targeting the wealthy Indian diaspora. See Sylviane A. Doiuf, 'Bollywood and Africa: A Love Story', New York Public Library, Blogs, 6 December 2011, http://www.nypl.org/blog/2011/12/06/bollywood-and-africa-love-story (accessed on 20 January 2013).

19. The earliest African cinema was not popular but politically 'post-colonial' and intended to create an indigenous culture after the colonial past. For example, films by Senegal's Ousmane Sembène, such as *Xala* (1975), often satirized the new ruling class. Nollywood is popular cinema which has no political or cultural agenda.

20. A nation which takes pride in the capacity of a few of its citizens to outspend Europeans or a handful of its criminals to out-torture the Russian mafia cannot be an inclusive one.

15

The Sporting Nation after *Lagaan*

Iqbal (2005), *Chak De India* (2007), and
Paan Singh Tomar (2012)

Lagaan (2001) and Sports Nationalism

Ashutosh Gowariker's *Lagaan* (2001) was not the first Hindi film to
deal with sports but it was perhaps the first to make a connection in
cinema between sports and Indian nationalism—a connection which
has since become commonplace. Before *Lagaan*, Prakash Jha's *Hip
Hip Hurray* (1984) dealt with college football and Mansoor Khan's
Jo Jeeta Wohi Sikandar (1992) also dealt with a college-level sport,
bicycle racing. An obsessive association between cricket and the
Nation was perhaps made only in the 1990s, with not even India's
Prudential Cup triumph of 1983[1] in Britain leading immediately
to it, although cricket was perhaps more popular than hockey, the
national game. Cricket's growing popularity in the 1990s has been
attributed to the growth of private television channels.[2] But the
1990s also marks the period when new economy businesses started
growing and Anglophone Indians began to become economically
important and an association can be tentatively made between

cricket nationalism and Anglophone India. Another factor is that unlike football and hockey, cricket was a predominantly middle-class game in India after Independence.[3] Although Anglophone India has now expanded beyond the domain of the traditional middle-class, there is still evidence to suggest that stadium spectatorship in cricket is primarily the domain of the Anglophone classes. While cricket fever has spread far outside the metropolises, its associations remain largely Anglophone and this is suggested by the products endorsed by cricketers.[4] Other indicators are the gradual disappearance of slogans in languages other than English among those displayed at cricket matches[5] as well as the proficiency in English quickly acquired by cricketing stars who initially appear ill at ease with the language.

Before moving on to *Lagaan*, it will help to reiterate the argument (made in the Introduction) that the economic liberalization of 1991–2 gave rise to a streak of nationalism in Hindi cinema of which the most important film is *Border* (1998). As already observed, the end of Nehruvian socialism depleted Hindi cinema's subject matter: the conflict in the narrative—instead of being within the Nation—was pushed to its boundaries, that is, towards patriotism/nationalism. When the boundary is in space, the adversary is Pakistan and when it is in time, the adversaries are the British. The sports nationalism of *Lagaan* may have extended the anti-Pakistan militarism of *Border* but there is also evidence that the audience which responded to *Lagaan* was not quite the same as the one that responded to the anti-Pakistan nationalism of *Gadar: Ek Prem Katha* (2001), which came out along with *Lagaan*. Gowariker's film was a hit in the metropolises, while *Gadar* did well even in the B and C centres.[6] Moreover, *Lagaan* was positioned as a global artefact and carefully marketed in the run up to the Oscars—which is an Anglophone fetish in India—and its collections abroad were substantially higher than those of *Gadar*[7] although, overall, *Gadar* collected over three times as much as *Lagaan*.

Apart from its marketing side, *Lagaan* used many of the narrative devices of Hollywood till then foreign to Hindi cinema. To mention a few, the story had a definite duration (three months) denoted through a deadline,[8] point of view was employed although still fleetingly, and the film began with a voice over by Amitabh Bachchan recalling Satyajit Ray's *Shatranj Ke Khiladi* (1977). Ray has been, internationally, the most respected of India's film-makers and this is significant. Most importantly, *Lagaan*'s narrative—for much of the film—is structured as a chain of causes and effects in the manner of classical Hollywood cinema. All these factors certainly helped the film earn itself a nomination for the Best Foreign Film Oscar. But if the film was positioned as a global artefact, it still remained a vehicle for nationalism.

It has been convincingly argued that rather than being an exemplar of globalization, sports is actually a means of resisting the culturally global and articulating difference.[9] If this is conceded, it can be proposed that the classes most affected by globalization are likely to be more receptive to sports nationalism in India. Judging from the relative successes of *Lagaan* and *Gadar* in the same year, non-Anglophone India is perhaps more receptive to the anti-Pakistan variety of militant nationalism, while sports (cricket) nationalism seems, generally, to belong more securely to the territory of the Anglophone Indian. This is a broad hypothesis and has been made to facilitate the examination of three films about the sporting nation. The first film chosen is Nagesh Kukunoor's *Iqbal* (2005), which is also about cricket, although it is different from *Lagaan*.

Iqbal

Iqbal tells the story of Iqbal (Shreyas Talpade), a deaf and mute boy, who dreams of playing cricket for India. He is discouraged by his father who thinks that Iqbal's dreams are unproductive. Instead, he wants Iqbal to help him tend to the crops and become a farmer like him, which is a more reliable profession. The film begins with Iqbal's pregnant mother watching cricket on television with other villagers and the period is apparently around the time of the Prudential Cup triumph. Kapil Dev, India's captain then, is her hero and he becomes Iqbal's idol as well.

Iqbal is not a blatantly nationalistic film and anticipates Mani Rathnam's *Guru* (2007) rather than follow *Lagaan*, though *Guru* is not about cricket but business. It celebrates Iqbal's talent at cricket because the boy teaches himself pace bowling on a field all by himself. But unlike Gurukanth Desai in *Guru*, he does not 'aspire', and his younger sister Khadija (Shweta Prasad) helps him by speaking about his cricketing prowess to Guruji (Girish Karnad), a former cricketer, who runs a cricket academy. Cricket academies are usually located in the cities but this one is uncharacteristically located in a rustic area close to where Iqbal lives. Guruji is sceptical until he sees Iqbal bowling and accepts him as a pupil. Iqbal does well but comes into conflict with the mean-spirited Kamal, the star batsman at the academy, and after an insulting altercation, bowls Kamal a bouncer and knocks him down. Kamal's father is a local rich man and Iqbal is expelled from the academy.

Iqbal makes several narrative choices which need to be examined. The first one is to make its protagonist a rustic and a second is to make him Muslim. At a point in the film, someone explains to Iqbal's father (who is not a cricket lover) that cricket brings Indians together and there is perhaps a clue in this. Since cricket is largely a game associated with urban India, the film makes Iqbal's father a farmer. Secondly, the cricketing loyalty of Muslims in India is an issue constantly brought up because it is alleged frequently that they cheer for Pakistan at cricket games.[10] The primary purpose of the film, therefore, appears to be to use cricket as a way of defining an inclusive nation. Its secondary purpose will become clearer in due course.

In Iqbal's village wanders a drunkard named Mohitji (Naseeruddin Shah), once a great cricketer who did not live up to his potential. Iqbal approaches him to mentor him. Mohitji declines initially but, on seeing Iqbal's potential, helps him out and gradually also gets over his dependence on drink. Iqbal's father is against this but the boy trains secretly and improves. Mohitji tries to get Iqbal into a Ranji Trophy (played between Indian states) team and is eventually able to get him into the lowly ranked Andhra team. Iqbal's efforts see the Andhra team climbing in the rankings and Iqbal gets noticed by the media and the selectors. But it is at this time that the truth about Guruji's machinations emerges. Mohit was once Guruji's favourite pupil but Guruji destroyed Mohit's chances when it suited him. In the final of the Ranji Trophy, Iqbal is pitted against Kamal and Guruji tries to bribe him with Rs 25 lakh to perform badly so that Kamal is selected for the national team. If Iqbal refuses, Guruji threatens to ensure that he will never play for the national team. Iqbal's father needs the money badly to bail him out of his financial mess and extricate his lands from the clutches of the bank where they are mortgaged. Iqbal is tempted but, at the last moment, an agent offers him a better deal; Iqbal gets Kamal's wicket and Andhra win the finals for the first time. The film ends with Iqbal donning the national colours—blue—bowling his first over in an international cricket game.

It is in the second part of *Iqbal* that its similarity to *Guru* becomes clearer. Guruji in the film is the entrenched power—like Arzaan Contractor in *Guru*—who favours the influential and powerful. Mohit is himself apparently part of the landed aristocracy because he lives in a dilapidated mansion in which the furniture is covered by cobwebs. But the more important allusion is that cricket was once the terrain of the feudal aristocracy[11] and run on feudal lines by people like Guruji. The 'agent' who assists Iqbal get lucrative contracts (and pays him Rs 50 lakh) is therefore a representative of Indian global enterprise, which represents a level playing field in which ability and talent are the only qualities respected. Iqbal donning the Indian colors at the conclusion of the film has virtually the same connotations as Gurukanth Desai vowing to build a global industrial giant in *Guru*.

The sense of the Nation being once pulled down by traditional structures is not a new one and the film shows the same faith in global enterprise paving the way for a strong India like several other films, such as *Bunty Aur Babli*, *Guru*, and even *3 Idiots*, in which Rancho has a large number of industrial patents to his credit. A factor of importance in the film is the absence of information about

Iqbal's father's financial condition and how it came about. The family has been living well and there is an unexplained deterioration in the man's fortunes. When Iqbal bails him out later—out of his bonus from the agent—there is a suggestion that the farmers' lot has no traditional remedy and that their problems need amelioration through sources outside the traditional. The father's resistance to Iqbal playing cricket may therefore allegorize traditional India's resistance to the non-traditional, that is, to globalization.[12] If cricket allegorizes global enterprise, then the latter could be the agent to rescue traditional India from its financial quagmire, is perhaps the covert implication.

At this point it may be interesting to examine why Iqbal is made deaf and mute in the film because this disability plays no part in the film's plot. My own sense of it is that he had to be given a handicap but one which would not prevent him from playing international cricket for India and earning the huge sums of money required to be invoked to make sport-as-global-activity attractive. At the same time, giving him no handicap at all would have necessarily made him 'aspire', that is, he would be thought to have been attracted by the lure of cricket as enterprise (as most young men playing cricket are) for the film to successfully invoke the Nation.

An observation which needs to be made here is that while 'enterprise' may have seen India dominating world cricket financially (that is, BCCI, dominating the International Cricket Council [ICC]), it has been noted in the international media that Indian teams have not often seen themselves on the winning side[13] despite the earnings of Indian cricket being, by far, the largest in the world. If Indian cricket has done well because of its domestic appeal and not because of its international performances in tournaments/games—given *Iqbal*'s allegorical aspect—this is tantamount to Indian enterprise pretending to be globally competitive but taking shelter in its local moorings. The next film to be examined, Shimit Amin's *Chak De India* (2007), may shed more light on this.

Chak De India

Chak De India is about hockey but its protagonist is a Muslim and the film explicitly invokes the issue of the 'loyalty' of Muslims that *Iqbal* is only implicit about. The film begins with India's captain, Kabir Khan (Shahrukh Khan), in the finals of the World Cup when he is unable to convert a penalty stroke into a goal and Pakistan wins. A journalist spots Kabir Khan shaking hands with a Pakistan player after the match and the media instantly alleges that Kabir Khan 'played for Pakistan'. He is also hounded out of his ancestral home by irate hockey fans and dubbed a traitor. Kabir Khan quits hockey for seven years and is virtually a forgotten man when he reappears.

Mr Tripathi (Anjan Srivastav), the head of India's Hockey Association, meets with Kabir Khan's friend and hockey advocate Uttamaji, to discuss the Indian women's hockey team. Tripathi argues the team has no future but Uttamaji is of the view that Kabir Khan wants to coach the team. Though initially sceptical, Tripathi ultimately agrees to this arrangement. Khan thus finds himself in charge of a group of sixteen young women from various sections of India who are divided by their own individual prejudices. While Komal Chautala from Haryana conflicts with Preeti Sabarwal from Chandigarh, Balbir Kaur from Punjab has a short temper and bullies Rani Dispotta and Soimoi Kerketa, belonging to remote villages in Jharkhand. Mary Ralte from Mizoram and Molly Zimik from Manipur are both treated as 'foreigners' because they are racially more Mongoloid. The team's captain, Vidya Sharma, is asked to choose between hockey and the wishes of her husband's family, while Preeti's boyfriend, Abimanyu Singh, vice-captain of the Indian cricket team, is threatened by her involvement in the team.

The film is able to catch the squabbling between the women convincingly and their antagonism to Kabir Khan's demands for hard training quickly surfaces. The mischief maker is the most experienced player Bindiya Naik, who resents the fact that Vidya has been made captain. Kabir cannot manage her machinations and their relationship reaches its nadir when Bindiya makes defiantly sexual overtures. Left with no other option, Kabir Khan resigns his position but, on the last day, at lunch in a restaurant, the girls are harassed by male onlookers and there is a brawl in which the girls come up trumps. That this is their first demonstration of 'teamwork' is Kabir Khan's expressed comment; the girls understand their need for him and he rejoins. Their newly found unity is, however, challenged by Mr Tripathi who suddenly decides that the women's team will not go to Australia for the World Championship. Kabir Khan, however, forces him to agree to a challenge match with the men's team on the condition that if the girls win, they will be allowed to go to Australia. The girls lose the match but their courageous performance is praised by the men's team and this forces Tripathi to change his mind and send them to Down Under.

There is only one way in which the film can go from here—which is the team working its way to victory in Australia, and this takes up a large part of the remainder. The film draws from *Lagaan* in the sense that we watch the tournament/games as we would a spectator sport and the intricacies of the story are virtually abandoned. The only fiction revolves around how the hostile Bindiya Naik is finally made a team player. Since this last part of the film involving the tournament is so like watching an actual spectator sport, it may be more useful to discuss why women's hockey should engage the film. The Indian women's hockey team won the gold in the Commonwealth Games of 2002 but the best they have done in a world tournament is to achieve the fourth rank in 1974. The film is about women's hockey but it deliberately makes men's cricket look bad when Abhimanyu Singh casts aspersions on hockey as a game and displays arrogance. He is also served right when Preeti rejects him in full public view at the conclusion of the film. This furnishes us with a clue as to the film's inspiration: if we look back at the men's Cricket World Cup of 2007 (the year of the film's making) we find that India and Pakistan, the favourites, did not even make it to the 'Super Eight', while Bangladesh and Ireland, among the lowest ranked cricketing nations did so. This imparts new meaning to the Indo-Pakistan rivalry that

Chak De India begins with and the films discourse can now be read as the need for India to become competitive at the global level without countering only Pakistan. Sports nationalism has, therefore, a slightly different significance in *Chak De India* from that in *Iqbal*.

Another factor of importance in the film is its decrying of the Hockey Federation, a government body. This decrying of state institutions is not in evidence in *Iqbal* but parallels the sentiments expressed in films like *Rang De Basanti* (2006), *Traffic Signal* (2007), and *Kaminey* (2009) in which government servants are acting for personal gain. Apart from Mr Tripathi being presented as a typically cynical government official, the film is scornful of government incentives like flats for sportspersons, the insinuation being that they are counterproductive. This should be seen alongside the view of the signing bonus of Rs 50 lakh that Iqbal gets which is looked at as a true indication of sporting merit. *Iqbal* and *Chak De India* were made by different film-makers but they can be regarded as the utterances by the same public—to which rewarding by the market is apparently of greater value than recognition by the Indian state.

Paan Singh Tomar

If *Iqbal* and *Chak De India* are made to be inspirational and therefore employ a rose-tinted visual aesthetic, Tigmanshu Dhulia's *Paan Singh Tomar*, the biopic of an actual athlete-turned-dacoit, tries for a much more grimy appeal. Paan Singh Tomar was a soldier in the army who held the national record in the steeplechase for over a decade. Subedar Tomar hailed from the Chambal valley and when his conflict with a relative could not be resolved and he found the police more sympathetic to his foe, he (like many others) turned dacoit and began to rob and kidnap for ransom in the Chambal belt. After he had brutally gunned down nine people of a village for being police informers, the law turned on him with a vengeance and Tomar was killed in an encounter in 1981.

The film more or less sticks to this story except that it is caught between being authentic and taking sides with its protagonist. In the film, Paan Singh (Irrfan Khan) becomes an athlete because athletes in the military are entitled to better rations. After being unsuccessful in the Tokyo Asian Games because he wears spiked shoes to which he is not accustomed (he takes his shoes off in the middle of the race, runs barefoot but still accredits himself honourably), he attains the highpoint of his career by winning the steeplechase in an international military athletic meet. After his retirement from the army, Paan Singh is offered the job of a coach but back home his cousin has usurped his land and the law is unsympathetic. The collector asks those involved to 'resolve their disputes amicably' but ignores Tomar's plea to confiscate his adversary's licenced guns. When the police inspector is similarly unhelpful—despite evidence of Paan Singh's doings as a national athlete and hero—and the protagonist's nephew and mother are assaulted, he turns dacoit (or 'rebel' as he would have it) and begins kidnapping rich men and merchants for ransom.

Paan Singh's story is related in a flashback motivated by a journalist interviewing Paan Singh and the account we get is his account.[14] The narrative can be broadly divided into two sections, the first one dealing with his submission to military hierarchy and the second, with his resistance to the state. Paan Singh emerges as a different person in the second section. The justification for his submission is that being in the military is serving the Nation ('Mother' as Paan Singh phrases it). In order to keep this patriotic view of the military feasible the film overlooks the Sino-Indian War of 1962. It names the 1965 war with Pakistan in which Paan Singh was not allowed to participate and one can think of no reason for the omission of the Sino-Indian War except the inconvenience of military defeat to a film professing patriotism.

The readiness with which a man accustomed to obedience rebels against authority in civilian life is the first aspect that should strike the viewer in the latter part of the film. This part pertains to the early 1970s when the police were still highly respected in Hindi cinema in films like *Zanjeer* (1973). While the argument that the police were corrupt and incompetent even in the 1970s cannot be disallowed, their filmic portrayal at the time should be factored in to understand how they were regarded by the public. Seen in this light, *Paan Singh Tomar* is imposing the attitudes of its times on historical material inimical to them.

The film announces before the title sequence that it is fiction 'inspired by actual events' which means that it has taken some liberty with facts. An aspect of the film which also deserves comment is the fact that it sees no difference between Paan Singh's version of his life and the truth. Paan Singh is initially shown as a 'simple rustic' but his principal adversary is his own scheming cousin and simplicity is evidently not the intrinsic quality of the villager. When he is unable to deal with the cousin through straightforward means, he lodges a complaint. The argument placed before the police inspector (who is unsympathetic) is not that Paan Singh is legally on the right side but that he is a national hero in sport. Since the director does not delineate his own position from Paan Singh's, we may surmise that he is in agreement with his protagonist about national heroes needing to be treated preferentially, that is, that the law should be partisan if the situation so warrants. Since the story of the film is largely told through an interview to a journalist the film arranges it so that the protagonist answers for some of his nefarious acts—like the cold-blooded killing of the nine informers. His explanation is that while the nine were unarmed, they were not 'innocent'. At the same time, the film rebukes the state for not being strong enough. The highpoint here is Paan Singh making an unclothed police officer salute his own uniform.

Paan Singh Tomar, it is evident, is uncertain about its position on the citizen's relationship to state authority. Unlike a host of other films (including *Chak De India*) which see nothing worthwhile coming out of state action, it nominally wishes for the state to be stronger. The collector's hesitation to intervene in Paan Singh's dispute with his cousin is evidence of the weakness of the state being the film's primary grievance. Since it chooses an aesthetic close to realism, it can even be seen as criticism of official law enforcement. But an issue is whether using informers against a kidnapper and extortionist is not legitimate strategy for law enforcement and if it is, whether the film can side so uncritically with Paan Singh. The film appears, therefore, not to have resolved these contradictions.

If, seen cumulatively, the film's patriotic discourse favours love of the Nation and the concurrent spurning of the state, the film's protagonist must not be confused with the real Paan Singh. The actual athlete-turned-dacoit did remarkably well on the track but this does not mean that he was patriotic: one can win races without feeling anything for the Nation. While he fought the police to be eventually gunned down, there is also no evidence that he despised the Indian state. Being 'anti-state' is a polemical position which may not be embraced by all those who break the law. While one may be 'anti-state' for several reasons (including radical ones), in Hindi cinema it is also the call of those who seek the further withdrawal of the state from the public space to make way for enterprise. We have already seen *Chak De India* castigating state-run sports bodies for being apathetic and *Iqbal* lauding agents for paying out signing bonuses to talented sportsmen; *Paan Singh Tomar* only continues the discourse. But when the film identifies the military and Indian sports with the Nation, my own sense of the choice is that unlike the state, with which citizens interact on a daily basis, these are institutions whose inner workings remain opaque and this may account for why they are still respected by Hindi cinema.[15]

A characteristic shared by *Iqbal*, *Chak De India*, and *Paan Singh Tomar* is that they allow no room for romance/heterosexual attachments, which is normally unimaginable in Hindi cinema. Paan Singh Tomar is given a wife but she is already present when the film begins and there is no indication at the time of his death that he is even thinking of her. This is significant considering that almost every Hindi film concludes with the bringing together of male and female protagonist even if they are both dying as in *Haqeeqat* (1964) in which they face the Chinese army holding hands. There is a clue in this as to why there is no romance in any of the films and this has to do with the male and the female protagonists also having to be united by the expressed sentiments of the film. If *Lagaan* allows for a romance—unlike the other three films this chapter deals with—it is not promoting sports nationalism. The game is a mere occasion in the Nation's fight against colonialism[16] and the film is therefore able to provide for a romance. But in the three films dealt with here, the Nation is *embodied* in sport. Iqbal's love could only have been for someone in the same position vis-à-vis the sporting Nation and Kabir Khan would need to have romances with all sixteen hockey players. Since all women players worship the Nation equally, there would be an unacceptable asymmetry in his loving only one woman player. These observations can be rephrased appropriately to include *Paan Singh Tomar* because the film is not bemoaning injustice as much as decrying the marginalization of a patriot. Since his wife is not shown to share in his achievements or sentiments, Paan Singh recalling her in his final hour would perhaps mitigate his fervour.

The sense of the Nation being *embodied in an activity* is a new one because, previously, the activity was only a means of serving the people of the Nation. The farmer in *Upkar* (1967) is a patriot because farmers produce food for the people. Accordingly, the villain in the film is someone who hoards food grains to profit at the people's expense. Soldiers are, similarly, patriots in *Border* and *Haqeeqat* because they defend the people against an invading foreign army. When these war films show us the wives and families of the soldiers at war, the implication is partly that these are the people the soldiers are protecting. I compared *Iqbal* to *Guru* earlier and that film ends with an Indian businessman dreaming of building a world class industry. This is presented as a patriotic act and *Guru*, essentially, sees Indian business as embodying India[17] in the same way that sport embodies it in the three films discussed. My proposition here is that these later films see a patriotic act as done *on behalf of the Nation* (as an abstraction) with little sense of the Nation being composed of a public that should be benefited by its onward progress. This is because the state as an inclusive overarching structure is undermined by them.

Increasingly, it is being asserted, that the state needs to play no role in maintaining the Nation, that private activity can do it just as well if not better. A factor that needs to be considered here is whether the Nation should not be a more inclusive one than the one which is being thus fostered. An Indian businessman acquiring the largest steel plant in the world may be a matter for national pride but will the 'Nation' that feels this pride be as inclusive as it should be? The sentiment that cricket unifies the Nation is often expressed (as in *Iqbal*) but one wonders if an activity which has no material benefits accruing to the public can become a unifying factor. If the Nation is not an inclusive one, one also wonders if it can survive in the long term. Will the discrediting of the state, therefore, not eventually destroy the Nation?

Notes

1. Cricket writers have attributed the cricket craze to this triumph. 'That evening, what used to be a mere sport was converted into a lucrative career option, and cricketers into default national icons. Soon enough the corporate world would take note and the rest of the world would follow.' Boria Majumdar, 'Opiate of the Masses or One in a Billion: Trying to Unravel the Indian Sporting Mystery', in K. Moti Gokulsing and Wimal Dissanayake (eds), *Popular Culture in a Globalised India* (London: Routledge, 2009), p. 241. But it is unlikely that the lucrative came to be fully realized until the advent of private television channels in the 1990s.

2. For instance, see Nalin Mehta, 'Batting for the Flag: Cricket, Television and Globalization in India', *Sports in Society: Cultures, Commerce, Media, Politics*, vol. 12, nos 4–5, 2009, pp. 579–99.

3. Some sense of the white-collar origins of India's cricketers may be got from the fact that while hockey and football were dominated by people from the military and industry, many of India's cricketers worked in public-sector banks. A useful account of the how the various classes traditionally flocked to different sports—from wrestling to cricket— can be found in Boria Majumdar, 'The Vernacular in Sports History', *Economic and Political Weekly*, vol. 37, no. 29, 20–26 July, 2002, pp. 3069–75.

4. Sachin Tendulkar is associated with Pepsi and Canon, Rahul Dravid with Reebok and Max Life Insurance. M.S. Dhoni has also become

increasingly Anglophone in the course of his career in endorsements. He was endorsing a Hindi newspaper, *Dainik Bhaskar*, until the newspaper could no longer afford him. See Ratna Bhushan and Vijaya Rathore, 'MS Dhoni Loses Five Brand Endorsements as His Popularity seems to Wane', Sports: Off the Field, *The Times of India*, 19 December 2012, http://timesofindia.indiatimes.com/ms-dhoni-loses-five-brand-endorsements-as-his-popularity-seems-to-wane/articleshow/17678622. cms (accessed on 20 June 2013)

5. Since Anglophone Indians are often more comfortable in their mother tongues than English but still try to speak English because of the authority associated with it, there is also a tendency for Hindi slogans to be written in the Latin script. The expanding use of the English language has seen Hindi words frequently being used but in the Latin script as in advertising copy. Another factor to be considered is that India–Pakistan matches have different status and have more Hindi slogans. A sense of this can be gained from the website www.indian cricketfans.com. See http://www.indiancricketfans.com/showthread. php?t=158335 (accessed on 31 December 2012).

6. While *Lagaan* did best in the metropolises, *Gadar* also did exceedingly well at B and C centres. It still runs well at rerun theatres in Madhya Pradesh, Bihar, Uttar Pradesh, and Rajasthan, that is, in semi-urban India. See '*Gadar: Ek Prem Katha: 10 Years On*' and 'Celebrating *Lagaan*: 10 Years On', India-Forums, 15 June 2011, http://www.india-forums.com/forum_posts.asp?TID=1707522 (accessed on 31 December 2012).

7. See Suhel Johar, '*Lagaan, Gadar*: Harbinger of Good Times', www. smashhits.com, http://ww.smashits.com/lagaan-gadar-harbinger-of-good-times/bollywood-gossip-1264.html (accessed on 31 December 2012).

8. Duration is usually connoted through appointments and deadlines in films from Hollywood. In *Lagaan*, the deadline of three months represents the time allowed to the teams to prepare for the game. David Bordwell, 'The Classical Hollywood Style', in David Bordwell, Janet Staiger, and Kristin Thompson, *The Classical Hollywood Cinema: Film Style and Mode of Production to 1960* (London: Routledge & Kegan Paul, 1985), p. 48.

9. See David Rowe, 'Sport and the Repudiation of the Global', *International Review for the Sociology of Sport*, vol. 38, no. 3, September 2003, pp. 281–94.

10. Here are some references (taken from various websites) which bring up this issue: http://www.rediff.com/news/interview/remembering-omar-khalidi/20101130.htm; http://kafila.org/2012/12/28/seeing-pakistan-from-juhapura-zahir-janmohamed/; and http://yuvadesh.in/105/Beyond-Cheering-For-Muslim-Brotherhood (accessed on 2 January 2012).

11. Some of these aristocrats were K.S. Ranjitsinhji, K.S. Duleepsinhji, Vijayananda Gajapathi Raju, the Maharajkumar of Vizianagram (popularly known as Vizzy), and the Nawab of Pataudi (both Sr and Jr).

12. It is difficult to see the father's resistance as other than allegorical because people know the value of cricket as a money earner. M.S. Dhoni, India's captain, is a local hero in Jharkhand, best known as a state dominated by tribal population. Since Dhoni's rise began at around the time the film was made, *Iqbal* could even have been inspired by Dhoni (who was once a railway ticket examiner in Kharagpur).

13. See Alex Perry, 'Crazy for Cricket', *TIME*, Sunday, 6 March 2006, http://www.time.com/time/magazine/article/0,9171,1170023,00.html (accessed on 2 January 2013).

14. Character memory motivates the flashback as in classical Hollywood cinema but what we subsequently see is not restricted to point of view. See David Bordwell, 'The Classical Hollywood Style', pp. 42–3.

15. The BCCI has since then become embroiled in several scandals as has the military. For instance, see Jason Burke, 'IPL Money-laundering Scandal Threatens Indian Government', Sport-IPL, *The Guardian*, 23 February 2010, http://www.guardian.co.uk/sport/2010/apr/23/ipl-ministers-scandal-india-investigation (accessed on 10 January 2013). Also see 'Indian Army's Top Corruption Scandals', *SiliconIndia*, 27 March 2012, http://www.siliconindia.com/news/general/Indian-Armys-Top-Corruption-Scandals-nid-110443-cid-1.html (accessed on 10 January 2013).

16. The actual issue in *Lagaan* is taxation during a period of drought. At stake in the wager around the game of cricket being played is the prospect of taxes being waived if the Indians beat the British.

17. It is significant that in *Guru*, the protagonist's wife, played by Aishwarya Rai, shares the platform with him when he is being attacked/interrogated by the state for his questionable doings. She is effectively sharing in his achievements because she is with him when he is attacked.

Conclusion

Collapsing State, Dissolving Nation

A Divided Cinema

This enquiry into the politics of the mainstream Hindi film in the new millennium began as an attempt to unravel the concerns of cinema but increasingly touched upon the implications of the political currents in India. As indicated in the Introduction, a case exists for popular cinema to be considered a series of utterances by the public which consumes it and, when we interpret cinema, we are primarily interpreting these utterances. Interpreting them is important because of the possible correlation between an influential section of the Indian public and Bollywood's constituency. Even though the two are not identical, they may be constituted similarly so that understanding one will help us understand the other; we could get a sense of the Nation's direction through this influential segment.

The method employed in this enquiry has been to examine a fair range of successful films made after 2000 by a variety of directors, stars, and producers and see if a pattern can be detected in their political discourses. Once the pattern is understood, it can then be interpreted to catch a sense of where the Nation stands and the direction in which it is being driven.

As may have been evident from the individual chapters, a distinct pattern in the discourses has emerged but rather than reflecting the attitudes of a dominant class, the terrain of Hindi cinema is perhaps like a 'contested site' claimed by two identifiable categories: a predominantly Anglophone one from the metropolitan sites and the other from the smaller towns and rural areas.[1] There are thus, broadly, two different kinds of films and it is the kind which addresses the non-Anglophone Indian (the second category above) which is closer to the earlier Hindi cinema. This is, of course, a working approximation because one cannot be certain that each cinema is consumed exclusively by a distinct group but the clear division in the discourses suggests social division along similar lines.

The meaning of mainstream Hindi cinema is not as clearly discernible as this book might have made it seem and there are other factors which have not been elaborated upon while choosing the films to interpret. If a Hindi film, for instance, is the remake of a regional language film, then one also finds motifs in it which are actually from Telugu or Tamil, or Malayalam cinema (as in *Bodyguard*, 2012, starring Salman Khan) and interpreting the motifs as those of a Hindi film need circumspection. The choice of the films examined may have influenced the understanding of the political currents as excavated by this book but the variety and number of films chosen is expected to have mitigated the possibility of an undesirable bias.

Every 'Indian' has several different concurrent identities—for example, national, religious, language, regional—which become pertinent in different contexts. The fact that regional language films exhibit entirely different motifs from Hindi cinema[2]—although they are sometimes consumed by the same individuals—suggests that different identities come into use depending on the context. To illustrate, since a Kannada speaker views a Hindi film and a Kannada film with different expectations, a different identity is apparently coming into play each time. The Hindi films dealt with in this book show evidences of addressing 'Indians'—and not spectators with other identities—but dubbed regional language films may not answer to this description.

The meaning derived from the various Hindi film texts in the book depends on a close reading of narrative texts and its juxtaposition with the broad issues in the historical world in the period contemporary to the release of the film.[3] But in order to make the reading reliable, the motifs selected for interpretation are those which find an echo in other films of the same period; 'meaning' is then arrived at by comparing them to representations of the same subject in other periods. Two aspects are clearly relevant here: the preponderance of a motif because of its political relevance and the anomaly[4] in the way the motif appears in the film because of the same issue now being regarded differently. For instance, the portrayal of the poor in *Peepli (Live)* (2010) bears comparison with that in *Traffic Signal* (2007) because both portrayals decline to find teleology in the lives they deal with. At the same time, there is an anomaly in the way farmers are represented in *Peepli (Live)* in comparison with *Upkar* (1967) and *Mother India* (1957) since farmers—who were once played heroically by stars like Nargis and Manoj Kumar, in whom a public projected itself—are treated in *Peepli (Live)* virtually as the subjects of visual anthropology.

There may be little evidence that mainstream Hindi cinema was ever consumed by a representative segment of the Indian public but it behaved as though it was addressed to 'India'. While it achieved this through its 'socialist' discourse after 1947 by admitting concern for the underprivileged into its narratives, there is also no evidence that its constituency narrowed after the economic liberalization of 1991–2 when its subjects became restricted to the affluent. If the world of films like *HAHK* (1994) is a hierarchical one constituted by the wealthy and their servants, so is the world of the Ramayana and the Mahabharata, but one cannot infer from this that the epics were consumed only by kings and princes. In the new millennium, however, Hindi films reveal biases which had not been in evidence earlier and it is these biases which restrict the Nation addressed by mainstream cinema.

Before going on to interpret the transformation of Hindi cinema in the new millennium, we should first examine the economic changes in India after 2000 especially those related to growth and wealth creation since the transformation of cinema owed to the creation of a new audience. While the growth of India's GDP increased in the 1990s, it hovered between 4 and 6 per cent in the period 1998–2003[5] and shot up to 8.5 per cent in 2004, continuing at around 8 per cent for the next few years. The political party at the centre was unseated in 2004 but it had already begun to celebrate the upbeat mood with the 'India Shining' campaign around the beginning of 2004. As suggested earlier, *Veer-Zaara* reflects the upbeat mood in 2004 but there is still inadequate evidence of Hindi cinema addressing a less inclusive Nation. Judging from the films examined in this book, the motifs marking the new cinema—crime as enterprise, the foregrounding of aspiration, the decrying of politics, and the weakened state—started to appear in 2005 in *Bunty Aur Babli*.[6] In *Dhoom* (2004) the motif of the indulgent law is yet to appear. The policeman, ACP Jai Dixit (Abhishek Bachchan), of *Dhoom* is the hero of both *Dhoom* and *Dhoom 2* (2006) but the bank robbers are eventually killed in the former while in the latter they are exalted. It would therefore appear that Hindi cinema transformed significantly after the Congress commenced to rule again in 2004 with Manmohan Singh installed as Prime Minister. The non-Congress government had also pushed the agenda of reform and one cannot say with certainty that Congress rule made a political difference but since Manmohan Singh was the actual architect of the reforms of 1991–2, his becoming Prime Minister may have raised the expectations of Indians in the metropolises for a speedier reforms and higher growth rates. To all appearances, therefore, while the Anglophone class addressed by the new cinema had evidently been gaining strength, Hindi cinema had not perceptibly responded to its presence until 2005.

Bunty Aur Babli may have been one of the first films to exhibit a motif associated with 'Anglophone' cinema—that of 'aspiration'—but the film to announce the new perspective was perhaps *Rang De Basanti*

(2006). This was the first mainstream film to openly decry politics and the state and a hypothesis explaining its extreme discourse is that it was precipitated by the National Rural Employment Guarantee Act (NREGA) announced in February 2005, widely perceived by industry as electoral populism[7] and expected to result in large-scale corruption.[8] Although the insinuation may be resisted, *Bunty Aur Babli* (2005) can be interpreted as being about young people from rural India who 'make their own way without seeking employment from the government'; the NREGA can be defined broadly as 'the government's scheme providing employment in rural India'. The protagonists may be fraudsters but the celebration by the film of their 'entrepreneurial success' justifies the interpretation.

Economic change is not a development to which popular culture can respond immediately and *HAHK*, which has been repeatedly cited as the first mainstream Hindi film to register the cultural effects of the economic liberalization announced in July 1991, was released only in August 1994. Only the endurance of many of the characteristics attributed to *HAHK* subsequently help us make the connection between the film and the economic reforms, which were also acknowledged as irreversible. By the same token, we may suppose that conditions existed for the creation of 'Anglophone' Hindi cinema about three years before we see actual evidence of it, that is, around 2002, which is shortly before information technology and business process outsourcing in India became globally visible.[9]

The primary consequence to Hindi cinema of the creation of an Anglophone and globally attuned audience with larger spending power was the reduced cultural gap between domestic and non-resident audiences, which had already been suggested by films like *Kal Ho Naa Ho* (2003),[10] and the increasing mismatch between audiences in the metropolises and semi-urban/rural India. As has been demonstrated in the course of this book, this eventually led to a division in Hindi cinema with different kinds of texts devised to address the different audiences. But the two kinds of cinema, when taken together, present a unified portrait of the Nation, the interpretation of which is the thrust of the last part of this book.

The Discourses as Social Evidence

If the division of Hindi cinema can be attributed to the advent of globalization which eventually divided audiences, the response to globalization is initially one of uniform alarm (*Raaz*, 2002; *Jism*, 2003). It is only when the alarm subsides that the new discourses become visible. The earliest of the new discourses pertains to 'aspiration' and the indulgence of the law towards the illegalities of the entrepreneurial class—apparently beginning with *Bunty Aur Babli*. In the earliest of the films, apparently, the law is still strong but indulgent. But into the millennium, it is seen to grow weaker and more ineffectual. In most films the 'law' is represented by the policeman but a distinction is quickly made between the two (signified and signifier) because these servants of the law soon serve themselves rather than the law, the portrayal reaching its apogee in *Kaminey* (2009). Since actual policemen benefit materially through their indulgence towards criminals, the corrupt law enforcers of the later film may be regarded as the natural outcome of the indulgent one in *Bunty Aur Babli*. The films may therefore reflect the laxity of the law as it encouraged entrepreneurship from 1991 onwards with the liberalization of the economy. Through its progressive 'withdrawal' from the public space, the state increasingly weakened its own apparatus since it unwittingly also empowered enterprise to subvert and corrupt it. It has been noted with regard to the economic liberalization of 1991 that the 'weakest government in modern Indian history undertook the most radical reform of the economy' since the Nehru era;[11] the same weakness of the government can perhaps be blamed for its disinclination to strengthen legality and enforcement while undertaking the reforms.

A pertinent question here is why such representations of the law appear only around 2005 and portrayed as a consequence of globalization if the weakening of the state was hastened in the early 1990s? There have been studies which suggest that both globalization and corruption have resulted in super-wealth[12] and there could be an association between the two but one doubts that this could have been registered by Hindi cinema, although the super-wealth of a few Indians became visible after 2000. Another explanation resides in the nature of Hindi cinema itself. Hindi cinema has never been 'mimetic' and has dealt with exemplary people and relationships and until the advent of globalization still tried to invoke traditional exemplars. But, as already indicated, traditional dharma has no means of dealing with the notion of criminality and/or illegality. It should be noted that once modernity no longer represented a threat in the 1960s, whatever had been held out as a threat—for example, bad modernity represented by the club dancer—was incorporated swiftly into popular cinema's ideal world. Where the club dancer of the 1950s performs in seedy spaces, the cabarets of the 1960s are glitzy and represent sophistication. My proposition here is that although the weakening of the state was hastened in the 1990s, illegality and indifference to the law were incorporated as desirable[13] into film narrative in the new millennium because it was part of the 'global way' and globalization was itself accepted. This may explain the celebratory attitude towards crime in *Kaminey* which sees it as an opportunity.

An aspect with some bearing on the weakening of the state is the representation of industry/business in Hindi cinema with it gradually gaining in approval. *Rang De Basanti* takes a relatively ambivalent view by lauding private television while castigating the arms contractor—that business can do both good and bad—but one finds business treated quite differently in *Corporate* (2006), *Guru* (2007), and *Fashion* (2008). *Corporate* distinguishes between the self-serving promoter and the 'corporate', with the latter actually becoming an object of loyalty. The justification is the 'shareholder' who is deliberately confused with the 'public'. We are familiar with the 'people' as an object of veneration but in this film and in *Guru*, the shareholders *are* the people. *Fashion* goes a step further by describing sordid happenings in the fashion industry but sugarcoating them and telling the story from the industry's side. If *Fashion* works as a 'corporate communication' for the fashion industry, *Om Shanti Om* (2007) can be partly understood as an advertisement for Bollywood as a brand. I suggested earlier that the empowerment of enterprise by the state led to the subversion of its apparatus by the former and progressively weakened it. The open endorsement of industry and business by Hindi cinema is evidence of its growing power in controlling opinion as the state correspondingly loses ground.

Another side to law enforcement not covered by the arguments offered earlier is the notion of culpability before the law. Films like *Page 3* (2005) regard extra-judicial killings with approval with the tacit assumption that the criminals thus dealt with belong to a designated 'criminal class'. Its converse is the suggestion in *Om Shanti Om* that the influential can legitimately enter into private arrangements outside the law to ameliorate the results of their acts. Increasingly, it would appear that rather than being disinterested, enforcement of the law is directed asymmetrically to the advantage of a more powerful class. Quite innocently, Hindi films regard this development with acceptance—as evidenced by the two films above—but also appear to lament it as in *Traffic Signal* when the murderers cannot be punished because they are powerful or influential.

Another aspect of importance pointed to by Anglophone cinema—notably in *Peepli (Live)* and *Traffic Signal*—is its constituency gradually coming to regard the marginalized as outside the grand narrative of the Nation's progress. The issue is not only a moral or philanthropic one, that is, that the well-off should carry those less fortunate along with them, because the poor have another role to play in the economy. There appears to be no admission in Hindi cinema, when celebrating enterprise, that Indian business being globally competitive can be associated with the low wage levels,[14] which are sustainable because of the relatively low cost of living in India. The suggestion here is that it is the persisting level of poverty in India which keeps the cost of living low. But Rancho, the gardener's son triumphing entirely on his own and becoming an inventor in *3 Idiots*, perhaps, embodies a hope that the poor 'will take care of themselves'.

An important discourse of Anglophone cinema which needs comment is its treatment of politicians. *Rang De Basanti* fires the first salvo against them when the defence minister accepts bribes from an arms contractor. After this portrayal, politicians are repeatedly shown as self-serving with their electoral planks being empty rhetoric as in *Kaminey*. More interesting, however, is the portrayal of the entrenched political class in *Raajneeti* (2010), which regards it as an aristocracy—since the characters are modelled on figures from the Mahabharata. The discourse in *Raajneeti* is that politics is a competitive game or business with all the energies of the players directed towards their rivals and not towards the electorate. When the rival leaders finally kill each other, the mantle passes to the apolitical daughter of a businessman, to 'govern' rather than 'play politics'. Most significant in this film is the portrayal of the electorate as composed of those in the slums and rural areas, with no will of their own and capable of being completely manipulated. One sees in this portrayal the lack of faith of the Anglophone Indian in the democratic process. If the electorate in *Raajneeti* is equated with the poor in *Peepli (Live)* and *Traffic Signal*, one begins to recognize that the electoral process is the only way in which the poor can remain implicated in the 'grand narrative of the Nation's progress' although the Anglophone Indian might prefer to see the marginalized, rather, as obstructing it. It is significant that seen from the non-Anglophone side (for example, in *Dabangg*, 2010) the political 'aristocrats' are people with little jurisdiction over the electorate they are supposedly 'manipulating'.

Before going on to scrutinize the other implications of the discourses in the second kind of cinema, an examination should be made of the meaning of Gandhi to the Anglophone class because Gandhi has represented the Indian political conscience and is the icon most summoned in relation to public morality. *Lage Raho Munnabhai* (2006) was widely hailed by the Anglophone public and NRI audiences—who have much in common. But if anything, this film, which was screened also at the United Nations, shows that Gandhian ethics, to the Anglophone Indian, has been divested of its political dimension and is regarded as a (perhaps) useful personal strategy to adopt in a milieu in which illegality is an attendant part of everyday life. The film also finds no apparent contradiction in oneself overlooking the law but employing 'Gandhian methods' against other people when they do likewise. It would appear that this 'Gandhian' strategy—which is an appeal to the adversary's better nature—is recommended because it is difficult to appeal to the state as arbiter.

A factor indicating that Anglophone cinema departs markedly from Hindi cinema as it was in the last century is the smaller reliance on the notion of 'tradition', which was a key way in which the Nation could be represented. Tradition was implicated in genealogy, which carried the same sanctity for Indian cinema that the nuclear family does for Hollywood. There has been a considerable weakening of genealogy as a morally binding force in Anglophone Hindi cinema and this has been associated with the new economy in India leading large sections of the populace to abandon their family's traditional occupations and being materially rewarded. One might even propose that it is this move which distinguishes the Anglophone Indian (as a category) from the non-Anglophone one because non-Anglophone cinema still valourizes tradition, although this should not be taken to imply that 'tradition' still has the same significance.

The two 'non-Anglophone' Hindi films examined in this book do not take the same position politically because *Rab Ne Bana Di Jodi* (2008) is moderate in its discourse, trying to be sympathetic to 'aspiration' even as it respects tradition. It does not, however, appear that this film more than marks a period of social transition and a more defining work (of the shape of things to come) is apparently *Dabangg*, which has had a huge following. 'Tradition' to *Dabangg* does not mean what it once did to Hindi cinema, when the notion was aligned with that of the Nation. If Anglophone cinema provides evidence of the rapidly weakening state, so does *Dabangg* although in a different way. *Dabangg* is set in a small town which is hierarchically organized but with caste being the dominant hierarchical criterion, as was not in evidence earlier. There is the sense to be gained in *Dabangg* that the state has ceded its authority to traditional structures of power. If anything, *Dabangg* provides evidence of the reappearance of feudalism, rendered stronger[15] because of the absence of legality and the weakening of state authority.

Anglophone cinema does not identify itself as 'Anglophone' and sees the 'other' only as the poor. Non-Anglophone cinema, which does not acknowledge the existence of Anglophone India, although it uses mispronounced English occasionally, has no special place for a category denoted as the 'poor'. It simply places them at the bottom of the social hierarchy with the provision that 'good people' will treat them kindly. The essential difference between Anglophone and non-Anglophone cinema is, perhaps, that the former is still infected by remnants of liberalism, while the latter is proceeding rapidly towards a sensibility that preceded democratic India—and perhaps even the late colonial period[16] although this proposition needs qualification. It has been suggested that caste politics in India is a direct result of modern politics and is not a throwback to traditional behaviour.[17] The efforts to weaken caste division in the Nehruvian era had caste groups responding to the new situation created by reverse discrimination (that is, reservation based on caste) and division did not simply fade away as had been hoped. Caste groups entered into vast electoral coalitions, mainly across north India. It may therefore be proposed that 'tradition' valourized in films like *Dabangg* has a more complex connotation.

As already indicated, the films registering the state's withdrawal in the 1990s still provide for emblems of moral authority, which was how the state was represented after Independence. In fact, the history of Hindi cinema after 1947 can be read as an ongoing register of the weakening moral authority of the state; at every instance of this weakening, cinema finds other ways to affirm the Nation with reduced assistance from the state, 'tradition' perhaps representing the last bastion until it falls in the new millennium with the advent of the Anglophone film. The last phase of Hindi cinema dealt with in this book, essentially, marks efforts to find new ways of affirming the Nation, *Zindagi Na Milegi Dobara* (2011) by celebrating the prosperity of the wealthy classes and their capacity to spend and the films on sports by representing sporting achievements as patriotic acts. This is, essentially, identifying icons pertaining to private activity and attaching them to the Nation. An artist or a businessman could equally well be a national hero. The difficulty with the approach is that while such achievement has assisted in the creation of a national identity, this pertains only to that aspect of the identity which is directed outward, sometimes in relation to a single external stimulus.[18] There have been 'patriotic' films in Hindi which were directed outward like *Border* (1997, against Pakistan) and *Lagaan* (2001, against colonialism) but Hindi cinema also signified the Nation directed internally towards its own citizens and it is this latter kind of cinema which has assisted in the imaging of the Nation more than the former. However one may regard this evidence, it is difficult to see the imagined Nation as an enduring prospect.

Speculating on the State of the Nation

Understanding the state of the imagined Nation is rightly the purpose of this enquiry although the method employed is interpreting cinema rather than analyzing the implications of public developments. The logic is that popular cinema—in addressing audiences at the conscious and subconscious levels—can provide insights into the way of thinking of the 'public' although it may be restricted to major segments without encompassing the entire populace.

Judging from the information yielded by the films, the end of 'Nehruvian socialism'—regardless of socialism's effectiveness in actually providing equity—had far-reaching consequences upon the cultural and social fabric of the Nation. While it had a beneficial economic outcome, it has lent so much power to enterprise that the machinery of the state was steadily undermined and subverted. 'Corruption' is universally lamented in India but its implications are rarely acknowledged. Corruption is, essentially, the subversion of the machinery of the state to private ends, and the corruption of the state machinery is both the cause and the effect of the illegalities overlooked in the conduct of enterprises. The strengthening of private enterprise without the concurrent strengthening of systems of enforcement has evidently had this detrimental effect. The state is hence progressively less than able to deliver its services—whether justice, health, education, or welfare—and 'withdrawing' further will only heighten its incapacity further.

If the dividing line between politicians and entrepreneurs is being steadily obliterated, this is perhaps the natural consequence of 'economic reform' being the only long-term political agenda. It is to be asked, since the long-term agenda is pre-determined, whether policy initiatives which originate democratically in the needs/ wishes of the electorate are possible at all. But since politics is less 'bottom-up' (the wishes of the electorate being represented at the top) than 'top-down' (the spoils of politics being passed downward), patronage has become the key issue. The similarity between politics and business has consequently seen the constituency being viewed as a 'market' and top-level politicians are increasingly referred to as CEOs. But the similarity also justifies profit as a legitimate end in politics.

Globalization and its economic outcome have divided Indian society as never before, with a globally attuned public in the metropolises finding itself closer to the Western world than it is to rural India. Since economic liberalization has been interpreted as licenced Darwinism, this (largely Anglophone) public has shut out the rest of India from its consciousness except as the Nation's baggage. At the same time, those in the semi-urban or rural areas are falling back to dependence on traditional power structures to which the weak state has lent authority. Economic liberalization was expected to create 'trickle-down' benefits to the marginalized but much of the 'trickle-down' affluence has further strengthened these informal power structures. The scenario is strikingly feudal but where feudal power once resided in the ownership of land, land is a depleting resource and its ownership may not confer the greatest degree of power. Power therefore comes out of political patronage, connections with state authority, and one's hereditary position in caste hierarchy.

On examining the history of Hindi cinema we find national issues being represented through characters or relationships of various kinds and the Nation has, in effect, been 'delivered' to audiences by farmers, lawyers, doctors, policemen, teachers, dam construction engineers, judges, war heroes, and perhaps most enduringly, fathers and mothers. Each of these often has a different relationship with the Nation and, as instances, teachers, doctors, and dam construction engineers are emblems of the modern Nation in the 1950s. But as we move down chronologically, we discover them progressively abandoned as emblems: those representing modernity after the Nehruvian era, the policemen and judges when the state machinery became discredited, and so on. The last to go were the fathers and mothers when young people in the new economy businesses abandoned their family callings. These developments, it can be argued, represent the Nation losing its attributes but the question is whether something which has lost all its attributes can continue to exist. If it exists as an empty shell, will it not exist only in relation to something outside it? Hence, sports can perhaps only ensure that the Nation exists in relation to other sporting countries rather than as an entity to which its own citizens belong.

Whichever the way in which one regards this reading of the mainstream film, it has bleak implications. But making it plausible is the fact that it is not a prognosis that cinema has willingly offered but information yielded despite itself, since its surface discourse has been celebratory. It is perhaps this celebratory aspect of the mainstream Hindi film—when the underlying predicament is the Nation dissolving—that gives one the greatest cause for disquiet because it reflects the outlook of influential segments of the Indian public.

Notes

1. For a broad examination of audience segmentation from the target audience and territory-wise distribution, see Derek Bose, *Brand Bollywood: A New Global Entertainment Order* (New Delhi: Sage, 2006), p. 26.

2. The most successful model for Kannada cinema in the new millennium, for instance, is that of the man from a small town who migrates to

Bangalore, lives in shabby surroundings, becomes a dreaded gangland thug but continues to live squalidly until he is killed in an encounter, usually by a low-ranking policeman. See M.K. Raghavendra, 'Meanings of the City', *Caravan*, vol. 3, no. 10, 1 October 2011. http://caravanmagazine.in/arts/meanings-city (accessed on 20 October 2013).

3. When we say we 'understand' a narrative, we have found a satisfactory relationship between the fictional world of the film and the real world. See Robert Scholes, James Phelan and Robert Kellogg, *The Nature of Narrative* (New York: Oxford University Press, 1966), p. 82.

4. As Noël Carroll proposes, film interpretation finds its natural calling in dealing with the deviation, with what violates the norm or re-imagines it. Noël Carroll, 'Prospects for Film Theory: A Personal Assessment', in David Bordwell and Noël Carroll (eds), *Post-Theory: Reconstructing Film Studies* (Madison: University of Wisconsin Press, 1996), p. 43.

5. See 'GDP Growth under Various Governments', DalalStreet.Biz, 9 June 2008, http://www.dalalstreet.biz/stocktips/2008/06/gdp-growth-under-various-governments/ (accessed on 24 January 2013).

6. This conclusion is based on an examination of the super hits and hits in 2004 and 2005. See http://www.boxofficeindia.com/showProd.php?itemCat=210&catName=MjAwNA== (accessed on 24 January 2013).

7. For instance, see 'NREGA Is Like a Cash Distribution Scheme: Kiran Shaw', *The Hindu Business Line*, 24 November 2012, http://www.thehindubusinessline.com/industry-and-economy/economy/article2656525.ece?homepage=true&css=print (accessed on 24 January 2012). In 2009, the defeat of the Left was also partly blamed on its abandoning its traditional position and following neo-liberalist economic policies. Significantly, its losing its bastions in West Bengal and Kerala was also attributed to its poor performance under the NREGA. Deepankar Basu, 'The Left and the 15th Lok Sabha Elections,' *Economic and Political Weekly*, vol. 44, no. 22, 20 May 2009, pp. 10–14.

8. See N. Chandra Mohan, 'Loot for Work Programme?' Opinion, *Outlook*, 11 August 2005, http://www.outlookindia.com/article.aspx?228227 (accessed on 24 January 2012).

9. A clue to when the new economy in India became globally visible may be sought in the first use of the word 'Bangalored', which refers to people who have been laid off from a multinational because their job

has been moved to India. This word has apparently been in use since 2003. See Michael Quinion, 'Bangalored', World Wide Words, 14 August 2004, http://www.worldwidewords.org/turnsofphrase/tp-ban1. htm (accessed on 24 January 2013).

10. It has been noted by researchers that the non-residents in films like *Kal Ho Naa Ho* do not reflect the reality of NRIs but rather are the reflection of the homeland's perception of NRIs. Still, the film in question was an enormous success not only in the country but also abroad. See Brian Hu, 'Bollywood Dreaming: *Kal Ho Naa Ho* and the Diasporic Spectator', *Post-Script: Essays in Film and the Humanities*, vol. 25, 2006, http://www.freepatentsonline.com/article/Post-Script/172833462.html (accessed on 25 January 2013).

11. Sudipta Kaviraj, *The Trajectories of the Indian State: Politics and Ideas* (Ranikhet: Permanent Black, 2010), p. 256.

12. Benno Torgler and Marco Piatti, 'Extraordinary Wealth, Globalization and Corruption', Centre for Research in Economics, Management and the Arts, Working Paper No. 2009–04, CREMA, Basel, http://ww.crema-research.ch/papers/2009-04.pdf (accessed on 29 March 2014).

13. A disconnect between Hinduism as a religion and morality has been noted by commentators like Nirad C. Chaudhuri.

> The worldly orientation of the entire religious life of the Hindus can be seen in its manifold expressions, but it cannot be said that according to this belief, the material and moral order of the universe is maintained by their religion or their gods. What is clear is that the Hindu gods could give to their worshippers what the world contained, but had no part to play in maintaining the existence of the world, nor were they responsible for the moral behaviour of men. In fact, help from religion was sought for all purposes, moral or immoral. Religion and morality ran along parallel courses.

> Nirad C. Chaudhuri, *Hinduism: A Religion to Live By* (New York: Oxford University Press, 1979), p. 15. This offers an explanation for why illegality was not resisted as 'untraditional'.

14. Some studies reveal that while wage levels have generally increased in India industry, the share of wages in value addition have come down. This suggests higher mechanization and lower dependence on labour. But the issue being raised has to do not only with actual wage levels

but with the indirect effect of poverty, keeping the cost of living down. For instance, see Hina Sidhu, 'Share of Wages and Competitiveness in Indian Industry', *Indian Journal of Industrial Relations*, vol. 43, no. 2, October 2007, pp. 170–90.

15. If one takes *Andaz* (1949) and *Awaara* (1951) as providing instances of entrenched feudalism (based on M. Madhava Prasad's definition of the 'feudal family romance'), 'feudal power' in both films submits to state authority when it is judged in the courtroom. In *Dabangg*, state authority has submitted to feudal power because the policeman hero identifies himself by his caste (Brahmin) and triumphs as 'Pandeyji', which announces his caste. To provide a contrary instance, it was the villain (a policeman played by Amrish Puri) who did likewise in J.P. Dutta's *Batwara* (1988) when he declared he was a 'Thakur first and a policeman afterwards'.

16. This may appear an extreme assertion but the colonial cinema of the 1940s in India was termed 'reformist' because it upheld social reform, taking up issues like women's emancipation, caste prejudice, superstition, labour reform, and so on, in right earnest. See M.K. Raghavendra, *Seduced by the Familiar: Narration and Meaning in Indian Popular Cinema* (New Delhi: Oxford University Press, 2008), p. 86.

17. Kaviraj, *Trajectories of the Indian State*, p. 34.

18. For instance, Scottish football fans find their identity primarily defined in relation to England while English fans see theirs defined in relation to the rest of the football world. If England were absent from the World Cup, English fans would support Scotland, but this would not be reciprocated by the Scots. See the Introduction in Alan Bairner, *Sport, Nationalism, and Globalization: European and North-American Perspectives* (Albany: SUNY Press, 2001), p. xiv.

Bibliography

Abraham, Janaki, 'Veiling and the Production of Gender and Space in a Town in North India: A Critique of the Public/Private Dichotomy', *Indian Journal of Gender Studies*, vol. 17, no. 2, June 2010.

Amanullah, Arshad and Aijaz Gul, 'Cinema in Pakistan: History, Present Scenario and Future Prospects', in Meenakshi Bharat and Nirmal Kumar (eds), *Filming the Line of Control: Indo-Pak Relationships through the Cinematic Lens* (New Delhi: Routledge, 2008).

Arnes, Roy, *Third World Film Making and the West* (Berkeley, CA: University of California Press, 1987).

Bairner, Alan, *Sport, Nationalism, and Globalization: European and North-American Perspectives* (Albany: SUNY Press, 2001).

Barthes, Roland, *Mythologies* (London: Paladin, 1973).

Basu, Deepankar, 'The Left and the 15th Lok Sabha Elections', *Economic and Political Weekly*, vol. 44, no. 22, 20 May 2009.

Baudrillard, Jean, 'Simulacra and Simulations', in *Selected Writings* (Stanford, CA: Stanford University Press, 1988).

Bertelsen, Eve, '"Serious Gourmet Shit": Quentin Tarantino's *Pulp Fiction*', *Journal of Literary Studies*, vol. 15, nos 1–2, 1999.

Besley, Timothy J., Rohini Pandey, and Vijayendra Rao, 'Political Selection and the Quality of Government: Evidence from South India', Centre for Economic Policy Research Discussion Paper No. 5201, Social Science Research Network, August 2005.

Bharucha, Rustom, 'Utopia in Bollywood: *Hum Aapke Hain Koun..!'*
Economic and Political Weekly, vol. 30, no. 15, 15 April 1995.

Bordwell, David, *Narration in the Fiction Film* (London: Methuen, 1985).

———, *Inference and Rhetoric in the Interpretation of Cinema* (Cambridge, MA: Harvard University Press, 1989).

———, 'The Classical Hollywood Style', in David Bordwell, Janet Staiger, and Kristin Thompson, *The Classical Hollywood Cinema: Film Style and Mode of Production to 1960* (London: Routledge & Kegan Paul, 1985).

Bose, Derek, *Brand Bollywood: A New Global Entertainment Order* (New Delhi: Sage, 2006).

Brooks, Peter, *The Melodramatic Imagination: Balzac, Henry James, Melodrama, and the Mode of Excess* (New York: Columbia University Press, 1985).

Byrski, M. Christopher, 'Sanskrit Drama as an Aggregate of Model Situations', in Rachel Van M. Baumer and James R. Brandon (eds), *Sanskrit Drama in Performance* (New Delhi: Motilal Banarsidass, 1993).

Carey, James W., *Communication as Culture: Essays on Media and Society* (Winchester, MA: Unwin Hyman, 1989).

Carroll, Noël, 'As the Dial Turns: Notes on Soap Operas', in *Theorizing the Moving Image* (New York: Cambridge University Press, 1996).

———, 'Prospects for Film Theory: A Personal Assessment', in David Bordwell and Noël Carroll (eds), *Post-Theory: Reconstructing Film Studies* (Madison: University of Wisconsin Press, 1996).

Chakravarty, Ambar, '*Taare Zameen Par* and Dyslexic Savants', *Annals of Indian Academy of Neurology*, vol. 12, no. 2, April–June 2009.

Chandra, Kanchan, *Why Ethnic Parties Succeed: Patronage and Ethnic Headcounts in India* (New York: Cambridge University Press, 2004).

Chatterjee, Gayatri, *Mother India* (New Delhi: Penguin, 2002).

Chatterjee, Partha, *The Nation and Its Fragments: Colonial and Post-colonial Histories* (New Delhi: Oxford University Press, 1997).

———, *The Politics of the Governed: Reflections on Popular Politics in Most of the World* (New York: Columbia University Press, 2004).

Chakravarty, Sumita S., *National Identity in Indian Popular Cinema, 1947–1987* (New Delhi: Oxford University Press, 1998).

Cham, Mbye Babucar, 'Film Production in West Africa', in John D.H. Downing (ed.), *Film and Politics in the Third World* (New York: Praeger, 1987).

Chaudhuri, Nirad C., *Hinduism: A Religion to Live By* (New York: Oxford University Press, 1979).

Choi, Jinhee, 'National Cinema: The Very Idea', in Noël Carroll and Jinhee Choi (eds), *Philosophy of Film and Motion Pictures* (Oxford: Blackwell, 2006).

Cieko, Anne Tereska, 'Introduction', in Anne Tereska Cieko (ed.), *Contemporary Asian Cinema: Popular Culture in a Global Frame* (New York: Berg, 2006).

Corbridge, Stuart, 'Cartographies of Loathing and Desire: The Bharatiya Janata Party, the Bomb, and the Political Spaces of Hindu Nationalism', Yale H. Ferguson and R.J. Barry Jones (eds), *Political Space: Frontiers of Change and Governance in a Globalizing World* (New York: State University of New York Press, Albany, 2002).

Coward, Rosalind, *Female Desire* (London: Paladin, 1984).

Danto, Arthur C., 'Deep Interpretation', in *The Philosophical Disenfranchisement of Art* (New York: Columbia University Press, 1986).

Desai, Lord Meghnad, *Nehru's Hero: Dilip Kumar in the Life of India* (Delhi: Roli, 2004).

Deutsch, Eliot, 'Reflections on Some Aspects of the Theory of Rasa', in Rachel M. Van Baumer and James R. Brandon (eds), *Sanskrit Drama in Performance* (Delhi: Motilal Banarsidass, 1993).

Dhareshwar, Vivek and R. Srivatsan, '"Rowdy-Sheeters": An Essay on Subalternity and Politics', in Shahid Amin and Dipesh Charkrabarty (eds), *Subaltern Studies IX: Writings on South Asian History and Society* (New Delhi: Oxford University Press, 1996).

Dixon, Wheeler Winston (ed.), *Film Genre 2000: New Critical Essays* (Albany, NY: State University of New York Press, 2000).

Dudrah, Rajinder, 'Borders and Border Crossings in *Main Hoon Na* and *Veer-Zara*', in Meenakshi Bharat and Nirmal Kumar (eds), *Filming the Line of Control: Indo-Pak Relationships through the Cinematic Lens* (New Delhi: Routledge, 2008).

Dumont, Louis, *Homo Hierarchicus: The Caste System and Its Implications* (New Delhi: Oxford University Press, 1998).

Dwyer, Rachel, 'Shooting Stars: The Indian Film Magazine *Stardust*', in Rachel Dwyer and Christopher Pinney (eds), *Pleasure and the Nation: The History, Politics and Consumption of Public Culture in India* (New Delhi: Oxford University Press, 2001).

Dwyer, Rachel, 'Bollywood Bourgeoise', *India International Centre Quarterly*, vol. 33, nos 3/4, 'India 60', Winter 2006–Spring 2007.

Featherstone, Mike, 'Localism, Globalism, Cultural Identity', in Rob Wilson and Wimal Dissanayake (eds), *Global Local: Cultural Production and the Transnational Imaginary* (Durham: Duke University Press, 1996).

Federation of Indian Chambers of Commerce and Industry (FICCI), *Indian Entertainment Industry: Envisioning for Tomorrow*, March 2001, prepared by Arthur Andersen.

Gazdar, Mushtaq, *Pakistani Cinema 1947–1997* (Karachi: Oxford University Press, 1997).

Gerould, Daniel, 'Russian Formalist Theories of Melodrama', *Journal of American Culture*, no. 1, 1978.

Gilmour, Heather, 'Different, Except in a Different Way: Marriage, Divorce and Gender in the Hollywood Comedy of Remarriage', *Journal of Film and Video*, vol. 50, no. 2, Summer 1998.

Gopalan, Lalitha, *Cinema of Interruptions: Action Genres in Contemporary Indian Cinema* (New Delhi: Oxford University Press, 2002).

Guha, Ranajit, 'The Prose of Counter-Insurgency', in Ranajit Guha and Gayatri Chakravorty Spivak, *Selected Subaltern Studies* (New York: Oxford University Press, 1988).

Guhathakurta, Meghna, 'Families, Displacement', in Ghislaine Glasson Deschaumes and Rada Ivekovic (eds), *Divided Countries, Separated Cities: The Modern Legacy of Partition* (New Delhi: Oxford University Press, 2003).

Gupta, Amit, *Global Security Watch- India* (Santa Barbara: Praeger, 2012).

Harvey, Sylvia, 'Woman's Place: The Absent Family of Film Noir', in E. Ann Kaplan (ed.), *Women in Film Noir* (London: British Film Institute, 1980).

Hogan, Patrick Colm, *Understanding Indian Movies: Culture, Cognition and Cinematic Imagination* (Austin: University of Texas Press, 2008).

Hu, Brian, 'Bollywood Dreaming: *Kal Ho Naa Ho* and the Diasporic Spectator', *Post-Script: Essays in Film and the Humanities*, vol. 25, 2006.

The Indian Outbound Travel Market with Special Insight into Europe as a Destination (Madrid: World Tourism Organization, 2009).

Jameson, Frederic, 'World Literature in the Age of Multinational Capitalism', in Clayton Koelb and Virgil Lokke (eds), *The Current in Criticism* (West Lafayette, Ind.: Purdue University Press, 1987).

Jameson, Frederic, 'Postmodernism and Consumer Society', in E. Ann Kaplan (ed.), *Postmodernism and Its Discontents* (London: Verso, 1988).

Jha, Subhash K., 'The ABC of Revolutionary Films', *Deccan Herald*, 26 February 2006.

Johnston, Claire, 'Double Indemnity', in E. Ann Kaplan (ed.), *Women in Film Noir* (London: British Film Institute, 1980).

Kakar, Sudhir, 'The Ties That Bind: Family Relationships in the Mythology of Hindi Cinema', *India International Centre Quarterly Special Issue*, vol. 8, no. 1, March 1980.

————, *Intimate Relations: Exploring Indian Sexuality* (New Delhi: Penguin, 1989).

Kapur, Devesh and Pratap Bhanu Mehta, 'Indian Higher Education Reform: From Half-baked Socialism to Half-baked Capitalism', Center for International Development at Harvard University, Working Paper No. 108, September 2004.

Kaviraj, Sudipta, *The Trajectories of the Indian State: Politics and Ideas* (Ranikhet: Permanent Black, 2010).

Kazmi, Fareed, *The Politics of India's Conventional Cinema: Imaging a Universe and Subverting a Multiverse* (New Delhi: Sage, 1999).

Khan, Shahnaz, 'Nationalism and Hindi Cinema: Narrative Strategies in *Fanaa*', *Studies in South Asian Film and Media*, vol. 1, no. 1, 1 May 2009.

Khilnani, Sunil, *The Idea of India* (New Delhi: Penguin, 1998).

Koelb, Clayton and Virgil Lokke (eds), *The Current in Criticism* (West Lafayette, Ind.: Purdue University Press, 1987).

Krishnan, Rajan and M.S.S. Pandian, 'The Brahmin and the Citizen: Shankar's *Anniyan*', *Economic and Political Weekly*, vol. 41, nos 27–8, 8–15 July 2006.

Lannoy, Richard, *The Speaking Tree: A Study of Indian Culture and Society* (London: Oxford University Press, 1971).

Lelyveld, David, 'Talking the National Language: Hindi/Urdu/Hindustani in Indian Broadcasting and Cinema', in Sujata Patel, Jasodhara Bagchi, and Krishna Raj (eds), *Thinking Social Science in India: Essays in Honour of Alice Thorner* (Delhi: Sage, 2002).

Lent, John A., *The Asian Film Industry* (London: Christopher Helm, 1990).

Lerche, K., 'Agricultural Labourers, the State and Agrarian Transition in Uttar Pradesh', *Economic and Political Weekly*, vol. 33, no. 13, 26 March 1998.

Lothspeich, Pamel, 'The Mahabharata's Imprint on Contemporary Literature and Film', in K. Moti Gokulsing and Wimal Dissanayake (eds), *Popular Culture in a Globalised India* (London: Routledge, 2009).

Lutze, Lothar, 'Interview with Raj Khosla', in Lothar Lutze and Beatrix Pfleiderer (eds), *The Hindi Film: Agent and Re-agent of Cultural Change* (Delhi: Manohar, 1985).

————, 'Bharata to Bombay: Change and Continuity in Hindi Film Aesthetics', in Lothar Lutze and Beatrix Pfleiderer (eds), *The Hindi Film: Agent and Re-agent of Cultural Change* (Delhi: Manohar, 1985).

Lyman, Stanford M., 'The Road to Anhedonia: Patterns of Emotional Conflict in American Films, 1930–1988', in David D. Franks and Viktor Gelas (eds), *Social Perspectives on Emotion: A Research Annual*, vol. 1 (Greenwich, Conn.: Jai Press, 1992).

Macdonell, Arthur A., *A History of Sanskrit Literature* (New Delhi: Munshiram Manoharlal, 1958).

Majumdar, Boria, 'The Vernacular in Sports History', *Economic and Political Weekly*, vol. 37, no. 29, 20–26 July 2002.

————, 'Opiate of the Masses or One in a Billion: Trying to Unravel the Indian Sporting Mystery', in K. Moti Gokulsing and Wimal Dissanayake (eds), *Popular Culture in a Globalised India* (London: Routledge, 2009).

Mankekar, P., 'Brides Who Travel: Gender, Transnationalism and Nationalism in Hindi Film', *Positions: Asia Critique*, vol. 7, no. 3, Winter 1999.

Marriott, McKim, 'Caste Ranking and Food Transactions: A Matrix Analysis', in Milton B. Singer and Bernard S. Cohn (eds), *Structure and Change in Indian Society* (New Jersey: Transaction Publishers, 1968).

Mazumdar, Ranjani, *Bombay Cinema: An Archive of the City* (Raniketh: Permanent Black, 2007).

McKeon, Michael, *The Origins of the English Novel (1600–1740)* (Baltimore: Johns Hopkins University Press, 1987).

Mehta, Nalin, 'Batting for the Flag: Cricket, Television and Globalization in India', *Sports in Society: Cultures, Commerce, Media, Politics*, vol. 12, nos 4–5, 2009.

————, 'Breaking News, Indian Style: Politics, Democracy and Indian News Television', in K. Moti Gokulsing and Wimal Dissanayake (eds), *Popular Culture in a Globalised India* (London: Routledge, 2009).

Mishra, Vijay, 'Towards a Theoretical Critique of Bombay Cinema', *Screen*, vol. 26, nos 3–4, 1985.

Mishra, Vijay, *Bollywood Cinema: Temples of Desire* (London: Routledge, 2002).

———, 'The Texts of *Mother India*', in *Bollywood Cinema: Temples of Desire* (London: Routledge, 2002).

Monaco, James, *How to Read a Film: The Art, Technology, Language, History and Theory of Film and Media* (New York: Oxford University Press, 1981).

Mukherji, Rahul, 'The Political Economy of India's Economic Reforms', *Asian Economic Policy Review*, vol. 3, no. 2, December 2008.

Nanda, Ritu, *Raj Kapoor Speaks* (New Delhi: Viking, 2002).

Nandy, Ashis, 'The Hindi Film: Ideology and First Principles', *India International Centre Quarterly*, vol. 8, no. 1, 1981.

———, *The Intimate Enemy: Loss and Recovery of Self under Colonialism* (New Delhi: Oxford University Press, 1983).

Neele, Steve, *Genre and Hollywood* (London: Routledge, 2000).

Niranjana, Tejaswini, 'Integrating Whose Nation? Tourists and Terrorists in *Roja*', *Economic and Political Weekly*, vol. 24, no. 3, 15 January 1994.

Orsini, Francesca, *The Hindi Public Sphere, 1920–1940: Language and Literature in the Age of Nationalism* (New Delhi: Oxford University Press, 2002).

Pal, Joyojeet, 'Between Goddesses, Vamps and Software Engineers: Women and Jobs in Tamil Cinema in an Era of Economic Liberalization', *Phalanx: A Quarterly Review for Continuing Debate*, July 2011.

Pandey, Gyanendra, *Remembering Partition: Violence, Nationalism and History in India* (Cambridge: Cambridge University Press, 2001).

Pandian, M.S.S., 'Nation as Nostalgia: Ambiguous Spiritual Journeys of Vengal Chakkarai', *Economic and Political Weekly*, vol. 38, nos 51/52, 27 December 2003.

Pfleiderer, Beatrix, 'An Empirical Study of Urban and Semi-urban Audience Reactions to Hindi Film', in Lothar Lutze and Beatrix Pfleiderer (eds), *The Hindi Film: Agent and Re-agent of Cultural Change* (New Delhi: Manohar, 1985).

Prasad, M. Madhava, *Ideology of the Hindi Film: A Historical Construction* (New Delhi: Oxford University Press, 1999).

Radway, Janice, *Reading the Romance: Women, Patriarchy and Popular Literature* (London: Verso, 1987).

Raghavendra, M.K., 'Structure and Form in Indian Popular Film Narrative', in Vinay Lal and Ashis Nandy (eds), *Fingerprinting Popular Culture: The*

Mythic and the Iconic in Indian Cinema (New Delhi: Oxford University Press, 2006).

———, *Seduced by the Familiar: Narration and Meaning in Indian Popular Cinema* (New Delhi: Oxford University Press, 2008).

———, *Bipolar Identity: Region, Nation and the Kannada Language Film* (New Delhi: Oxford University Press, 2011).

———, 'Nation and Transgression: Ideology and the Horror Film in India and Pakistan', *Phalanx: A Quarterly Review for Continuing Debate*, no. 6, July 2011.

———, 'The Reinterpretation of Historical Trauma: Three Films about Partition', in Sukalpa Bhattacharjee and C. Joshua Thomas (eds), *Society, Representation and Textuality: The Critical Interface* (New Delhi: Sage, 2013).

Rajadhyaksha, Ashish, 'Viewership and Democracy in the Cinema', in Ravi S. Vasudevan (ed.), *Making Meaning in Indian Cinema* (New Delhi: Oxford University Press, 2000).

———, 'The "Bollywoodization" of Indian Cinema: Cultural Nationalism in a Global Arena', *Inter-Asia Cultural Studies*, vol. 4, no. 1, April 2003.

———, *Indian Cinema in the Time of Celluloid: From Bollywood to the Emergency* (New Delhi: Tulika, 2009).

———, 'The Cinema Effect I and II', in *Indian Cinema in the Time of Celluloid: From Bollywood to the Emergency* (New Delhi: Tulika, 2009), pp. 84–132.

Rajadhyaksha, Ashish and Paul Willemen, *Encyclopedia of Indian Cinema* (New Delhi: Oxford University Press, 1995).

Rampal, Kuldip R., 'Asia: The Hollywood Factor', in Lee Artz and Yahya R. Kamalipour (eds), *The Media Globe: Trends in International Mass Media* (Lanham: Rowman and Littlefield, 2006).

Rao, Shakuntala, 'Accountability, Democracy, and Globalization: A Study of Broadcast Journalism in India', *Asian Journal of Communication*, vol. 18, no3, August 2008.

Rao, T.S. Sathyanarayana and V.S.T. Krishna, 'Wake Up Call from "Stars on the Ground"', *Indian Journal of Psychiatry*, vol. 50, no. 1, January–March 2008.

Real, Michael R., *Exploring Media Culture: A Guide* (Thousand Oaks: Sage, 1996).

Reddy, V. Vamshi Krishna, 'Ram Gopal Varma, Bombay and Globalization', *Asian Cinema*, vol. 22, no. 2, 2013.

Rowe, David, 'Sport and the Repudiation of the Global', *International Review for the Sociology of Sport*, vol. 38, no. 3, September 2003.

Roy, R.M. (ed.), *Sangeet Natak Akademi Film Seminar Report* (New Delhi: Sangeet Natak Akademi, 1956).

Runkle, Susan, 'Bollywood, Beauty and the Construction of "International Standards" in Post-liberalization Bombay', *Sagar: South Asia Research Journal*, University of Texas at Austin, vol. 11, 2004.

Scholes, Robert, 'Narration and Narrativity in Film', in Gerald Mast and Marshall Cohen (eds), *Film Theory and Criticism: Introductory Readings*, 3rd edition (New York: Oxford University Press, 1985).

Scholes, Robert, James Phelan, and Robert Kellogg, *The Nature of Narrative* (New York: Oxford University Press, 1966).

Sidhu, Hina, 'Share of Wages and Competitiveness in Indian Industry', *Indian Journal of Industrial Relations*, vol. 43, no. 2, October 2007.

Steene, Gwenda Vander, 'Bollywood Films and African Audiences', in Anjali Gera Roy and Chua Beng Huat (eds), *Travels of Bollywood Cinema: From Bombay to LA* (New Delhi: Oxford University Press, 2012).

Stern, Susannah R., 'Self-Absorbed, Dangerous and Disengaged: What Popular Films Tell Us about Teenagers', *Mass Communication and Society*, vol. 8, no. 1, 2005.

Tan, Jee-Peng and Alain Mingat, *Education in Asia: A Comparative Study of Cost and Financing* (Washington, DC: World Bank Publications, 1992).

Thapar, Romila, *A History of India*, vol. 1 (Harmondsworth: Penguin, 1966).

Thomas, Rosie, 'Indian Cinema: Pleasures and Popularity', *Screen*, vol. 26, nos 3–4, 1985.

Todorov, Tsvetan, *The Fantastic: A Structural Approach to a Literary Genre*, translated from French by Richard Howard (Ithaca, NY: Cornell University Press, 1975).

———, *The Poetics of Prose* (Oxford: Blackwell, 1997).

Uricchio, William, 'The Batman's Gotham City™: Story, Ideology, Performance', in Jorn Ahrens and Arno Meteling (eds), *Comics and the City: Urban Space in Print, Picture and Sequence* (London: The Continuum International Publishing, 2010).

Valicha, Kishore, *The Moving Image: A Study of Indian Cinema* (Hyderabad: Orient Longman, 1988).

Vasudev, Aruna, *The New Indian Cinema* (New Delhi: Macmillan, 1986).

Vasudevan, Ravi S., 'The Melodramatic Mode and Commercial Hindi Cinema', *Screen*, vol. 30, no. 3, 1989.

————, 'Shifting Codes, Dissolving Identities: The Hindi Social Film of the 1950s as Popular Culture', in Ravi S. Vasudevan (ed.), *Making Meaning in Indian Cinema* (New Delhi: Oxford University Press, 2000).

————, 'An Imperfect Public: Cinema and Citizenship in the Third World', in *Sarai Reader 1: The Public Domain* (Delhi: Sarai, The New Media Initiative, 2001).

————, 'Bombay and Its Public', in Rachel Dwyer and Christopher Pinney (eds), *Pleasure and the Nation: The History, Politics and Consumption of Popular Culture in India* (New Delhi: Oxford University Press, 2001).

————, *The Melodramatic Public: Film Form and Spectatorship in Indian Cinema* (Ranikhet: Permanent Black, 2010).

Virdi, Jyotika, *The Cinematic ImagiNation: Indian Popular Films as Social History* (Delhi: Permanent Black, 2003).

Viswamohan, Aysha Iqbal, 'English in Filmsongs from India: An Overview', *English Today*, vol. 27, no. 3, September 2011.

Viswanath, Gita, 'The Multiplex: Crowd, Audience and the Genre Film', *Economic and Political Weekly*, vol. 42, no. 32, 11 August 2007.

Vitali, Valentina, *Hindi Action Cinema: Industries, Narratives, Bodies* (New Delhi: Oxford University Press, 2008).

Wilson, Ron, 'The Left-handed Form of Human Endeavor: The Crime Films of the 1990s', in Wheeler Winston Dixon (ed.), *Film Genre 2000: New Critical Essays* (Albany, NY: State University of New York Press, 2000).

Wood, Robin, 'An Introduction to the American Horror Film', in Bill Nichols (ed.), *Movies and Methods*, vol. 2 (Calcutta: Seagull, 1993).

Zavarzadeh, Mas'ud, *Seeing Films Politically* (Albany: SUNY Press, 1991).

Subject Index

Bhandarkar, Madhur 98–9, 106–7, 110, 111, 114, 129, 158n10
Bharatiya Janata Party (BJP) 32–3, 38–9, 137, 140 (*see also* 'Akhand Bharat' [undivided India])
Board of Control for Cricket in India (BCCI) 159n12, 214, 224n15
Bollywood films xiii–xv, xiii–xv, xxiv, 87, 206n5, 231–2
  as cultural artefact 90
  decline of popularity in Africa 208n18
  events in London 90
  global success as business model 90
  politics of xxx–xxxii
  and *Slumdog Millionaire* 93
  star physique in 92
Bombay cinema/film industry 79, 188n1
Bombay Dreams (musical) xiv–xv
Bombay riots, in *Bombay* 75
border crossings 37
Bordwell, David 14, 128n9
Brooks, Peter xix

Cannes film festival 59–60
caper film 70, 80n8
CEO, the politician as, in film 155–7, 237
character memory 224n14
Chatterjee, Partha 153, 190n20
Chidambaram, P. 158n11
childhood sequences as defining moments 177
Chaudhuri, Nirad C. 95n4, 240n13

civil society 153
classical screenwriting 124
club dancer in Hindi films, motif of 20, 231
colonialism 45, 221, 236
comedies, romantic in Hindi cinema 54–5
commercial cinemas of India xv, 89
community, Hindi film 47–51
Congress party/government 31, 33, 38, 137, 158n11
  transformation in Hindi cinema after regaining power in 2004 228
'control raj' 126
corporate/business sector 156
corporate communication, film as 113
corruption in Hindi cinema xxxi, 48–9, 123–5, 151, 229–30, 236
counterculture movement in the US 51n2
cricket's/cricketing
  fever outside metropolises 210
  growing popularity in 1990s 209
  loyalty of Muslims in India 212
  writers 222n1
criminal in Hindi cinema 68–9
criminalized politician in Hindi cinema 145

daku (dacoit) 160, 168n2
  film 160
deep interpretation xii–xiii
deregulation 126
devotion in Hindi films 5, 10n11

feudalism, in *Dabangg* 234–5, 241n15

feudal power, Nehru's efforts against 138

Film Inquiry Commission Report of 1951 188n1

friendship, three-way, in Hindi films 198–9

funding institutions 155–6

Gandhigiri in *Lage Raho Munna Bhai* xxxi, 58, 59, 62–5

Gandhi, Indira 20, 28, 46, 69, 123, 175

gangland wars xxv

GDP growth, India's 228

Ghatak, Ritwik 137–8

'global', the, and the 'modern' 19–22

globalization 237

and Hindi cinema xxvi–xxviii

impact in India xi

governance 155–6

Green Revolution depicted in Hindi films 138–9, 161

heterosexual love 195

hierarchy and comedy in Hindi cinema 54–7

Hindi 'B' films 5, 8 (*see also* mythological films)

aesthetics 24n6

low-budget commercial movie 1

and mainstream Hindi cinema, thematic difference between 3

reasons for rise of 2

Hinduism 27, 95n4

as religion and morality, disconnect between 240n13

Hirani, Rajkumar 130

Hollywood films xiv, xxxiii, xxxviiin37, 12, 15, 21, 24n10, 111–12, 124, 188n1, 198

classical xxxiv, 211, 224n14

mimetic nature of 83

nuclear family sacred in 206n5

screenwriting manuals 66n7, 128n9

honour killings in Haryana 192n33 (*see also khap panchayats* in Haryana)

horror film/cinema, Hindi 1, 3, 8, 11n13

hyperreality 92–3

ideology of Hindi cinema xxx

'Imaginasia' xv

India and Pakistan, relationship between 27

'India Shining' campaign by BJP 39, 228

India's war with Pakistan in 1965 and 1971 28

Indian cinema, popularity of in Nigeria and Senegal 205

information technology (IT) industry, turnover of 52n9

International Cricket Council (ICC) 214

Jameson, Frederic xviii, 108, 127n4

jati 191n25

in *Dabangg* 182–7

joint family xxii, 15, 206n5

national heroes, representations in films 48

national institutions for preservation of culture 89

national issues represented in Hindi cinema through relationships/characters 237–8

National Rural Employment Guarantee Act (NREGA) 2005 229

Nehru, Jawaharlal xvi, 138, 142n16

Nehruvian
era 235, 238
modernity 4, 169n9
radical economic reforms since 230
socialism xviii, xxiv, 29, 51, 79, 124, 210, 236

new economy in India 47, 239n9 (*see also* 'Bangalored')

Nigerian films, characters in 205

noir, American 12, 15, 21–2

'Nollywood' 205, 207n16, 208n19

non-Anglophone cinema/Hindi films 172–3, 226, 234–5

non-Anglophone India 211

non-resident Indians (NRIs) 171, 189n6, 240n10

nuclear family 206n5, 234

Oscars, marketing of *Lagaan* prior to 210–11

Padukone, Deepika 86

pan-national cinema xxiii, 37

parental presence in Hindi cinema 176–7

parenthood in earlier Hindi cinema 198

Parsi theatre, use of romance by xvi (*see also* Hindi cinema) .

Partition in films xix, 27–8, 31–2, 37

pastiche or blank parody 86, 127n4

Patel, Sardar Vallabhbhai 138

patriotism in films, periods of 22, 28–9, 33, 210, 218, 236

petty criminal, motif of 68–9

philanthropy and responsibility 106–9

Phoolan Devi (bandit queen) 80n6

politician(s) xxxi, 49–50, 73, 78, 88, 104, 119, 121–2, 155–7, 232, 237
Anglophone 155
English-speaking 155
in Hindi cinema 145–6

politics
electoral (*see* electoral politics)
as exclusive domain of a political class 150–5
representation in Hindi cinema 47–51
opportunism in 156
as soap opera 148–50

politics, film stars entering 152

popular cinema as utterance xii

post-liberalization period, Hindi cinema in 29

post-Marxist theory xii

Prasad, M. Madhava xvi, xxxivn5

primary education represented in films 136, 140

private enterprise xxvii, 236–7

Film Index

About the Author

M.K. Raghavendra is a film scholar and a founder-editor of *Phalanx*, a web journal dedicated to debate. He received the National Award (the *Swarna Kamal*) for best film critic in the year 1997. He was awarded a two-year Homi Bhabha Fellowship in 2000–1 to research Indian popular film narrative as well as a Goethe Insitut Fellowship in 2000 to study post-war German cinema. He has authored books on academic film criticism, such as *Bipolar Identity: Region, Nation, and the Kannada Language Film* (Oxford University Press, 2011), *50 Indian Film Classics* (HarperCollins, 2009), and *Seduced by the Familiar: Narration and Meaning in Indian Popular Cinema* (Oxford University Press, 2008). His academic essays on Indian cinema find a place in Indian and international anthologies. *Seduced by the Familiar* and *50 Indian Film Classics* have been recognized among the best books on cinema from around the world by FIPRESCI (Fédération Internationale de la Presse Cinématographique), the International Federation of Film Critics. His most recent book *Directors Cut: 50 Major Filmmakers of the Modern Era* (Collins) came out in June 2013.